ALSO BY MICHAEL HOFMANN

POETRY
K.S. in Lakeland
Approximately Nowhere

PROSE
Behind the Lines

EDITOR (with James Lasdun)
After Ovid: New Metamorphoses

TWENTIETH-CENTURY
GERMAN POETRY

TWENTIETH-CENTURY

GERMAN POETRY

AN ANTHOLOGY

EDITED BY Michael Hofmann

FARRAR, STRAUS AND GIROUX

NEW YORK

FARRAR, STRAUS AND GIROUX
19 Union Square West, New York 10003

Introduction and selection copyright © 2005 by Michael Hofmann
Printed in the United States of America
Originally published (without the German text) in 2005 by Faber and Faber
    Limited, Great Britain, as *The Faber Book of 20th-Century German Poems*
Published in the United States by Farrar, Straus and Giroux
First American edition, 2006

Owing to limitations of space, all acknowledgments for permission to reprint
previously published material can be found on pages 503–509.

Library of Congress Cataloging-in-Publication Data
Twentieth-century German poetry / an anthology / edited by Michael
Hofmann.— 1st American ed.
       p.   cm.
    English and German.
    Originally published as The Faber Book of 20th-Century German Poems:
    London : Faber and Faber, 2005.
    Includes bibliographical references and index.
    ISBN-13: 978-0-374-10535-8 (hardcover : alk. paper)
    ISBN-10: 0-374-10535-9 (hardcover : alk. paper)
    1. German poetry—20th century—Translations into English.   I. Title:
20th century German poetry.   II. Hofmann, Michael, 1957 Aug. 25–

PTI 160.E5T84   2006
831´.9108—dc22

                                                                    2006006873

Designed by Cassandra J. Pappas

www.fsgbooks.com

10 9 8 7 6 5 4 3 2 1

CONTENTS

CONTENTS

CONTENTS

CONTENTS

Night Song of the Fish

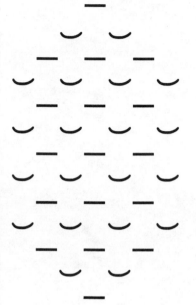

[The deepest German poem]

Who had the best poets in the twentieth century? For their size of population, the Irish and the Poles, absolutely, without hesitation. And under open rules? Well, then it's more like the usual suspects, the Americans and the Russians, the Spanish (particularly if you throw in Latin America)—and (beefed up by the Austrians and the Swiss, and a few Czechs and Balts and Romanians) the Germans. I don't think I'm being biased here, except inasmuch as I am able to read the stuff at all. If you're a monoglot in English, you have to struggle mightily to make your Mercator look any better adjusted or more adequately representative than the famous *New Yorker* map of the States. ("Do you mean *foreign* poetry?" exclaims a coiled, repugnant Larkin, asked if he read poetry in translation. As if English poetry in (English!) translation might be acceptable.) To answer the question fairly and properly, you'd have to be a thoroughgoing polyglot; and I'm only a bi-glot. But here's my case anyway.

Rilke, first—whatever else one thinks of him—is at least as good a poet as there has ever been, in point of skill, originality and expression. Brecht, it can be argued, took poetry into the twentieth century. He is even, perhaps, its single most crucial figure; certainly, he would be my choice. That notion was first suggested to me by Daniel Weissbort's brilliant collection of the poetry of World War II, Holocaust, Diaspora, and totalitarian division of Europe, *The Poetry of Survival*, which begins with Brecht. Where now, I've come to think, without Brecht, would there have been poetry as a living counter-force in socio-political reality, where else would the poetry of dissent and fear and protest and rebuke and pleasure have ever begun? Unlike, say, T. S. Eliot or Paul Valéry or García Lorca, the idea of Brecht is heartening and inspiring even if you have never read him. He represents utility, and private opposition; *"Seid Sand, nicht das Öl im Getriebe der Welt"* ("Be sand, not oil, in the machinery of the world"), as Günter Eich famously and Brecht-ishly said. And if you have read him, I'm sure that with the *ur*-cool of his "my brother Shelley" *schtick*, and his great "Motto" ("In the dark times/Will there also be singing?/Yes, there will also be singing/About the dark times."), his example has made poetry more possible anywhere in the world. If I were a poet in Asia or Africa or Latin America, he is the one "old world" poet I would go to. He synthesized, improbably, Kipling, Rimbaud, Waley, the Bible and later Horace to make something utterly and radically new. The prevailing British view of him as an arid theorist of drama (you keep the house-lights on, there's no proper acting, and someone writes things down on a blackboard), and the author of a few baffling but conniving plays, excruciatingly boring but now happily debunked, is as bad and thoroughgoing a misrepresentation as any ever perpetrated.

Gottfried Benn, his great counter-pole, and for thirty or forty years the other great German poet (they both died in the summer of 1956, Brecht in East Berlin, Benn in West Berlin), is one of the consummate poets of the century: the poet of private griefs and musics, of monologue, of fascination. What all the mid-century American poets—Lowell, Bishop, Jarrell, Berryman, Roethke, Snodgrass—half-officially set themselves to be, "heartbreaking," Benn simply is. There is no one harder, and no one softer. Both Brecht and Benn, incidentally, are depleted in translation. Rilke at times puts up quite a plausible showing—I have sometimes referred to him, derisively, as an American poet (but that's mainly a comment on his adoptedness there)—but the subtlety and elegance of Brecht, and the extraordinary, inspissated jargon-glooms of middle-period Benn are barely possible. There's a near-thirty-year gap between "Express Train" and "Chopin" in the present selection, in which Benn wrote things I would certainly have liked to represent, but they are short-lined, tightly rhyming octaves of techno-collages. I simply would have had no idea what to do with a line like *"Banane, yes, Banane,"* which seems to me great and zany poetry, in equal parts hilarious and gravely majestic. Anyway, there's the basis of a century there. Add on the unaccountable and grievous Celan and Sachs and Bachmann and Inge Müller. Add on Hans Magnus Enzensberger, a contemporary and an observer and a participant like Auden or MacNiece, and also a Renaissance of one. Add on Expressionism—a universal literary movement in one country—add on the strange, state-sponsored, but then, at its best, state-biting poetry of East Germany for the better part of fifty years, and you get something not so much formidable as unexpectedly irresistible.

The next thing about German twentieth-century poetry is how closely it is bound up with Germany's villainous history. Benn—who also wrote formidable and hauntingly beautiful prose—speaks of the generation that tramped to war with Rilke's *"Wer spricht von Sieg? Überstehn ist alles."* ("Who speaks of victory? Surviving is all") on their lips. Quite a few of the poets died in the war, or were left permanently affected (Stadler, Trakl, van Hoddis); Benn himself, a medical doctor, was at HQ in Brussels during the First World War, and was with the Army again in the Second (he was compiling statistics on suicide), describing it as "the aristocratic form of emigration." The end of World War II is marked by Ernst Jandl's poem—one of the best and most widely known "concrete poems" there are. Celan and Nelly Sachs wrote obliquely and more straightforwardly about the death camps; Bobrowski was first inspired to write by the Russian landscape he saw as a prisoner-of-war; Eich wrote about being a prisoner of the Americans. Theodor Adorno's—again—vastly well-known remark about poetry being impossible after Auschwitz drew an oblique reply from Brecht, which drew a more direct one from Celan, and—a little like poetry in Poland (Herbert and Rozewicz)—a bitter and cleansed and haunted poetry sprang up again in Germany in the postwar years, with the "Gruppe 47" and others. (Those football players of the "Gruppe 47," as Celan, the unco-optable individualist, witheringly said; but I have to say, mostly they meant well, and did good.)

The false prospectus of "really existent Socialism" was increasingly criticized in the East (there was an uprising in '54, anticipating that in Hungary in '56, which had to be brutally put down); Brecht, who had sworn never to do anything to harm the cause of Communism, didn't publish or otherwise circulate poems like "Changing the Wheel" or "The Solution," but he was at least moved to write them. Meanwhile, the horrid materialism of the "Economic Miracle" and the "fake Fifties" (Grass's phrase) was attacked in the West, by Enzensberger and others. In the Sixties, the Federal Republic (West Germany) came increasingly under American influence, Pop culture; Rolf Dieter Brinkmann translated Frank O'Hara and got himself run over in Soho, on Old Compton Street. The more left-wing writers—Germany's *soixante-huitards*—decided that poetry and literature in general were hopelessly bourgeois, and gave them up; after a time, most of them came back. In the East, there was almost a new natural career progression as writers began, wrote critically of the state, and found themselves shunted off to the West (Wolf Biermann's was the most celebrated case, in November 1976, but this relatively discreet and unpleasantly effective practice continued for at least a decade). As in Brecht's time, a word or phrase could still have immense carry: I think of two titles: Uwe Kolbe's *"Hineingeboren"* ("Born Into It"—i.e., East Germany), and Durs Grünbein's *"Grauzone morgens"* ("Mornings in the Grayzone"—i.e., once again, East Germany). As the century ended, a re-unified country was looking at itself and its neighbours in new ways (Grass, Grünbein, Göritz).

The other thing that maybe separates German poets from those of other countries is how many of them do other things. There were painters like Klee, Schwitters, Arp, and Grosz. Christoph Meckel and Günter Grass are very accomplished graphic artists. Brecht and Heiner Müller and now Durs Grünbein are all playwrights. Benn was a doctor, and Trakl a pharmacist. Grass, evidently, is far better known as a novelist; but Werfel also had a huge bestseller with *The Song of Bernadette*, while Rilke, Brecht, Bobrowski, Bachmann, Born, Braun, Krüger and Beyer have all written novels. Günter Eich was an admired writer of radio plays; Celan translated poetry from Russian, French, English, and other languages; Bartsch and Müller adapted Shakespeare; Enzensberger and Sartorius, each in his generation, compiled anthologies of world poetry; Krüger is the most important German publisher. Benn and Enzensberger and Grünbein are all prolific essayists. I enumerate this, in such detail, to demonstrate how much the poets here are "in the world"; "pure poets" and ivory tower-ites are elsewhere.

Possibly related to this is a streak of rebelliousness in many of the poems against what one might think of as a German temperament. It is the reverence for America of George Grosz (who once, as a child, copied out a Fenimore Cooper novel by hand), or for Poland of Johannes Bobrowski's "Report"; it is the startling low comedy of Rilke's tailor-king (in a spectacular translation by Don Paterson) and Enzensberger's beautiful praise ("precise/and perculiarly cheerful"—the antithesis of anything *typisch deutsch*) for William Carlos Williams; it is Günter Grass's worry about the standard-issue copy of Hölderlin in the soldier's knapsack, and Reiner Kunze's about the tyrannical imposition of a more than literal "Beethoven"; it is the persistent concreteness of Brecht ("Truth is always concrete" was one of his great sayings, which he kept appropriately pinned to the wall), and the moving simplicity of Celan's very late—and impossible—instruction to himself, that he "learn to live." It is the undiminished truculence of Heiner Müller and Volker Braun—even after the "*Wende*" and the reabsorption of the East. It is Eich's "I have always loved nettles,/and only now learned/of their usefulness" and part of Pastior's wonderful portmanteau, "riennevapluperfect." It is the scepticism of Brecht's "*Und nach uns wird komnen: nichts Nennenswertes*" in "Of Poor B.B.": "And after us there will come: really nothing worth mentioning"— a line, incidentally, that is echoed at the end of Enzensberger's "Fetish" ("*und nicht weiter/nennenswert*" in the original) and more explicity cited in Volker Braun's "O Chicago! O Dialectic!" That sort of moody or whimsical or sophisticated rejection is of course explicitly against the whole tenor of Rilke's *Ninth Duino Elegy*, in which he makes poets responsible for naming and telling.

In a wider way, it is an inevitable—but also a deliberately fostered— aspect of the selection that many of the poems here appeal to, or celebrate, or attempt to take forward the example of other poets, both within and beyond Germany, within and beyond the limits of this book. Hence Lasker-Schüler's portrait of Grosz (a former lover), Benn's Shakespeare, Bobrowski's Trakl, Kunert's Koeppen, Heiner Müller's Brecht, Kunze's Bobrowski, Bartsch's Enzensberger (with its allusions to the latter's great, and unfortunately not very excerptible, long poem, *The Sinking of the Titanic*), Sartorius's Cavafy, Krüger's Ernst Meister; even, in its utterly elliptical way, Grünbein's Vallejo.

This book aims to be at once readable, objective, and unfair. There are inevitable omissions and distortions—on the whole, I don't want to apologize for them. I didn't want to leave out great poets (Rilke, Brecht) just because one can find them elsewhere, or great poems either ("Orpheus. Eurydice. Hermes," which Joseph Brodsky nominated as possibly the greatest poem of the century; "Poor B.B." and "To Those Born Later"; "Morgue"; "Inventory"; "Deathfugue"—in John Felstiner's challenging retro-translation). I tried to take seriously the anthology-as-island. Therefore, one way or another, the poems here are meant to travel: they are great in the original, or good in English, or there is nothing like them in either language, or in many cases perhaps all three. When I first read through what I had assembled, it seemed to me that it was both true to itself and not unassimilable to an English readership. Historically, I don't think twentieth-century German poetry has had much effect on English and American poetry except, in a shallow and mistaken way, for Celan and Rilke. But there is much that might. Jakob van Hoddis's work has a slapstick feel—like a Feininger drawing—on top of Expressionism's end-of-the-world aura. Robert Lowell's Werfel translation sounds altogether more like his own poetry of fifteen years later (and indeed contains a phrase that appeared in *Life Studies*). Hans Magnus Enzensberger's "At Thirty-three" and "The Holiday" both come out of a 1979 book called *Die Furie des Verschwindens*, which, had it been in English, would surely have made even greater waves. I can imagine the delight of Charles Simic (whom Enzensberger has translated into German) at the asperities of Günter Eich, or the drastic economy of Inge Müller. Benn's poems from the 1940s read like fifty years later. Many of the works here are both international and English—and that at a time when too few English poems are international.

I would like to thank Bill Donahue, Barbara Honrath, the indefatigable Hauke Hückstädt and his estimable Göttingen assistants, Wiebke Herrmann and Henrike Rohloff; thanks also to Ludwig Krapf and Eliot Weinberger for their respective *empfindlich* bits of help. "Like being handed a lantern, or a spiked stick," as the poet said, or rather, the poets said.

TWENTIETH-CENTURY
GERMAN POETRY

George Grosz

Manchmal spielen bunte Tränen
In seinen äschernen Augen.

Aber immer begegnen ihm Totenwagen,
Die verscheuchen seine Libellen.

Er ist abergläubig—
—Ward unter einem bösen Stern geboren—

Seine Schrift regnet,
Seine Zeichnung: Trüber Buchstabe.

Wie lange im Fluß gelegen
Blähen seine Menschen sich auf,

Mysteriöse Verlorene mit Quabbenmäulern
Und verfaulten Seelen.

Fünf träumende Totenfahrer
Sind seine silbernen Finger.

Aber nirgendwo ein Licht im verirrten Märchen
Und doch ist er ein Kind,

Der Held aus dem Lederstrumpf;
Mit dem Indianerstamm auf Duzfuß.

Sonst haßt er alle Menschen,
Sie bringen ihm Unglück.

Aber George Grosz liebt sein Mißgeschick
Wie einen anhänglichen Feind.

George Grosz

Sometimes coloured tears play
In his ashen eyes.

He is forever encountering funeral processions
Which scatter his dragonflies.

He is superstitious—
Born under a bad star—

His writing rains,
His drawings: gloomy alphabets.

His people are bloated,
As though they'd long lain in rivers,

Mysterious missing persons with fish-mouths
And mouldering souls.

His silver fingers
Are five dreamy undertakers.

Nowhere is there a light in his lost *Märchen*,
But he remains a boy at heart,

A Fenimore Cooper hero;
On first-name terms with a tribe of Indians.

Apart from them, he hates everyone,
They bring him bad luck.

But George Grosz loves his fate
Like a trusty enemy.

Und seine Traurigkeit ist dionysisch,
Schwarzer Champagner seine Klage.

Kein Mensch weiß, wo er herkam;
Ich weiß, wo er landet.

Er ist ein Meer mit verhängtem Mond,
Sein Gott ist nur scheintot.

ELSE LASKER-SCHÜLER

And his sadness is Dionysian,
Black champagne his plaints.

No one knows where he came from;
I know where he ends up.

He is a sea with a dim moon above it,
His god is only playing dead.

   Michael Hofmann

Herbsttag

Herr: es ist Zeit. Der Sommer war sehr groß.
Leg deinen Schatten auf die Sonnenuhren,
und auf den Fluren laß die Winde los.

Befiehl den letzten Früchten voll zu sein;
gib ihnen noch zwei südlichere Tage,
dränge sie zur Vollendung hin und jage
die letzte Süße in den schweren Wein.

Wer jetzt kein Haus hat, baut sich keines mehr.
Wer jetzt allein ist, wird es lange bleiben,
wird wachen, lesen, lange Briefe schreiben
und wird in den Alleen hin und her
unruhig wandern, wenn die Blätter treiben.

RAINER MARIA RILKE, 1875–1926

Autumn Day

Lord, it is time. The summer was too long.
Lay now thy shadow over the sundials,
and on the meadows let the winds blow strong.

Bid the last fruit to ripen on the vine;
allow them still two friendly southern days
to bring them to perfection and to force
the final sweetness in the heavy wine.

Who has no house now will not build him one.
Who is alone now will be long alone,
will waken, read, and write long letters
and through the barren pathways up and down
restlessly wander when dead leaves are blown.

    C. F. MacIntyre

Spanische Tänzerin

Wie in der Hand ein Schwefelzündholz, weiß,
eh es zur Flamme kommt, nach allen Seiten
zuckende Zungen streckt—: beginnt im Kreis
naher Beschauer hastig, hell und heiß
ihr runder Tanz sich zuckend auszubreiten.

Und plötzlich ist er Flamme, ganz und gar.

Mit einem Blick entzündet sie ihr Haar
und dreht auf einmal mit gewagter Kunst
ihr ganzes Kleid in diese Feuersbrunst,
aus welcher sich, wie Schlangen die erschrecken,
die nackten Arme wach und klappernd strecken.

Und dann: als würde ihr das Feuer knapp,
nimmt sie es ganz zusamm und wirft es ab
sehr herrisch, mit hochmütiger Gebärde
und schaut: da liegt es rasend auf der Erde
und flammt noch immer und ergiebt sich nicht—.
Doch sieghaft, sicher und mit einem süßen
grüßenden Lächeln hebt sie ihr Gesicht
und stampft es aus mit kleinen festen Füßen.

RAINER MARIA RILKE

The Spanish Dancer

The audience in the cup of her hand,
she is a struck match: sparks,
darting tongues, and then the white flare
of phosphorus and the dance ignites
a charm of fire, uncoiling, spreading fast.

And suddenly she is all flame.

She is brazen: glancing round and shamelessly
setting her hair alight, turning her dress
to a seething inferno, from which she stretches
long white arms, and castanets, like rattlesnakes
woken, startled to their ratcheting and clack.

And just as quick, as if constricted
by the sheath of fire, she gathers it up
and casts it off in one high gesture,
and looks down: it lies there raging on the ground,
shed flame stubbornly alive.
Radiant, chin tilted in salute, she dispatches it
with a steely fusillade of feet:
stamps it, pounds it, stamps it out.

Robin Robertson

Blaue Hortensie

So wie das letzte Grün in Farbentiegeln
sind diese Blätter, trocken, stumpf und rauh,
hinter den Blütendolden, die ein Blau
nicht auf sich tragen, nur von ferne spiegeln.

Sie spiegeln es verweint und ungenau,
als wollten sie es wiederum verlieren,
und wie in alten blauen Briefpapieren
ist Gelb in ihnen, Violett und Grau;

Verwaschnes wie an einer Kinderschürze,
Nichtmehrgetragnes, dem nichts mehr geschieht:
wie fühlt man eines kleinen Lebens Kürze.

Doch plötzlich scheint das Blau sich zu verneuen
in einer von den Dolden, und man sieht
ein rührend Blaues sich vor Grünem freuen.

RAINER MARIA RILKE

Blue Hydrangea

Like the green that cakes in a pot of paint,
these leaves are dry, dull and rough
behind this billow of blooms whose blue
is not their own but reflected from far away
in a mirror dimmed by tears and vague,
as if it wished them to disappear again
the way, in old blue writing paper,
yellow shows, then violet and gray;

a washed-out color as in children's clothes
which, no longer worn, no more can happen to:
how much it makes you feel a small life's brevity.
But suddenly the blue shines quite renewed
within one cluster, and we can see
a touching blue rejoice before the green.

William Gass

Vor dem Sommerregen

Auf einmal ist aus allem Grün im Park
man weiß nicht was, ein Etwas, fortgenommen;
man fühlt ihn näher an die Fenster kommen
und schweigsam sein. Inständig nur und stark

ertönt aus dem Gehölz der Regenpfeifer,
man denkt an einen Hieronymus:
so sehr steigt irgend Einsamkeit und Eifer
aus dieser einen Stimme, die der Guß

erhören wird. Des Saales Wände sind
mit ihren Bildern von uns fortgetreten,
als dürften sie nicht hören was wir sagen.

Es spiegeln die verblichenen Tapeten
das ungewisse Licht von Nachmittagen,
in denen man sich fürchtete als Kind.

RAINER MARIA RILKE

Before Summer Rain

Suddenly, from all the green around you,
something—you don't know what—has disappeared;
you feel it creeping closer to the window,
in total silence. From the nearby wood

you hear the urgent whistling of a plover,
reminding you of someone's *Saint Jerome*:
so much solitude and passion come
from that one voice, whose fierce request the downpour

will grant. The walls, with their ancient portraits, glide
away from us, cautiously, as though
they weren't supposed to hear what we are saying.

And reflected on the faded tapestries now:
the chill, uncertain sunlight of those long
childhood hours when you were so afraid.

Stephen Mitchell

Orpheus. Eurydike. Hermes

Das war der Seelen wunderliches Bergwerk.
Wie stille Silbererze gingen sie
als Adern durch sein Dunkel. Zwischen Wurzeln
entsprang das Blut, das fortgeht zu den Menschen,
und schwer wie Porphyr sah es aus im Dunkel.
Sonst war nichts Rotes.

Felsen waren da
und wesenlose Wälder. Brücken über Leeres
und jener große graue blinde Teich,
der über seinem fernen Grunde hing
wie Regenhimmel über einer Landschaft.
Und zwischen Wiesen, sanft und voller Langmut,
erschien des einen Weges blasser Streifen,
wie eine lange Bleiche hingelegt.

Und dieses einen Weges kamen sie.

Voran der schlanke Mann im blauen Mantel,
der stumm und ungeduldig vor sich aussah.
Ohne zu kauen fraß sein Schritt den Weg
in großen Bissen; seine Hände hingen
schwer und verschlossen aus dem Fall der Falten
und wußten nicht mehr von der leichten Leier,
die in die Linke eingewachsen war
wie Rosenranken in den Ast des Ölbaums.
Und seine Sinne waren wie entzweit:
indes der Blick ihm wie ein Hund vorauslief,
umkehrte, kam und immer wieder weit
und wartend an der nächsten Wendung stand,—
blieb sein Gehör wie ein Geruch zurück.
Manchmal erschien es ihm als reichte es
bis an das Gehen jener beiden andern,
die folgen sollten diesen ganzen Aufstieg.

RAINER MARIA RILKE

Orpheus. Eurydice. Hermes

That was the so unfathomed mine of souls.
And they, like silent veins of silver ore,
were winding through its darkness. Between roots
welled up the blood that flows on to mankind,
like blocks of heavy porphyry in the darkness.
Else there was nothing red.

But there were rocks
and ghostly forests. Bridges over voidness
and that immense, grey, unreflecting pool
that hung above its so far distant bed
like a grey rainy sky above a landscape.
And between meadows, soft and full of patience,
appeared the pale strip of the single pathway,
like a long line of linen laid to bleach.

And on this single pathway they approached.

In front the slender man in the blue mantle,
gazing in dumb impatience straight before him.
His steps devoured the way in mighty chunks
they did not pause to chew; his hands were hanging,
heavy and clenched, out of the falling folds,
no longer conscious of the lightsome lyre,
the lyre which had grown into his left
like twines of rose into a branch of olive.
It seemed as though his senses were divided:
for, while his sight ran like a dog before him,
turned round, came back, and stood, time and again,
distant and waiting, at the path's next turn,
his hearing lagged behind him like a smell.
It seemed to him at times as though it stretched
back to the progress of those other two
who should be following up this whole ascent.

Dann wieder wars nur seines Steigens Nachklang
und seines Mantels Wind was hinter ihm war.
Er aber sagte sich, sie kämen doch;
sagte es laut und hörte sich verhallen.
Sie kämen doch, nur wärens zwei
die furchtbar leise gingen. Dürfte er
sich einmal wenden (wäre das Zurückschaun
nicht die Zersetzung dieses ganzen Werkes,
das erst vollbracht wird), müßte er sie sehen,
die beiden Leisen, die ihm schweigend nachgehn:

Den Gott des Ganges und der weiten Botschaft,
die Reisehaube über hellen Augen,
den schlanken Stab hertragend vor dem Leibe
und flügelschlagend an den Fußgelenken;
und seiner linken Hand gegeben: *sie*.

Die So-geliebte, daß aus einer Leier
mehr Klage kam als je aus Klagefrauen;
daß eine Welt aus Klage ward, in der
alles noch einmal da war: Wald und Tal
und Weg und Ortschaft, Feld und Fluß und Tier;
und daß um diese Klage-Welt, ganz so
wie um die andre Erde, eine Sonne
und ein gestirnter stiller Himmel ging,
ein Klage-Himmel mit entstellten Sternen—:
Diese So-geliebte.

Sie aber ging an jenes Gottes Hand,
den Schritt beschränkt von langen Leichenbändern,
unsicher, sanft und ohne Ungeduld.
Sie war in sich, wie Eine hoher Hoffnung,
und dachte nicht des Mannes, der voranging,
und nicht des Weges, der ins Leben aufstieg.

RAINER MARIA RILKE

Then once more there was nothing else behind him
but his climb's echo and his mantle's wind.
He, though, assured himself they still were coming;
said it aloud and heard it die away.
They still were coming, only they were two
that trod with fearful lightness. If he durst
but once look back (if only looking back
were not undoing of this whole enterprise
still to be done), he could not fail to see them,
the two light-footers, following him in silence:

The god of faring and of distant message,
the travelling-hood over his shining eyes,
the slender wand held out before his body,
the wings around his ankles lightly beating,
and in his left hand, as entrusted, *her*.

She, so belov'd, that from a single lyre
more mourning rose than from all women-mourners,—
that a whole world of mourning rose, wherein
all things were once more present: wood and vale
and road and hamlet, field and stream and beast,—
and that around this world of mourning turned,
even as around the other earth, a sun
and a whole silent heaven full of stars,
a heaven of mourning with disfigured stars:—
she, so beloved.

But hand in hand now with that god she walked,
her paces circumscribed by lengthy shroudings,
uncertain, gentle, and without impatience.
Wrapt in herself, like one whose time is near,
she thought not of the man who went before them,
nor of the road ascending into life.

Sie war in sich. Und ihr Gestorbensein
erfüllte sie wie Fülle.
Wie eine Frucht von Süßigkeit und Dunkel,
so war sie voll von ihrem großen Tode,
der also neu war, daß sie nichts begriff.

Sie war in einem neuen Mädchentum
und unberührbar; ihr Geschlecht war zu
wie eine junge Blume gegen Abend,
und ihre Hände waren der Vermählung
so sehr entwöhnt, daß selbst des leichten Gottes
unendlich leise, leitende Berührung
sie kränkte wie zu sehr Vertraulichkeit.

Sie war schon nicht mehr diese blonde Frau,
die in des Dichters Liedern manchmal anklang,
nicht mehr des breiten Bettes Duft und Eiland
und jenes Mannes Eigentum nicht mehr.

Sie war schon aufgelöst wie langes Haar
und hingegeben wie gefallner Regen
und ausgeteilt wie hundertfacher Vorrat.

Sie war schon Wurzel.
Und als plötzlich jäh
der Gott sie anhielt und mit Schmerz im Ausruf
die Worte sprach: Er hat sich umgewendet—
begriff sie nichts und sagte leise: *Wer?*

Fern aber, dunkel vor dem klaren Ausgang,
stand irgend jemand, dessen Angesicht
nicht zu erkennen war. Er stand und sah,
wie auf dem Streifen eines Wiesenpfades
mit trauervollem Blick der Gott der Botschaft

RAINER MARIA RILKE

Wrapt in herself she wandered. And her deadness
was filling her like fullness.
Full as a fruit with sweetness and with darkness
was she with her great death, which was so new
that for the time she could take nothing in.

She had attained a new virginity
and was intangible; her sex had closed
like a young flower at the approach of evening,
and her pale hands had grown so disaccustomed
to being a wife, that even the slim god's
endlessly gentle contact as he led her
disturbed her like a too great intimacy.

Even now she was no longer that blonde woman
who'd sometimes echoed in the poet's poems,
no longer the broad couch's scent and island,
nor yonder man's possession any longer.

She was already loosened like long hair,
and given far and wide like fallen rain,
and dealt out like a manifold supply.

She was already root.
And when, abruptly,
the god had halted her and, with an anguished
outcry, outspoke the words: He has turned round!—
she took in nothing, and said softly: Who?

But in the distance, dark in the bright exit,
someone or other stood, whose countenance
was indistinguishable. Stood and saw
how, on a strip of pathway between meadows,
with sorrow in his look, the god of message

sich schweigend wandte, der Gestalt zu folgen,
die schon zurückging dieses selben Weges,
den Schritt beschränkt von langen Leichenbändern,
unsicher, sanft und ohne Ungeduld.

RAINER MARIA RILKE

turned silently to go behind the figure
already going back by that same pathway,
its paces circumscribed by lengthy shroudings,
uncertain, gentle, and without impatience.

   J. B. Leishman

Der König von Münster

Der König war geschoren;
nun ging ihm die Krone zu weit
und bog ein wenig die Ohren,
in die von Zeit zu Zeit

gehässiges Gelärme
aus Hungermäulern fand.
Er saß, von wegen der Wärme,
auf seiner rechten Hand,

mürrisch und schwergesäßig.
Er fühlte sich nicht mehr echt:
der Herr in ihm war mäßig,
und der Beischlaf war schlecht.

RAINER MARIA RILKE

The King of Munster*

His Highness had been scalped;
his crown, now too big, pinned
his lugs down like a whelp's.
From time to time, the sound
of hunger-stoked alarm
would reach them on the wind.
He sat, to keep it warm,
upon his stitching-hand,
fat-arsed, bald and snivelling.
He knew himself unmanned;
the king in him was shrivelling
and he couldn't get a stand.

Don Paterson

*The King of Munster: John of Leyden, a former Munster tailor who became leader of that city's Anabaptist uprisings of 1534–1535. He was beheaded in 1536.

"Ausgesetzt auf den Bergen des Herzens"

Ausgesetzt auf den Bergen des Herzens. Siehe, wie klein dort,
siehe: die letzte Ortschaft der Worte, und höher,
aber wie klein auch, noch ein letztes
Gehöft von Gefühl. Erkennst du's?
Ausgesetzt auf den Bergen des Herzens. Steingrund
unter den Händen. Hier blüht wohl
einiges auf; aus stummem Absturz
blüht ein unwissendes Kraut singend hervor.
Aber der Wissende? Ach, der zu wissen begann
und schweigt nun, ausgesetzt auf den Bergen des Herzens.
Da geht wohl, heilen Bewußtseins,
manches umher, manches gesicherte Bergtier,
wechselt und weilt. Und der große geborgene Vogel
kreist um der Gipfel reine Verweigerung.—Aber
ungeborgen, hier auf den Bergen des Herzens . . .

RAINER MARIA RILKE

"Exposed on the cliffs of the heart"

Exposed on the cliffs of the heart. Look, how tiny down there,
look: the last village of words and, higher,
(but how tiny) still one last
farmhouse of feeling. Can you see it?
Exposed on the cliffs of the heart. Stoneground
under your hands. Even here, though,
something can bloom; on a silent cliff-edge
an unknowing plant blooms, singing, into the air.
But the one who knows? Ah, he began to know
and is quiet now, exposed on the cliffs of the heart.
While, with their full awareness,
many sure-footed mountain animals pass
or linger. And the great sheltered bird flies, slowly
circling, around the peak's pure denial.—But
without a shelter, here on the cliffs of the heart . . .

Stephen Mitchell

Die neunte Elegie

Warum, wenn es angeht, also die Frist des Daseins
hinzubringen, als Lorbeer, ein wenig dunkler als alles
andere Grün, mit kleinen Wellen an jedem
Blattrand (wie eines Windes Lächeln)—: warum dann
Menschliches müssen—und, Schicksal vermeidend,
sich sehnen nach Schicksal? . . .
                          Oh, nicht, weil Glück ist,
dieser voreilige Vorteil eines nahen Verlusts.
Nicht aus Neugier, oder zur Übung des Herzens,
das auch im Lorbeer wäre . . .
Aber weil Hiersein viel ist, und weil uns scheinbar
alles das Hiesige braucht, dieses Schwindende, das
seltsam uns angeht. Uns, die Schwindendsten. Einmal
jedes, nur einmal. Einmal und nichtmehr. Und wir auch
einmal. Nie wieder. Aber dieses
einmal gewesen zu sein, wenn auch nur einmal:
irdisch gewesen zu sein, scheint nicht widerrufbar.

Und so drängen wir uns und wollen es leisten,
wollens enthalten in unseren einfachen Händen,
im überfüllteren Blick und im sprachlosen Herzen.
Wollen es werden. Wem es geben? Am liebsten
alles behalten für immer . . . Ach, in den andern Bezug,
wehe, was nimmt man hinüber? Nicht das Anschaun, das hier
langsam erlernte, und kein hier Ereignetes. Keins.
Also die Schmerzen. Also vor allem das Schwersein,
also der Liebe lange Erfahrung,—also
lauter Unsägliches. Aber später,
unter den Sternen, was solls: die sind besser unsäglich.
Bringt doch der Wanderer auch vom Hange des Bergrands
nicht eine Hand voll Erde ins Tal, die allen unsägliche, sondern
ein erworbenes Wort, reines, den gelben und blaun
Enzian. Sind wir vielleicht hier, um zu sagen: Haus,
Brücke, Brunnen, Tor, Krug, Obstbaum, Fenster,—

RAINER MARIA RILKE

The Ninth Elegy

Why, when this span of life might be fleeted away
as laurel, a little darker than all
the surrounding green, with tiny waves on the border
of every leaf (like the smile of a wind):—oh, why
have to be human, and, shunning Destiny,
long for Destiny? . . .

                         Not because happiness really
exists, that precipitate profit of imminent loss.
Not out of curiosity, not just to practise the heart,
that could still be there in laurel . . .
But because being here is much, and because all this
that's here, so fleeting, seems to require us and strangely
concerns us. Us the most fleeting of all. Just once,
everything, only for once. Once and no more. And we, too,
once. And never again. But this
having been once, though only once,
having been once on earth—can it ever be cancelled?

And so we keep pressing on and trying to perform it,
trying to contain it within our simple hands,
in the more and more crowded gaze, in the speechless heart.
Trying to become it. To give it to whom? We'd rather
hold on to it all for ever . . . But into the other relation,
what, alas! do we carry across? Not the beholding we've here
slowly acquired, and no here occurrence. Not one.
Sufferings, then. Above all, the hardness of life,
the long experience of love; in fact,
purely untellable things. But later,
under the stars, what use? the more deeply untellable stars?
Yet the wanderer too doesn't bring from mountain to valley
a handful of earth, of for all untellable earth, but only
a word he has won, pure, the yellow and blue
gentian. Are we, perhaps, *here* just for saying: House,
Bridge, Fountain, Gate, Jug, Fruit tree, Window,—

höchstens: Säule, Turm . . . aber zu sagen, verstehs,
oh zu sagen so, wie selber die Dinge niemals
innig meinten zu sein. Ist nicht die heimliche List
dieser verschwiegenen Erde, wenn sie die Liebenden drängt,
daß sich in ihrem Gefühl jedes und jedes entzückt?
Schwelle: was ists für zwei
Liebende, daß sie die eigne ältere Schwelle der Tür
ein wenig verbrauchen, auch sie, nach den vielen vorher
und vor den künftigen . . . , leicht.

Hier ist des Säglichen Zeit, hier seine Heimat.
Sprich und bekenn. Mehr als je
fallen die Dinge dahin, die erlebbaren, denn,
was sie verdrängend ersetzt, ist ein Tun ohne Bild.
Tun unter Krusten, die willig zerspringen, sobald
innen das Handeln entwächst und sich anders begrenzt.
Zwischen den Hämmern besteht
unser Herz, wie die Zunge
zwischen den Zähnen, die doch,
dennoch die preisende bleibt.

Preise dem Engel die Welt, nicht die unsägliche, ihm
kannst du nicht großtun mit herrlich Erfühltem; im Weltall,
wo er fühlender fühlt, bist du ein Neuling. Drum zeig
ihm das Einfache, das, von Geschlecht zu Geschlechtern gestaltet,
als ein Unsriges lebt neben der Hand und im Blick.
Sag ihm die Dinge. Er wird staunender stehn; wie du standest
bei dem Seiler in Rom, oder beim Töpfer am Nil.
Zeig ihm, wie glücklich ein Ding sein kann, wie schuldlos und unser,
wie selbst das klagende Leid rein zur Gestalt sich entschließt,
dient als ein Ding, oder stirbt in ein Ding—, und jenseits
selig der Geige entgeht. Und diese, von Hingang
lebenden Dinge verstehn, daß du sie rühmst; vergänglich,
traun sie ein Rettendes uns, den Vergänglichsten, zu.

RAINER MARIA RILKE

possibly: Pillar, Tower? . . . but for *saying*, remember,
oh, for such saying as never the things themselves
hoped so intensely to be. Is not the secret purpose
of this sly Earth, in urging a pair of lovers,
just to make everything leap with ecstasy in them?
Threshold: what does it mean
to a pair of lovers, that they should be wearing their own
worn threshold a little, they too, after the many before,
before the many to come, . . . as a matter of course!

Here is the time for the Tellable, *here* is its home.
Speak and proclaim. More than ever
things we can live with are falling away, for that
which is oustingly taking their place is an imageless act.
Act under crusts, that will readily split as soon
as the doing within outgrows them and takes a new outline.
Between the hammers lives on
our heart, as between the teeth
the tongue, which, in spite of all,
still continues to praise.

Praise this world to the Angel, not the untellable: you
can't impress him with the splendour you've felt; in the cosmos
where he more feelingly feels you're only a novice. So show him
some simple thing, refashioned by age after age,
till it lives in our hands and eyes as a part of ourselves.
Tell him *things*. He'll stand more astonished: as you did
beside the roper in Rome or the potter in Egypt.
Show him how happy a thing can be, how guileless and ours;
how even the moaning of grief purely determines on form,
serves as a thing, or dies into a thing,—to escape
to a bliss beyond the fiddle. These things that live on departure
understand when you praise them: fleeting, they look for
rescue through something in us, the most fleeting of all.

Wollen, wir sollen sie ganz im unsichtbarn Herzen verwandeln
in—o unendlich—in uns! wer wir am Ende auch seien.

Erde, ist es nicht dies, was du willst: unsichtbar
in uns erstehn?—Ist es dein Traum nicht,
einmal unsichtbar zu sein?—Erde! unsichtbar!
Was, wenn Verwandlung nicht, ist dein drängender Auftrag?
Erde, du liebe, ich will. Oh glaub, es bedürfte
nicht deiner Frühlinge mehr, mich dir zu gewinnen, einer,
ach, ein einziger ist schon dem Blute zu viel.
Namenlos bin ich zu dir entschlossen, von weit her.
Immer warst du im Recht, und dein heiliger Einfall
ist der vertrauliche Tod.
Siehe, ich lebe. Woraus? Weder Kindheit noch Zukunft
werden weniger . . . Überzähliges Dasein
entspringt mir im Herzen.

RAINER MARIA RILKE

Want us to change them entirely, within our invisible hearts,
into—oh, endlessly—into ourselves! Whosoever we are.

Earth, is it not just this that you want: to arise
invisibly in us? Is not your dream
to be one day invisible? Earth! invisible!
What is your urgent command, if not transformation?
Earth, you darling, I will! Oh, believe me, you need
no more of your spring-times to win me over: a single one,
ah, one, is already more than my blood can endure.
Beyond all names I am yours, and have been for ages.
You were always right, and your holiest inspiration
is Death, that friendly Death.
Look, I am living. On what? Neither childhood nor future
are growing less . . . Supernumerous existence
wells up in my heart.

J. B. Leishman and Stephen Spender

Sonette an Orpheus II, 4

O dieses ist das Tier, das es nicht giebt.
Sie wußtens nicht und habens jeden Falls
—sein Wandeln, seine Haltung, seinen Hals,
bis in des stillen Blickes Licht—geliebt.

Zwar *war* es nicht. Doch weil sie's liebten, ward
ein reines Tier. Sie ließen immer Raum.
Und in dem Raume, klar und ausgespart,
erhob es leicht sein Haupt und brauchte kaum

zu sein. Sie nährten es mit keinem Korn,
nur immer mit der Möglichkeit, es sei.
Und die gab solche Stärke an das Tier,

daß es aus sich ein Stirnhorn trieb. Ein Horn.
Zu einer Jungfrau kam es weiß herbei—
und war im Silber-Spiegel und in ihr.

RAINER MARIA RILKE

The Unicorn

This, then, is the beast that has never actually been:
not having seen one, they prized in any case
its perfect poise, its throat, the straightforward gaze
it gave them back—so straightforward, so serene.

Since it had never been, it was all the more
unsullied. And they allowed it such latitude
that, in a clearing in the wood,
it raised its head as if its essence shrugged off mere

existence. They brought it on, not with oats or corn,
but with the chance, however slight,
that it might come into its own. This gave it such strength

that from its brow there sprang a horn. A single horn.
Only when it met a maiden's white with white
would it be bodied out in her, in her mirror's full length.

Paul Muldoon

Wasser

Wasser
darauf Wellen,
darauf ein Boot,
darauf ein Weib,
darauf ein Mann.

PAUL KLEE, 1879–1940

Water

Water,
topped by waves,
topped by a boat,
topped by a woman,
topped by a man.

Harriet Watts

Fahrt über die Kölner Rheinbrücke bei Nacht

Der Schnellzug tastet sich und stößt die Dunkelheit entlang.
Kein Stern will vor. Die ganze Welt ist nur ein enger, nachtumschienter
    Minengang,
Darein zuweilen Förderstellen blauen Lichtes jähe Horizonte reißen—
    Feuerkreis
Von Kugellampen, Dächern, Schloten, dampfend, strömend . . . nur
    sekundenweis . . .
Und wieder alles schwarz. Als führen wir ins Eingeweid der Nacht zur
    Schicht.
Nun taumeln Lichter her . . . verirrt, trostlos vereinsamt . . . mehr und
    sammeln sich . . . und werden dicht.
Gerippe grauer Häuserfronten liegen bloß, im Zwielicht bleichend,
    tot—etwas muß kommen . . . o, ich fühl es schwer
Im Hirn. Eine Beklemmung singt im Blut. Dann dröhnt der Boden
    plötzlich wie ein Meer:
Wir fliegen, aufgehoben, königlich durch nachtentrissne Luft, hoch
    übern Strom. O Biegung der Millionen Lichter, stumme Wacht,
Vor deren blitzender Parade schwer die Wasser abwärts rollen. Endloses
    Spalier, zum Gruß gestellt bei Nacht!
Wie Fackeln stürmend! Freudiges! Salut von Schiffen über blauer See!
    Bestirntes Fest!
Wimmelnd, mit hellen Augen hingedrängt! Bis wo die Stadt mit letzten
    Häusern ihren Gast entläßt.
Und dann die langen Einsamkeiten. Nackte Ufer. Stille. Nacht.
    Besinnung. Einkehr. Kommunion. Und Glut und Drang.
Zum Letzten, Segnenden. Zum Zeugungsfest. Zur Wollust. Zum Gebet.
    Zum Meer. Zum Untergang.

ERNST STADLER, 1883–1914

On Crossing the Rhine Bridge at Cologne by Night

The express train gropes and thrusts its way through darkness. Not a star
    is out.
The whole world's nothing but a mine-road the night has railed about
In which at times conveyors of blue light tear sudden horizons: fiery
    sphere
Of arc-lamps, roofs and chimneys, steaming, streaming—for seconds
    only clear,
And all is black again. As though we drove into Night's entrails to the
    seam.
Now lights reel into view . . . astray, disconsolate and lonely . . . more . . .
    and gather . . . and densely gleam.
Skeletons of grey housefronts are laid bare, grown pale in the twilight,
    dead—something must happen . . . O heavily
I feel it weigh on my brain. An oppression sings in the blood. Then all at
    once the ground resounds like the sea:
And royally upborne we fly through air from darkness wrested, high up
    above the river. O curve of the million lights, mute guard at the sight
Of whose flashing parade the waters go roaring down. Endless line
    presenting arms by night!
Surging on like torches! Joyful! Salute of ships over the blue sea! Star-
    jewelled, festive array!
Teeming, bright-eyed urged on! Till where the town with its last houses
    sees its guest away.
And then the long solitudes. Bare banks. And Silence. Night. Reflection.
    Self-questioning. Communion. And ardor outward-flowing.
To the end that blesses. To conception's rite. To pleasure's
    consummation. To prayer. To the sea. To self's undoing.

Michael Hamburger

aus **Morgue**

KLEINE ASTER

Ein ersoffener Bierfahrer wurde auf den Tisch gestemmt.
Irgendeiner hatte ihm eine dunkelhellila Aster
zwischen die Zähne geklemmt.
Als ich von der Brust aus
unter der Haut
mit einem langen Messer
Zunge und Gaumen herausschnitt,
muß ich sie angestoßen haben, denn sie glitt
in das nebenliegende Gehirn.
Ich packte sie ihm in die Brusthöhle
zwischen die Holzwolle,
als man zunähte.
Trinke dich satt in deiner Vase!
Ruhe sanft,
kleine Aster!

GOTTFRIED BENN, 1886–1956

from Morgue

I. LITTLE ASTER

A drowned truck-driver was propped on the slab.
Someone had stuck a lavender aster
between his teeth.
As I cut out the tongue and the palate,
through the chest
under the skin,
with my long knife,
I must have touched the flower, for it slid
into the brain lying next.
I packed it into the cavity of the chest
among the excelsior
as it was sewn up.
Drink yourself full in your vase!
Rest softly,
little aster!

Babette Deutsch

SCHÖNE JUGEND

Der Mund eines Mädchens, das lange im Schilf gelegen hatte,
sah so angeknabbert aus.
Als man die Brust aufbrach, war die Speiseröhre so löcherig.
Schließlich in einer Laube unter dem Zwerchfell
fand man ein Nest von jungen Ratten.
Ein kleines Schwesterchen lag tot.
Die andern lebten von Leber und Niere,
tranken das kalte Blut und hatten
hier eine schöne Jugend verlebt.
Und schön und schnell kam auch ihr Tod:
Man warf sie allesamt ins Wasser.
Ach, wie die kleinen Schnauzen quietschten!

GOTTFRIED BENN

II. LOVELY CHILDHOOD

The mouth of a girl who had long lain among the reeds looked gnawed
    away.
As the breast was cut open, the gullet showed full of holes.
Finally in a cavity below the diaphragm
a nest of young rats was discovered.
One little sister lay dead.
The others thrived on liver and kidneys,
drank the cold blood and
enjoyed a lovely childhood here.
And sweet and swift came their death also:
They were all thrown into the water together.
Oh, how the little muzzles squeaked!

Babette Deutsch

Nachtcafé

824: Der Frauen Liebe und Leben.
Das Cello trinkt rasch mal. Die Flöte
rülpst tief drei Takte lang: das schöne Abendbrot.
Die Trommel liest den Kriminalroman zu Ende.

Grüne Zähne, Pickel im Gesicht
winkt einer Lidrandentzündung.

Fett im Haar
spricht zu offenem Mund mit Rachenmandel
Glaube Liebe Hoffnung um den Hals.

Junger Kropf ist Sattelnase gut.
Er bezahlt für sie drei Biere.

Bartflechte kauft Nelken,
Doppelkinn zu erweichen.

B-moll: die 35. Sonate.
Zwei Augen brüllen auf:
Spritzt nicht das Blut von Chopin in den Saal,
damit das Pack drauf rumlatscht!
Schluß! He, Gigi!—

Die Tür fließt hin: Ein Weib.
Wüste ausgedörrt. Kanaanitisch braun.
Keusch. Höhlenreich. Ein Duft kommt mit.
                              Kaum Duft.
Es ist nur eine süße Vorwölbung der Luft
gegen mein Gehirn.

Eine Fettleibigkeit trippelt hinterher.

GOTTFRIED BENN

Night Café

824: Lives and Loves of Women.
The cello takes a quick drink. The flute
belches expansively for three beats: good old dinner.
The timpani is desperate to get to the end of his thriller.

Mossed teeth and pimple face
wave to incipient stye.

Greasy hair
talks to open mouth with adenoids
Faith Love Hope round her neck.

Young goitre has a crush on saddlenose.
He treats her to onetwothreee beers.

Sycosis brings carnations
to melt the heart of double chin.

B flat minor: the 35th Sonata.
Two eyes yell:
stop hosing the blood of Chopin round the room
for that rabble to slosh around in!
Enough! Hey, Gigi!—

The door melts away: a woman.
Dry desert. Canaanite tan.
Chaste. Concavities. A scent accompanies her,
                    less a scent
than a sweet pressure of the air
against my brain.

An obesity waddles after.

   Michael Hofmann

D-Zug

Braun wie Kognak. Braun wie Laub. Rotbraun. Malaiengelb.
D-Zug Berlin-Trelleborg und die Ostseebäder.

Fleisch, das nackt ging.
Bis in den Mund gebräunt vom Meer.
Reif gesenkt, zu griechischem Glück.
In Sichel-Sehnsucht: Wie weit der Sommer ist!
Vorletzter Tag des neunten Monats schon!

Stoppel und letzte Mandel lechzt in uns.
Entfaltungen, das Blut, die Müdigkeiten,
die Georginennähe macht uns wirr.

Männerbraun stürzt sich auf Frauenbraun:

Eine Frau ist etwas für eine Nacht.
Und wenn es schön war, noch für die nächste!
Oh! Und dann wieder dies Bei-sich-selbst-Sein!
Diese Stummheiten! Dies Getriebenwerden!

Eine Frau ist etwas mit Geruch.
Unsägliches! Stirb hin! Resede.
Darin ist Süden, Hirt und Meer.
An jedem Abhang lehnt ein Glück.

Frauenhellbraun taumelt an Männerdunkelbraun:

Halte mich! Du, ich falle!
Ich bin im Nacken so müde.
Oh, dieser fiebernde süße
letzte Geruch aus den Gärten.

GOTTFRIED BENN

Express Train

Brown as cognac. Brown as leaves. Red-brown. Malayan yellow.
Express train Berlin-Trelleborg and the Baltic Sea resorts.

Flesh, that went naked.
Tanned to the very lips by the sea.
Deeply ripe, for Grecian pleasure.
And yearning for the scythe: how long the summer seems!
Almost the end of the ninth month already!

Stubble and the last almond thirst in us.
Unfoldings, the blood, the weariness,
The nearness of dahlias confuses us.

Man-brown hurls itself upon woman-brown:

A woman is something for a night.
And if it was good, for the next night too!
Oh, and then again this being by oneself!
These silences! This letting oneself drift!

A woman is something with fragrance.
Unspeakable. Dissolve. Reseda.
In her the south, shepherd and sea.
On every slope a pleasure lies.

Woman-light-brown reels towards man-dark-brown:

Hold me, dear; I'm falling.
I'm so weary at the neck.
Oh, this feverish sweet
Last fragrance blown from the gardens.

   Michael Hamburger

Chopin

Nicht sehr ergiebig im Gespräch,
Ansichten waren nicht seine Stärke,
Ansichten reden drum herum,
wenn Delacroix Theorien entwickelte,
wurde er unruhig, er seinerseits konnte
die Notturnos nicht begründen.

Schwacher Liebhaber;
Schatten in Nohant,
wo George Sands Kinder
keine erzieherischen Ratschläge
von ihm annahmen.

Brustkrank in jener Form
mit Blutungen und Narbenbildung,
die sich lange hinzieht;
stiller Tod
im Gegensatz zu einem
mit Schmerzparoxysmen
oder durch Gewehrsalven:
man rückte den Flügel (Erard) an die Tür
und Delphine Potocka
sang ihm in der letzten Stunde
ein Veilchenlied.

Nach England reiste er mit drei Flügeln:
Pleyel, Erard, Broadwood,
spielte für zwanzig Guineen abends
eine Viertelstunde
bei Rothschilds, Wellingtons, im Strafford House
und vor zahllosen Hosenbändern;
verdunkelt von Müdigkeit und Todesnähe
kehrte er heim
auf den Square d'Orléans.

GOTTFRIED BENN

Chopin

Not much of a conversationalist,
ideas weren't his strong suit,
ideas miss the point,
when Delacroix expounded his theories
it made him nervous, he for his part
could offer no explanation of the Nocturnes.

A poor lover;
mere shadow in Nohant
where George Sand's children
rejected his attempts
at discipline.

His tuberculosis
took the chronic form,
with repeated bleeding and scarring;
a creeping death,
as opposed to one
in convulsions of agony
or by firing squad:
the piano (Erard) was pushed back against the door
and Delphine Potocka
sang him
a violet song in his last hour.

He took three pianos with him to England:
Pleyel, Erard, Broadwood,
for twenty guineas
he would give fifteen-minute recitals in the evenings
at the Rothschilds' and the Wellingtons', in Strafford House
to the assembled cummerbunds;
then, dark with fatigue and imminent death,
he went home
to the Square d'Orleans.

Dann verbrennt er seine Skizzen
und Manuskripte,
nur keine Restbestände, Fragmente, Notizen,
diese verräterischen Einblicke—
sagte zum Schluß:
"Meine Versuche sind nach Maßgabe dessen vollendet,
was mir zu erreichen möglich war."

Spielen sollte jeder Finger
mit der seinem Bau entsprechenden Kraft,
der vierte ist der schwächste
(nur siamesisch zum Mittelfinger).
Wenn er begann, lagen sie
auf e, fis, gis, h, c.

Wer je bestimmte Präludien
von ihm hörte,
sei es in Landhäusern oder
in einem Höhengelände
oder aus offenen Terrassentüren
beispielsweise aus einem Sanatorium,
wird es schwer vergessen.

Nie eine Oper komponiert,
keine Symphonie,
nur diese tragischen Progressionen
aus artistischer Überzeugung
und mit einer kleinen Hand.

GOTTFRIED BENN

Then he burned his sketches
and manuscripts,
didn't want any leftover scraps
betraying him—
at the end he said:
"I have taken my experiment
as far as it was possible for me to go."

Each finger was to play
to no more than its natural strength,
the fourth being the weakest
(twinned with the middle finger).
At the start, they occupied the keys
of E, F sharp, G sharp, B and C.

Anyone hearing
certain of his Preludes
in country seats or
at altitude,
through open French windows
on the terrace, say, of a sanatorium,
will not easily forget it.

He composed no operas,
no symphonies,
only those tragic progressions
from artistic conviction
and with a small hand.

Michael Hofmann

Kleines süßes Gesicht

Kleines süßes Gesicht,
eingesunken schon vor Vergängnis,
schneeblaß und tötlich,
Ausschütter großen Leids,
wenn du hingegangen
bald—

ach, wie wir spielten
entwicklungsvergessen,
Rück- und Weitblicke
abgefallen von unseren Rändern,
nichts lebend
außer dem Umkreis
unserer Laute!

Beschränkt! Doch dann
einmal der astverborgenen Männer
Oliven-Niederschlagen,
die Haufen gären.
Einmal Weine vom Löwengolf
in Rauchkammern, mit Seewasser beschönigt.
Oder Eukalyptus, Riesen, hundertsechsundfünfzig Meter hoch
und das zitternde Zwielicht in ihren Wäldern.
Einmal Cotroceni—
nicht mehr!

Kleines Gesicht
Schneeflocke
immer so weiß
und dann die Ader an der Schläfe
vom Blau der Traubenhyazinthe,
die ligurische,
die bisamartig duftet.

GOTTFRIED BENN

Little Sweet Face

Little sweet face,
shrunken already in transit,
snowy-, nearly deathly pale,
great outpouring of grief
when you shortly passed
away—

We played together
quite unmindful of our state of development
all looks back and out
cropped,
living, experiencing nothing
outside the charmed circle
of our own noises!

Hobbled—blinkered! But once,
the men beating the olive-trees, obscured by branches,
piles of fruit set to ripen.
Once, wine from the Gulf of Lions
in smoky vaults, accented with sea water.
Or giant eucalypts, 400 feet high,
and the trembling light under their crowns.
Once to Cotroceni—
once only.

Little face
snowflake
always so white
and the blue vein at the temple
Ligurian grape-hyacinth
blue,
musk-scented.

Michael Hofmann

Gewisse Lebensabende

I

Du brauchst nicht immer die Kacheln zu scheuern, Hendrickje,
mein Auge trinkt sich selbst,
trinkt sich zu Ende—
aber an anderen Getränken mangelt es—
dort die Buddhastatue,
chinesischen Haingott,
gegen eine Kelle Hulstkamp,
bitte!

Nie etwas gemalt
in Frostweiß oder Schlittschuhläuferblau
oder dem irischen Grün,
aus dem der Purpur schimmert—
immer nur meine Eintönigkeit,
mein Schattenzwang—
nicht angenehm,
diesen Weg so deutlich zu verfolgen.

Größe—wo?
Ich nehme den Griffel
und gewisse Dinge stehn dann da
auf Papier, Leinwand
oder ähnlichem Zunder—
Resultat: Buddhabronze gegen Sprit—
aber Huldigungen unter Blattpflanzen,
Bankett der Pinselgilde—:
was fürs Genre—!

. . . Knarren,
Schäfchen, die quietschen,
Abziehbilder
flämisch, rubenisch

GOTTFRIED BENN

The Evenings of Certain Lives

I

You needn't always be scrubbing the tiles, Hendrickje,
my eye drinks itself,
drinks itself dry—
but then it has no other liquor—
the statue of Buddha over there,
Chinese god of the bosk,
as against a good tot of Hulstkamp,
I ask you!

Never painted a thing
in frost-white or skater's blue
or in Irish green
with the purple flickering out of it—
only my own monotony always—
my coactive shadows—
it's not pleasant
to follow this bent with such distinctness.

Greatness—where?
I take my pencil
and certain things emerge, stand there
on paper, canvas
or similar tinder—
result: bronze Buddha as against hooch—
all those obeisances under indoor plants,
banquet of the dimwit daubers' guild—
give it to the genre painter!

. . . Rattles,
lambs bleating,
transfers,
Flemish, Rubenesque,

für die Enkelchen—!
(ebensolche Idioten—!)

Ah—Hulstkamp—
Wärmezentrum,
Farbenmittelpunkt,
mein Schattenbraun—
Bartstoppelfluidum um Herz und Auge—.

II

Der Kamin raucht,
—schnäuzt sich der Schwan vom Avon—
die Stubben sind naß,
klamme Nacht, Leere vermählt mit Zugluft—
Schluß mit den Gestalten,
übervölkert die Erde
reichlicher Pfirsichfall, vier Rosenblüten
pro anno—
ausgestreut,
auf die Bretter geschoben
von dieser Hand,
faltig geworden
und mit erschlafften Adern!

Alle die Ophelias, Julias,
bekränzt, silbern, auch mörderisch—
alle die weichen Münder, die Seufzer,
die ich aus ihnen herausmanipulierte—
die ersten Aktricen längst Qualm,
Rost, ausgelaugt, Rattenpudding—
auch Herzens-Ariel bei den Elementen.

GOTTFRIED BENN

for small grandchildren—
(likewise idiots!—)

Ah—Hulstkamp—
midpoint of warmth,
center of colors,
my shadow brown—
aura of unshaved bristle round heart and eye—

II

The fire is smoking
—the Swan of Avon blows his nose—
the tree-stumps are wet,
clammy night, emptiness suffused with draughts—
have done with characters,
earth overpopulated
by copious fall of peach, four rosebuds
pro anno—
strewn far and wide,
thrust on the boards
by this hand,
with its wrinkles now,
and its exhausted veins.

All the Ophelias, Juliets
wreathed, silvery, also murderous—
all the soft mouths, the sighs
I manipulated out of them—
the first actresses long since vapor,
rust, lixiviated, rats' pudding—
even the heart's Ariel off to the elements.

Die Epoche zieht sich den Bratenrock aus.
Diese Lord- und Läuseschädel,
ihre Gedankengänge,
die ich ins Extrem trieb—
meine Herren Geschichtsproduzenten
alles Kronen- und Szepteranalphabeten,
Großmächte des Weltraums
wie Fledermaus oder Papierdrachen!

Sir Goon schrieb neulich an mich:
"der Rest ist Schweigen":—
ich glaube, das ist von mir,
kann nur von mir sein,
Dante tot—eine große Leere
zwischen den Jahrhunderten
bis zu meinen Wortschatzzitaten—

aber wenn sie fehlten,
der Plunder nie aufgeschlagen,
die Buden, die Schafotte, die Schellen
nie geklungen hätten—:
Lücken—?? Vielleicht Zahnlücken,
aber das große Affengebiß
mahlte weiter
seine Leere, vermählt mit Zugluft—
die Stubben sind naß
und der Butler schnarcht in Porterträumen.

GOTTFRIED BENN

The age takes off its Sunday best.
These duke and desperado skulls,
their trains of thought
I drove to the extreme—
my history-making gentlemen
all illiterates of crown and sceptre,
major powers of space,
like flittermouse or paper kite!

Sir Goon recently wrote to me:
"The rest is silence."
I think I said that myself,
nobody else could have said it,
Dante dead—a great emptiness
between the centuries
up to the quotations from my vocabulary—

but if they were missing,
if all that stuff had never been turned out,
the booths and the gallowtrees, if the bells
had never jingled—:
gaps then? Gaps possibly in the teeth,
but the ape's great jaws
would go on grinding
their emptiness the draughts suffuse—
the tree-stumps are wet,
and the butler snores in his porter dreams.

  Christopher Middleton

Fragmente

Fragmente,
Seelenauswürfe,
Blutgerinnsel des zwanzigsten Jahrhunderts—

Narben—gestörter Kreislauf der Schöpfungsfrühe,
die historischen Religionen von fünf Jahrhunderten zertrümmert,
die Wissenschaft: Risse im Parthenon,
Planck rann mit seiner Quantentheorie
zu Kepler und Kierkegaard neu getrübt zusammen—

aber Abende gab es, die gingen in den Farben
des Allvaters, lockeren, weitwallenden,
unumstößlich in ihrem Schweigen
geströmten Blaus,
Farbe der Introvertierten,
da sammelte man sich
die Hände auf das Knie gestützt
bäuerlich, einfach
und stillem Trunk ergeben
bei den Harmonikas der Knechte—

und andere
gehetzt von inneren Konvoluten,
Wölbungsdrängen,
Stilbaukompressionen
oder Jagden nach Liebe.

Ausdruckskrisen und Anfälle von Erotik:
das ist der Mensch von heute,
das Innere ein Vakuum,
die Kontinuität der Persönlichkeit
wird gewahrt von den Anzügen,
die bei gutem Stoff zehn Jahre halten.

GOTTFRIED BENN

Fragments

Fragments,
soul flotsam,
coagulates of the twentieth century—

scars—break in flow from the dawn of creation,
the historical religions of five centuries in smithereens,
science: cracks in the Parthenon,
Planck running to Kepler and Kierkegaard
with the fresh murk of his quantum theory—

but there were evenings robed in the colours
of the Almighty, loose, flowing,
incontrovertible in the silence
of their streaming blues,
colour of introverts,
there I sat
hands propped on knees
like a farmer,
quietly nursing my drink
while the labourers played harmonicas—

and others
are driven by inner whorls,
convolutes,
architectonic compressions
or amours.

Crises of expression and spasms of eros:
that's the man of today,
the inside a vacuum,
the continuity of personality
provided by his suit,
which with stout cloth might be good for ten years.

Der Rest Fragmente,
halbe Laute,
Melodienansätze aus Nachbarhäusern,
Negerspirituals
oder Ave Marias.

GOTTFRIED BENN

The rest fragments,
mi-voix,
snatches of melody from next door,
Negro spirituals
or Ave Marias.

    Michael Hofmann

Blaue Stunde

I

Ich trete in die dunkelblaue Stunde—
da ist der Flur, die Kette schließt sich zu
und nun im Raum ein Rot auf einem Munde
und eine Schale später Rosen—du!

Wir wissen beide, jene Worte,
die jeder oft zu anderen sprach und trug,
sind zwischen uns wie nichts und fehl am Orte:
dies ist das Ganze und der letzte Zug.

Das Schweigende ist so weit vorgeschritten
und füllt den Raum und denkt sich selber zu
die Stunde—nichts gehofft und nichts gelitten—
mit ihrer Schale später Rosen—du.

II

Dein Haupt verfließt, ist weiß und will sich hüten,
indessen sammelt sich auf deinem Mund
die ganze Lust, der Purpur und die Blüten
aus deinem angeströmten Ahnengrund.

Du bist so weiß, man denkt, du wirst zerfallen
vor lauter Schnee, vor lauter Blütenlos,
totweiße Rosen Glied für Glied—Korallen
nur auf den Lippen, schwer und wundengroß.

Du bist so weich, du gibst von etwas Kunde,
von einem Glück aus Sinken und Gefahr
in einer blauen, dunkelblauen Stunde
und wenn sie ging, weiß keiner, ob sie war.

GOTTFRIED BENN

Blue Hour

I

I enter the deep blue hour—
here is the landing, the chain shuts behind
and now in the room only carmine on a mouth
and a bowl of late roses—you!

We both know, those words
that we both spoke and often offered others
are of no account and out of place between us:
this is everything and endgame.

Silence has advanced so far
it fills the room and seals it shut
the hour—nothing hoped and nothing suffered—
with its bowl of late roses—you.

II

Your face blurs, is white and fragile,
meanwhile there collects on your mouth
all of desire, the purple and the blossoms
from some ancestral flotsam stock.

You are so pale, I think you might disintegrate
in a snowdrift, in unblooming
deathly white roses, one by one—coral
only on your lips, heavy and like a wound.

You are so soft, you portend something
of happiness, of submersion and danger
in a blue, a deep blue hour
and when it's gone, no one knows if it was.

III

Ich frage dich, du bist doch eines andern,
was trägst du mir die späten Rosen zu?
Du sagst, die Träume gehn, die Stunden wandern,
was ist das alles: er und ich und du?

"Was sich erhebt, das will auch wieder enden,
was sich erlebt—wer weiß denn das genau,
die Kette schließt, man schweigt in diesen Wänden
und dort die Weite, hoch und dunkelblau."

GOTTFRIED BENN

III

I remind you, you are another's,
what are you doing bearing me these late roses?
You say dreams bleach, hours wander,
what is all this: he and I and you?

"What arises and arouses, it all comes to an end,
what happens—who exactly knows,
the chain falls shut, we are silent in these walls,
and outside is all of space, lofty and dark blue."

Michael Hofmann

Teils–teils

In meinem Elternhaus hingen keine Gainsboroughs
wurde auch kein Chopin gespielt
ganz amusisches Gedankenleben
mein Vater war einmal im Theater gewesen
Anfang des Jahrhunderts
Wildenbruchs "Haubenlerche"
davon zehrten wir
das war alles.

Nun längst zu Ende
graue Herzen, graue Haare
der Garten in polnischem Besitz
die Gräber teils-teils
aber alle slawisch,
Oder-Neiße-Linie
für Sarginhalte ohne Belang
die Kinder denken an sie
die Gatten auch noch eine Weile
teils-teils
bis sie weitermüssen
Sela, Psalmenende.

Heute noch in einer Großstadtnacht
Caféterrasse
Sommersterne,
vom Nebentisch
Hotelqualitäten in Frankfurt
Vergleiche,
die Damen unbefriedigt
wenn ihre Sehnsucht Gewicht hätte
wöge jede drei Zentner.

Aber ein Fluidum! Heiße Nacht
à la Reiseprospekt und

GOTTFRIED BENN

Par ci, par là

There were no Gainsboroughs hanging in my parents' house
and no one played Chopin
perfectly philistrous intellectual life
my father had been to the theatre once
in the early century
Wildenbruch's "Crested Lark"
that was our pabulum
there was nothing else.

All long gone now
grey hearts, grey hair
the garden in Polish hands
the graves *par ci, par là*
but all on the Slavic side
Oder-Neisse Line
inapplicable to the contents of coffins
the children continue to think about them
the spouses too for a while
par ci, par là
till it's time for them to move on
Selah, end of psalm.

Even now in the big city night
café terrace
summer stars
from the next door table
assessments
of hotels in Frankfurt
the ladies frustrated
if their desires had mass
they would each of them weigh twenty stone.

But the electricity in the air! Balmy night
à la travel brochure and

die Ladies treten aus ihren Bildern:
unwahrscheinliche Beauties
langbeinig, hoher Wasserfall
über ihre Hingabe kann man sich gar nicht erlauben
nachzudenken.

Ehepaare fallen demgegenüber ab,
kommen nicht an, Bälle gehn ins Netz,
er raucht, sie dreht ihre Ringe,
überhaupt nachdenkenswert
Verhältnis von Ehe und Mannesschaffen
Lähmung oder Hochtrieb.

Fragen, Fragen! Erinnerungen in einer Sommernacht
hingeblinzelt, hingestrichen,
in meinem Elternhaus hingen keine Gainsboroughs
nun alles abgesunken
teils-teils das Ganze
Sela, Psalmenende.

GOTTFRIED BENN

the girls step out of their pictures
improbable lovelies
legs up to here, a waterfall,
their surrender is something one daren't even begin
to contemplate.

Married couples by comparison disappoint,
don't cut it, fail to clear the net,
he smokes, she twists her rings,
worth considering
the whole relationship between marriage and creativity,
stifling or galvanizing.

Questions, questions! Scribbled nictitations
on a summer night,
there were no Gainsboroughs hanging in my parents' house
now everything has gone under,
the whole thing *par ci, par là,*
Selah, end of psalm.

    Michael Hofmann

Menschen getroffen

Ich habe Menschen getroffen, die,
wenn man sie nach ihrem Namen fragte,
schüchtern—als ob sie garnicht beanspruchen könnten,
auch noch eine Benennung zu haben—
"Fräulein Christian" antworteten und dann:
"wie der Vorname" sie wollten einem die Erfassung erleichtern,
kein schwieriger Name wie "Popiol" oder "Babendererde"—
"wie der Vorname"—bitte, belasten Sie Ihr Erinnerungsvermögen nicht!

Ich habe Menschen getroffen, die
mit Eltern und vier Geschwistern in einer Stube
aufwuchsen, nachts, die Finger in den Ohren,
am Küchenherde lernten,
hochkamen, äußerlich schön und ladylike wie Gräfinnen—
und innerlich sanft und fleißig wie Nausikaa,
die reine Stirn der Engel trugen.

Ich habe mich oft gefragt und keine Antwort gefunden,
woher das Sanfte und das Gute kommt,
weiß es auch heute nicht und muß nun gehn.

GOTTFRIED BENN

People Met

I have met people who, when asked what their names were,
Apologetically, as if they had no right to claim one's attention
Even with an appellation, would answer,
"Miss Vivian," then add, "just like the Christian name";
They wanted to make things easier, no complicated names
Like Popkiss or Umpleby-Dunball—
"Just like the Christian name"—so please do not burden your memory!

I have met people who grew up in a single room together with
Parents and four brothers and sisters; they studied by night,
Their fingers in their ears, beside the kitchen range;
They became eminent,
Outwardly beautiful, veritable *grandes dames*, and
Inwardly gentle and active as Nausicaa,
With brows clear as angels' brows.

Often I have asked myself, but found no answer,
Where gentleness and goodness can possibly come from;
Even today I can't tell, and it's time to be gone.

Christopher Middleton

Hör zu

Hör zu, so wird der letzte Abend sein,
wo du noch ausgehn kannst: du rauchst die "Juno,"
"Würzburger Hofbräu" drei, und liest die Uno,
wie sie der "Spiegel" sieht, du sitzt allein

an kleinem Tisch, an abgeschlossenem Rund
dicht an der Heizung, denn du liebst das Warme.
Um dich das Menschentum und sein Gebarme,
das Ehepaar und der verhaßte Hund.

Mehr bist du nicht, kein Haus, kein Hügel dein,
zu träumen in ein sonniges Gelände,
dich schlossen immer ziemlich enge Wände
von der Geburt bis diesen Abend ein.

Mehr warst du nicht, doch Zeus und alle Macht,
das All, die großen Geister, alle Sonnen
sind auch für dich geschehn, durch dich geronnen,
mehr warst du nicht, beendet wie begonnen—
der letzte Abend—gute Nacht.

GOTTFRIED BENN

Listen

Listen, this is what the last evening will be like
when you're still capable of going out: you're smoking your Junos,
quaffing your three pints of Wurzburger Hofbrau
and reading about the UN as reflected in the pages of the *Spiegel*,

you're sitting alone at your little table, the least possible company
beside the radiator, because you crave warmth.
All round you mankind and its mewling,
the couple and their loathsome hound.

That's all you are, you've no house or hill
to call your own, to dream in a sunny landscape,
from your birth to this evening
the walls around you were always pretty tightly drawn.

That's all you were, but Zeus and all the immortals,
the great souls, the cosmos and all the suns
were there for you too, spun and fed through you,
that's all you were, finished as begun—
your last evening—good night.

Michael Hofmann

Die Dämonen der Städte

Sie wandern durch die Nacht der Städte hin,
Die schwarz sich ducken unter ihrem Fuß.
Wie Schifferbärte stehen um ihr Kinn
Die Wolken schwarz vom Rauch und Kohlenruß.

Ihr langer Schatten schwankt im Häusermeer
Und löscht der Straßen Lichterreihen aus.
Er kriecht wie Nebel auf dem Pflaster schwer
Und tastet langsam vorwärts Haus für Haus.

Den einen Fuß auf einen Platz gestellt,
Den anderen gekniet auf einen Turm,
Ragen sie auf, wo schwarz der Regen fällt,
Panspfeifen blasend in den Wolkensturm.

Um ihre Füße kreist das Ritornell
Des Städtemeers mit trauriger Musik,
Ein großes Sterbelied. Bald dumpf, bald grell
Wechselt der Ton, der in das Dunkel stieg.

Sie wandern an dem Strom, der schwarz und breit
Wie ein Reptil, den Rücken gelb gefleckt
Von den Laternen, in die Dunkelheit
Sich traurig wälzt, die schwarz den Himmel deckt.

Sie lehnen schwer auf einer Brückenwand
Und stecken ihre Hände in den Schwarm
Der Menschen aus, wie Faune, die am Rand
Der Sümpfe bohren in den Schlamm den Arm.

Einer steht auf. Dem weißen Monde hängt
Er eine schwarze Larve vor. Die Nacht,
Die sich wie Blei vom finstern Himmel senkt,
Drückt tief die Häuser in des Dunkels Schacht.

GEORG HEYM

The Demons of the Cities

They wander through the cities night enshrouds:
The cities cower, black, beneath their feet.
Upon their chins like sailors' beards the clouds
Are black with curling smoke and sooty sleet.

On seas of houses their long shadow sways
And snuffs ranked street-lamps out, as with a blow.
Upon the pavement, thick as fog, it weighs,
And gropes from house to house, solid and slow.

With one foot planted on a city square,
The other knee upon a tower, they stand,
And where the black rain falls they rear, with blare
Of quickened Pan's-pipes in a cloud-stormed land.

About their feet circles a ritornelle
With the sad music of the city's sea,
Like a great burying-song. The shrill tones swell
And rumble in the darkness, changefully.

They wander to the stream that, dark and wide,
As a bright reptile with gold-spotted back,
Turns in the lanterned dark from side to side
In its sad dance, while heaven's stare is black.

They lean upon the bridge, darkly agog,
And thrust their hands among the crowds that pass,
Like fauns who perch above a meadow bog
And plunge lean arms into the miry mass.

Now one stands up. He hangs a mask of gloom
Upon the white-cheeked moon. The night, like lead
From the dun heavens, settles as a doom
On houses into pitted darkness fled.

Der Städte Schultern knacken. Und es birst
Ein Dach, daraus ein rotes Feuer schwemmt.
Breitbeinig sitzen sie auf seinem First
Und schrein wie Katzen auf zum Firmament.

In einer Stube voll von Finsternissen
Schreit eine Wöchnerin in ihren Wehn.
Ihr starker Leib ragt riesig aus den Kissen,
Um den herum die großen Teufel stehn.

Sie hält sich zitternd an der Wehebank.
Das Zimmer schwankt um sie von ihrem Schrei,
Da kommt die Frucht. Ihr Schoß klafft rot und lang
Und blutend reißt er von der Frucht entzwei.

Der Teufel Hälse wachsen wie Giraffen.
Das Kind hat keinen Kopf. Die Mutter hält
Es vor sich hin. In ihrem Rücken klaffen
Des Schrecks Froschfinger, wenn sie rückwärts fällt.

Doch die Dämonen wachsen riesengroß.
Ihr Schläfenhorn zerreißt den Himmel rot.
Erdbeben donnert durch der Städte Schoß
Um ihren Huf, den Feuer überloht.

GEORG HEYM

The shoulders of the cities crack. A gleam
Of fire from a roof burst open flies
Into the air. Big-boned, on the top beam
They sit and scream like cats against the skies.

A little room with glimmering shadows billows
Where one in labor shrieks her agony.
Her body lifts gigantic from the pillows.
And the huge devils stand about to see.

She clutches, shaking, at her torture-bed.
With her long shuddering cry the chamber heaves.
Now the fruit comes. Her womb gapes long and red,
And bleeding, for the child's last passage cleaves.

The devils' necks grow like giraffes'. The child
Is born without a head. The mother moans
And holds it. On her back, clammy and wild,
The frog-fingers of fear play, as she swoons.

But vast as giants now the demons loom.
Their horns in fury gore the bleeding skies.
An earthquake thunders in the cities' womb
About their hooves, where flint-struck fires rise.

Babette Deutsch and Avrahm Yarmolinsky

Umbra Vitae

Die Menschen stehen vorwärts in den Straßen
Und sehen auf die großen Himmelszeichen,
Wo die Kometen mit den Feuernasen
Um die gezackten Türme drohend schleichen.

Und alle Dächer sind voll Sternedeuter,
Die in den Himmel stecken große Röhren,
Und Zauberer, wachsend aus den Bodenlöchern,
Im Dunkel schräg, die ein Gestirn beschwören.

Selbstmörder gehen nachts in großen Horden,
Die suchen vor sich ihr verlornes Wesen,
Gebückt in Süd und West und Ost und Norden,
Den Staub zerfegend mit den Armen-Besen.

Sie sind wie Staub, der hält noch eine Weile.
Die Haare fallen schon auf ihren Wegen.
Sie springen, daß sie sterben, und in Eile,
Und sind mit totem Haupt im Feld gelegen,

Noch manchmal zappelnd. Und der Felder Tiere
Stehn um sie blind und stossen mit dem Horne
In ihren Bauch. Sie strecken alle Viere,
Begraben unter Salbei und dem Dorne.

Die Meere aber stocken. In den Wogen
Die Schiffe hängen modernd und verdrossen,
Zerstreut, und keine Strömung wird gezogen,
Und aller Himmel Höfe sind verschlossen.

Die Bäume wechseln nicht die Zeiten
Und bleiben ewig tot in ihrem Ende,
Und über die verfallnen Wege spreiten
Sie hölzern ihre langen Fingerhände.

GEORG HEYM

Umbra Vitae

The people on the streets draw up and stare,
While overhead huge portents cross the sky;
Round fanglike towers threatening comets flare,
Death-bearing, fiery-snouted where they fly.

On every roof astrologers abound,
Enormous tubes thrust heavenward; there are
Magicians springing up from underground,
Aslant in darkness, conjuring to a star.

Through night great hordes of suicides are hurled,
Men seeking on their way the selves they've lost;
Crook-backed they haunt all corners of the world,
And with their arms for brooms they sweep the dust.

They are as dust, keep but a little while;
And as they move their hair drops out. They run,
To hasten their slow dying. Then they fall,
And in the open fields lie prone,

But twitch a little still. Beasts of the field
Stand blindly round them, prod with horns
Their sprawling bodies till at last they yield,
Lie buried by the sage-bush, by the thorns.

But all the seas are stopped. Among the waves
The ships hang rotting, scattered, beyond hope.
No current through the water moves,
And all the courts of heaven are locked up.

Trees do not change, the seasons do not change.
Enclosed in dead finality each stands,
And over broken roads lets frigid range
Its palmless thousand-fingered hands.

Wer stirbt, der setzt sich auf, sich zu erheben,
Und eben hat er noch ein Wort gesprochen,
Auf einmal ist er fort. Wo ist sein Leben?
Und seine Augen sind wie Glas zerbrochen.

Schatten sind viele. Trübe und verborgen.
Und Träume, die an stummen Türen schleifen,
Und der erwacht, bedrückt vom Licht der Morgen,
Muß schweren Schlaf von grauen Lidern streifen.

GEORG HEYM

The dying man sits up, as if to stand,
Just one more word a moment since he cries,
All at once he's gone. Can life so end?
And crushed to fragments are his glassy eyes.

The secret shadows thicken, darkness breaks;
Behind the speechless doors dreams watch and creep.
Burdened by light of dawn the man that wakes
Must rub from greyish eyelids leaden sleep.

Christopher Middleton

Die Tote im Wasser

Die Masten ragen an dem grauen Wall
Wie ein verbrannter Wald ins frühe Rot,
So schwarz wie Schlacke. Wo das Wasser tot
Zu Speichern stiert, die morsch und im Verfall.

Dumpf tönt der Schall, da wiederkehrt die Flut,
Den Kai entlang. Der Stadtnacht Spülicht treibt
Wie eine weiße Haut im Strom und reibt
Sich an dem Dampfer, der im Docke ruht.

Staub, Obst, Papier, in einer dicken Schicht,
So treibt der Kot aus seinen Röhren ganz.
Ein weißes Tanzkleid kommt, in fettem Glanz
Ein nackter Hals und bleiweiß ein Gesicht.

Die Leiche wälzt sich ganz heraus. Es bläht
Das Kleid sich wie ein weißes Schiff im Wind.
Die toten Augen starren groß und blind
Zum Himmel, der voll rosa Wolken steht.

Das lila Wasser bebt von kleiner Welle.
—Der Wasserratten Fährte, die bemannen
Das weiße Schiff. Nun treibt es stolz von dannen,
Voll grauer Köpfe und voll schwarzer Felle.

Die Tote segelt froh hinaus, gerissen
Von Wind und Flut. Ihr dicker Bauch entragt
Dem Wasser groß, zerhöhlt und fast zernagt.
Wie eine Grotte dröhnt er von den Bissen.

GEORG HEYM

The Dead Girl in the Water

Masts tower against the sea-wall's grey
like a charred forest in the red of dawn,
black as slag. Where dead water turns
towards warehouses rotted with decay.

Returning tides beat with a muffled shock
along the quay. The city's nightfall slime
drifts like a skin of white upon the stream
to brush against the steamer in the dock.

Dust, fruit, paper clot and drift and spread
where pipes spill scourings from the city's swamp.
A white ball-dress comes now, in bloated pomp
a bare throat and a face as white as lead.

The body wallows up, inflates the dress
as if it were a white ship in the wind.
The lifeless eyes stare up, enormous, blind,
into a sky of cloud-pink rosiness.

The lilac water gently rocks and swells,
the wake stirred by the water-rats, who man
the white ship. Now it drifts serenely on,
writhing with grey heads and with sable pelts.

In bliss the dead girl rides the outward draw
of wind and tide, her swollen belly heaving,
big, hollowed out, all that the rats are leaving.
It murmurs like a grotto as they gnaw.

Sie treibt ins Meer. Ihr salutiert Neptun
Von einem Wrack, da sie das Meer verschlingt,
Darinnen sie zur grünen Tiefe sinkt,
Im Arm der feisten Kraken auszuruhn.

GEORG HEYM

She drifts into the ocean. Neptune hails
her from a wreck as the sea gulps her down
and she falls fathoms into depths of green
to rest her fill in the plump kraken's coils.

Anthony Hasler

Der Modedichter

Und nun ist Herbst.
Schon schleicht der Herbstpoet
Durchs rote Land,
Gehüllt in einen Kragenmantel,
Des Faltenwurf ein malerisch Gedicht.
Und mit todtraurigem Gesicht
Holt mit der schlanken, weißen Hand
Er hinterm Ohr
Den goldnen Bleistift vor.
Dann setzt er sich ins feuchte Gras;
Beileibe nicht, sonst würden ja
Am End die neuen Lackschuh naß.
Nein, auf der Holzbank kauernd
Und bang erschauernd
Im Vorgefühl des nahen, kalten Winters,
Starrt er die todesmüde Sonne an,
Die ihrem Grab entgegenhinkt,
Und kritzelt endlich sein Geschmier
Auf japanesisches Papier,
Das nach den letzten Rosen stinkt,
Und merkt nicht, wie die Kinder,
Die ihre Drachen
Hoch in den blauen Herbsttag steigen lassen,
Mit meiner, alten lieben Sonne um die Wette
Den jämmerlichen Wicht belachen.

GEORG HEYM

Poet à la Mode

Autumn is here.
The autumn poet creeps
through the red land
enshrouded in his heavy cloak,
its draping folds a poem to the eye.
And with face drear enough to die
he takes with white and slender hand
the golden pencil from
behind his ear.
Then he sits down in the damp grass—
certainly not, he mustn't let
his patent-leather shoes get wet.
No, huddled on a bench,
he shivers at the pinch
of winter's chill approach,
and watches the dead-weary sun
limping towards its tomb;
at last he scrawls his drivel down
on paper from Japan
stinking of the roses' latest bloom,
not seeing that the children
flying their kites
high in the blue autumn day
are vying with my dear old sun
to mock the wretched parasite.

Anthony Hasler

Weltende

Dem Bürger fliegt vom spitzen Kopf der Hut,
in allen Lüften hallt es wie Geschrei.
Dachdecker stürzen ab und gehn entzwei,
und an den Küsten—liest man—steigt die Flut.

Der Sturm ist da, die wilden Meere hupfen
an Land, um dicke Dämme zu zerdrücken.
Die meisten Menschen haben einen Schnupfen.
Die Eisenbahnen fallen von den Brücken.

End of the World

The bourgeois' hat flies off his pointed head,
the air re-echoes with a screaming sound.
Tilers plunge from roofs and hit the ground,
and seas are rising round the coasts (you read).

The storm is here, crushed dams no longer hold,
the savage seas come inland with a hop.
The greater part of people have a cold.
Off bridges everywhere the railroads drop.

Christopher Middleton

Traum des Bösen

Verhallend eines Gongs braungoldne Klänge—
Ein Liebender erwacht in schwarzen Zimmern
Die Wang' an Flammen, die im Fenster flimmern.
Am Strome blitzen Segel, Masten, Stränge.

Ein Mönch, ein schwangres Weib dort im Gedränge
Guitarren klimpern, rote Kittel schimmern.
Kastanien schwül in goldnem Glanz verkümmern;
Schwarz ragt der Kirchen trauriges Gepränge.

Aus bleichen Masken schaut der Geist des Bösen.
Ein Platz verdämmert grauenvoll und düster;
Am Abend regt auf Inseln sich Geflüster.

Des Vogelfluges wirre Zeichen lesen
Aussätzige, die zur Nacht vielleicht verwesen.
Im Park erblicken zitternd sich Geschwister.

Dream of Evil

A gong's brown-golden tones no longer loud—
A lover wakes in chambers growing dimmer,
His cheek near flames that in the window glimmer.
Upon the stream flash rigging, mast and shroud.

A monk, a pregnant woman in the crowd;
Guitars are strumming, scarlet dresses shimmer.
In golden gleam the chestnuts shrink and simmer;
The churches' mournful pomp looms black and proud.

The evil spirit peers from masks of white.
A square grows gloomy, hideous and stark;
Whispers arise on islands in the dark.

Lepers, who rot away perhaps at night,
Read convoluted omens of birdflight.
Siblings eye each other, trembling in the park.

Robert Firmage

De Profundis

Es ist ein Stoppelfeld, in das ein schwarzer Regen fällt.
Es ist ein brauner Baum, der einsam dasteht.
Es ist ein Zischelwind, der leere Hütten umkreist—
Wie traurig dieser Abend.

Am Weiler vorbei
Sammelt die sanfte Waise noch spärliche Ähren ein.
Ihre Augen weiden rund und goldig in der Dämmerung
Und ihr Schoß harrt des himmlischen Bräutigams.

Bei der Heimkehr
Fanden die Hirten den süßen Leib
Verwest im Dornenbusch.

Ein Schatten bin ich ferne finsteren Dörfern.
Gottes Schweigen
Trank ich aus dem Brunnen des Hains.

Auf meine Stirne tritt kaltes Metall.
Spinnen suchen mein Herz.
Es ist ein Licht, das in meinem Mund erlöscht.

Nachts fand ich mich auf einer Heide,
Starrend von Unrat und Staub der Sterne.
Im Haselgebüsch
Klangen wieder kristallne Engel.

GEORG TRAKL

De Profundis

It is a stubblefield, in which a black rain falls.
It is a brown tree, which stands there alone.
It is a hissing wind, which circles empty huts.
How sorrowful this evening.

Beyond the hamlet
Still the gentle orphan gleans her scanty grain.
Her eyes feed wide and golden in the twilight
And her womb trusts in the heavenly bridegroom.

Returning home,
The shepherds found the sweet corpse
Rotting in a thornbush.

I am a shadow far from darkened villages.
I drank
God's silence from the fountain in the grove.

Cold metal stands upon my brow;
Spiders seek my heart.
It is a light, which goes out in my mouth.

At night I found myself upon a heath,
Stiff with filth and stardust.
In the hazelbush
Crystal angels rang again.

Robert Firmage

Die Ratten

In Hof scheint weiß der herbstliche Mond.
Vom Dachrand fallen phantastische Schatten.
Ein Schweigen in leeren Fenstern wohnt;
Da tauchen leise herauf die Ratten

Und huschen pfeifend hier und dort
Und ein gräulicher Dunsthauch wittert
Ihnen nach aus dem Abort,
Den geisterhaft der Mondschein durchzittert

Und sie keifen vor Gier wie toll
Und erfüllen Haus und Scheunen,
Die von Korn und Früchten voll.
Eisige Winde im Dunkel greinen.

GEORG TRAKL

The Rats

Into the yard the autumn moon shines white.
From the roof's edge fantastic shadows fall,
In empty windows silence dwells;
The rats then quietly steal to the surface

And dart whistling hither and thither
And a horrid vaprous breath wafts
After them out of the sewer
Through which the ghostly moonlight trembles

And they brawl, maddened with greed
And crowd the house and barns
That are filled with corn and fruit.
Icy winds grizzle in the dark.

Alexander Stillmark

Landschaft

Septemberabend: traurig tönen die dunklen Rufe der Hirten
Durch das dämmernde Dorf; Feuer sprüht in der Schmiede.
Gewaltig bäumt sich ein schwarzes Pferd; die hyazinthenen Locken der
    Magd
Haschen nach der Inbrunst seiner purpurnen Nüstern.
Leise erstarrt am Saum des Waldes der Schrei der Hirschkuh
Und die gelben Blumen des Herbstes
Neigen sich sprachlos über das blaue Antlitz des Teichs.
In roter Flamme verbrannte ein Baum; aufflattern mit dunklen
    Gesichtern die Fledermäuse.

GEORG TRAKL

Landscape

September evening: mournfully the dark cries of the shepherds
Ring through the dusky village; fire spits in the forge.
A black horse rears up violently; the girl's hyacinthine locks
Snatch at the ardor of its crimson nostrils.
Softly the cry of the doe freezes at the edge of the forest
And the yellow blossoms of autumn
Bend speechlessly above the blue countenance of the pond.
In red flames a tree burned down; bats flap upward with dark faces.

Robert Firmage

Kindheit

Voll Früchten der Hollunder; ruhig wohnte die Kindheit
In blauer Höhle. Über vergangenen Pfad,
Wo nun bräunlich das wilde Gras saust,
Sinnt das stille Geäst; das Rauschen des Laubs

Ein gleiches, wenn das blaue Wasser im Felsen tönt.
Sanft ist der Amsel Klage. Ein Hirt
Folgt sprachlos der Sonne, die vom herbstlichen Hügel rollt.

Ein blauer Augenblick ist nur mehr Seele.
Am Waldsaum zeigt sich ein scheues Wild und friedlich
Ruhn im Grund die alten Glocken und finsteren Weiler.

Frömmer kennst du den Sinn der dunklen Jahre,
Kühle und Herbst in einsamen Zimmern;
Und in heiliger Bläue läuten leuchtende Schritte fort.

Leise klirrt ein offenes Fenster; zu Tränen
Rührt der Anblick des verfallenen Friedhofs am Hügel.
Erinnerung an erzählte Legenden; doch manchmal erhellt sich die Seele,
Wenn sie frohe Menschen denkt, dunkelgoldene Frühlingstage.

GEORG TRAKL

Childhood

Laden with berries the elderbush; placid the childhood
lived out in its blue hollow. The quiet branches are brooding
over the bygone path where lank, brownish grass
whips in the wind; a rustling of leaves

like blue water tumbling over rocks.
The blackbird's soft plaint. Speechless,
a shepherd follows the sun as it rolls from the autumnal hill.

A blue moment is nothing but soul.
A timid deer peeps out from the forest's edge, while ancient bells
and sunless hamlets merge tranquilly with the valley floor.

More pious now, you know the meaning of the dark years,
chill and autumn in lonely rooms;
and in sanctified blue, luminous footfalls echo away.

The soft rattle of an open casement; the sight of
a neglected graveyard on the hillside brings tears to the eyes.
Memories of once-told legends; but still the soul will sometimes lighten
when it recalls joyful people, burnt golden days of spring.

Michael Hofmann

Psalm II

Stille; als sänken Blinde an herbstlicher Mauer hin,
Lauschend mit morschen Schläfen dem Flug der Raben;
Goldne Stille des Herbstes, das Antlitz des Vaters in flackernder Sonne
Am Abend verfällt im Frieden brauner Eichen das alte Dorf,
Das rote Gehämmer der Schmiede, ein pochendes Herz.
Stille; in langsamen Händen verbirgt die hyazinthene Stirne die Magd
Unter flatternden Sonnenblumen. Angst und Schweigen
Brechender Augen erfüllt das dämmernde Zimmer, die zögernden
    Schritte
Der alten Frauen, die Flucht des purpurnen Munds, der langsam im
    Dunkel erlischt.

Schweigsamer Abend in Wein. Vom niedern Deckengebälk
Fiel ein nächtlicher Falter, Nymphe vergraben in bläulichen Schlaf.
Im Hof schlachtet der Knecht ein Lamm, der süße Geruch des Blutes
Umwölkt unsre Stirnen, die dunkle Kühle des Brunnens.
Nachtrauert die Schwermut sterbender Astern, goldne Stimmen im
    Wind.
Wenn es Nacht wird siehest du mich aus vermoderten Augen an,
In blauer Stille verfielen deine Wangen zu Staub.

So leise erlöscht ein Unkrautbrand, verstummt der schwarze Weiler im
    Grund
Als stiege das Kreuz den blauen Kalvarienhügel herab,
Würfe die schweigende Erde ihre Toten aus.

GEORG TRAKL

Psalm II

Silence; as if the blind were sinking down by an autumn wall,
Listening with wasted brows for the flight of ravens;
Golden stillness of autumn. Father's countenance in flickering sunlight.
At evening the old village decays in the peace of brown oaks,
The red hammering of the forge, a beating heart.
Silence; in her slow hands the maid hides her hyacinth brow
Beneath fluttering sunflowers. Fear and silence
Of eyes breaking in death fills the twilit room, the wavering steps
Of the old women, the flight of the crimson mouth that slowly goes out
   in the gloom.

Muted evening in wine. From the low roof beams
Dropped a nocturnal moth, a nymph buried in bluish sleep.
In the yard the farmhand slaughters a lamb, the sweet smell of blood
Enclouds our brows, the dark coolness of the well.
The melancholy of dying asters lingers in sadness, golden voices in the
   wind.
When night comes you look upon me with mouldering eyes,
In blue stillness your cheeks turned to dust.

So silently a fire for weeds goes out, the black hamlet in the valley grows
   still
As if the Cross were to descend the blue hill of Calvary,
The mute earth to cast out its dead.

Alexander Stillmark

Im Osten

Den wilden Orgeln des Wintersturms
Gleicht des Volkes finstrer Zorn,
Die purpurne Woge der Schlacht,
Entlaubter Sterne.

Mit zerbrochnen Brauen, silbernen Armen
Winkt sterbenden Soldaten die Nacht.
Im Schatten der herbstlichen Esche
Seufzen die Geister der Erschlagenen.

Dornige Wildnis umgürtet die Stadt.
Von blutenden Stufen jagt der Mond
Die erschrockenen Frauen.
Wilde Wölfe brachen durchs Tor.

GEORG TRAKL

Eastern Front

The wrath of the people is dark,
Like the wild organ notes of winter storm,
The battle's crimson wave, a naked
Forest of stars.

With ravaged brows, with silver arms
To dying soldiers night comes beckoning.
In the shade of the autumn ash
Ghosts of the fallen are sighing.

Thorny wilderness girdles the town about.
From bloody doorsteps the moon
Chases terrified women.
Wild wolves have poured through the gates.

Christopher Middleton

Grodek

Am Abend tönen die herbstlichen Wälder
Von tödlichen Waffen, die goldnen Ebenen
Und blauen Seen, darüber die Sonne
Düstrer hinrollt, umfängt die Nacht
Sterbende Krieger, die wilde Klage
Ihrer zerbrochenen Münder.
Doch stille sammelt im Weidengrund
Rotes Gewölk, darin ein zürnender Gott wohnt
Das vergoßne Blut sich, mondne Kühle;
Alle Straßen münden in schwarze Verwesung.
Unter goldnem Gezweig der Nacht und Sternen
Es schwankt der Schwester Schatten durch den schweigenden Hain,
Zu grüßen die Geister der Helden, die blutenden Häupter;
Und leise tönen im Rohr die dunkeln Flöten des Herbstes.
O stolzere Trauer! ihr ehernen Altäre
Die heiße Flamme des Geistes nährt heute ein gewaltiger Schmerz,
Die ungebornen Enkel.

GEORG TRAKL

Grodek

At evening the autumn woods resound
With deadly weapons, the golden plains
And blue lakes, the sun overhead
Rolls more darkly on; night embraces
Dying warriors, the wild lament
Of their broken mouths.
Yet silently red clouds, in which a wrathful god lives,
Gather on willow-ground
The blood that was shed, moon-coolness;
All roads flow into black decay.
Under the golden boughs of night and stars
Sister's shadow sways through the silent grove,
To greet the spirits of the heroes, the bleeding heads;
And softly the dark pipes of autumn sound in the reeds.
O prouder sorrow! You brazen altars,
The spirit's ardent flame today is fed by mighty grief,
The unborn generations.

Alexander Stillmark

Kaspar ist tot

weh unser guter kaspar ist tot.
wer verbirgt nun die brennende fahne im wolkenzopf und schlägt
täglich ein schwarzes schnippchen.
wer dreht nun die kaffeemühle im urfass.
wer lockt nun das idyllische reh aus der versteinerten tüte.
wer schneuzt nun die schiffe parapluis windeuter bienvaters
ozonspindeln und entgrätet die pyramiden.
weh weh weh unser guter kaspar ist tot. heiliger bimbam kaspar ist
tot.
die heufische klappern herzzerreissend vor leid in den
glockenscheunen wenn man seinen vornamen ausspricht. darum
seufze ich weiter seinen familiennamen kaspar kaspar kaspar.
warum hast du uns verlassen. in welche gestalt ist nun deine schöne
grosse seele gewandert. bist du ein stern geworden oder eine kette aus
wasser an einem heißen wirbelwind oder ein euter aus schwarzem licht
oder ein durchsichtiger ziegel an der stöhnenden trommel des felsigen
wesens.
jetzt vertrocknen unsere scheitel und sohlen und die feen liegen
halbverkohlt auf dem scheiterhaufen.
jetzt donnert hinter der sonne die schwarze kegelbahn und keiner
zieht mehr die kompasse und die räder der schiebkarren auf.
wer ißt nun mit der phosphoreszierenden ratte am einsamen
barfüßigen tisch.
wer verjagt nun den sirokkoko teufel wenn er die pferde verführen
will.
wer erklärt uns nun die monogramme in den sternen.
seine büste wird die kamine aller wahrhaft edlen menschen zieren
doch ist das kein trost und schnupftabak für einen totenkopf.

HANS ARP

Kaspar Is Dead

alas our good kaspar is dead.

who'll now hide the burning flag in the cloudpigtail and every day cock a
  black snook.

who'll now turn the coffeegrinder in the primeval tub.

who'll now lure the idyllic doe from the petrified paperbag.

who'll now blow the noses of ships parapluis windudders bee-fathers
  ozonespindles and who'll bone the pyramids.

alas alas alas our good kaspar is dead. saint dingdong kaspar is dead.

the grass-shark rattles his teeth heartrendingly in the bellbarns when his
  forename is spoken. therefore I shall go on sighing his familyname
  kaspar kaspar kaspar.

why hast thou forsaken us. into what form has thy great beautiful soul
  migrated. hast thou become a star or a chain of water hanging from a
  hot whirlwind or an udder of black light or a transparent tile on the
  groaning drum of the rocky essence.

now our tops and toes go dry and the fairies are lying halfcharred on the
  funeral pyre.

now the black skittle alley thunders behind the sun and nobody winds
  up the compasses and the pushcart wheels any more.

who'll now eat with the phosphorescent rat at the lonely barefoot table.

who'll now shoo away the siroccoco devil when he tries to ravish the
  horses.

who'll now elucidate for us the monograms in the stars.

his bust will grace the mantelpieces of all truly noble men but that's no
  consolation and snuff for a death's head.

Christopher Middleton

Die Raddadistenmaschine

Die Raddadistenmaschine ist für dich bestimmt. Sie ist durch eigenartige Zusammenstellung von Rädern, Achsen und Walzen mit Kadavern, Salpetersäure und Merz so konstruiert, daß du mit vollem Verstand hineingehst und vollständig ohne Verstand herauskommst. Das hat große Vorteile für dich. Lege dein Bargeld in einer Raddadistenkur an, du wirst es nie bereuen, du kannst überhaupt nicht mehr bereuen nach der Kur. Ob du reich oder arm bist, ist gleichgültig, die Raddadistenmaschine befreit dich sogar von dem Geld an sich. Als Kapitalist gehst du in den Trichter, passierst mehrere Walzen und tauchst in Säure. Dann kommst du mit einigen Leichen in nähere Berührung. Essig tröpfelt Kubismus dada. Dann bekommst du den großen Raddada zu sehen. (Nicht den Präsidenten des Erdballs, wie viele annehmen.) Raddada strahlt von Witz und ist bespießt mit einigen 100000 Nadelspitzen. Nachdem du dann hin und hergeschleudert bist, liest man dir meine neuesten Gedichte vor, bis du ohnmächtig zusammenbrichst. Dann wirst du gewalkt und raddadiert, und plötzlich stehst du als neu frisierter Antispießer wieder draußen. Vor der Kur graut dir vor dem Nadelör, nach der Kur kann dir nicht mehr grauen. Du bist Raddadist und betest zu der Maschine voll Begeisterung. —Amen.

The Dadarotator

The dadarotator is intended personally for you. It is a peculiar combination of rotators, spindles, and pistons, built with cadavers, nitric acid, and Merz in such a way that you enter it with complete understanding and emerge from it with none. This has great advantages for you. Invest your money in a dadarotator cure, you'll never regret it, after the treatment you'll never be able to regret anything. Rich or poor, whichever you are, it's all the same, the dadarotator frees you even from money *per se*. As a capitalist you go into the funnel, pass through several pistons, and plunge into acid. Then you come into contact with a corpse or two. Vinegar dribbles cubism dada. Then you get to see the Great Rotatory Dada. (Not the President of the Universe, as many suppose.) The dadarotator beams with wit and is pronged with about 100,000 needlepoints. After you've been flung back and forth, someone will read you my latest poems, until you collapse in a faint. Then comes the fulling and dadarotating, and suddenly there you are, with a fresh haircut, out in the open, an antibourgeois. Before the treatment the eye of the needle horrifies you, after it nothing can. You'll be a rotarydada and you'll pray to the machine like someone inspired. —Amen.

Christopher Middleton

"Es ist Herbst"

Es ist Herbst. Die Schwäne essen das Brot ihrer Herren mit
Tränen zusammengebacken. Einige matte Expressionisten
schreien nach Wein, denn es ist noch Wein genug da, aber es
gibt keinen Expressionismus mehr.
Es lebe der Kaiser, denn es gibt keinen Kaiser mehr. Uhren
uhren die Stunden fünfundzwanzigtausendmal.
Ich gleite.
Gleite Schlingen.
Kreischt eine Maschine.
Katzen hängen an der Wand.
Ein Jude geigt das Tier zum Fenster hinaus.
Heraus.
Es ist Herbst und die Schwäne herbsten auch.

KURT SCHWITTERS

"It is autumn"

It is autumn. Swans devour the bread of their masters held together by
    tears. A few feeble expressionists cry out for wine, for there's still
    enough wine, but no more Expressionism.
Long live the Kaiser, for there's no more Kaiser! Clocks clock the hours
    25 thousand times.
I glide.
Glide noose.
Clangs a machine.
Cats hang from the wall.
A Jew is fiddling the beast on out the window.
All the way out.
It is autumn, and the swans autumn also.

Harriet Watts

Gesetztes Bildgedicht (Composed Picture Poem)

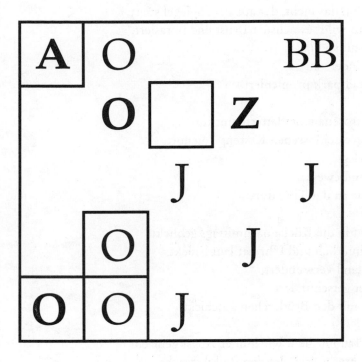

Der dicke Mann im Spiegel

Ach Gott, ich bin das nicht, der aus dem Spiegel stiert,
Der Mensch mit wildbewachsner Brust und unrasiert.
 Tag war heut so blau,
 Mit der Kinderfrau
Wurde ja im Stadtpark promeniert.

Noch kein Matrosenanzug flatterte mir fort
Zu jenes strengverschlossenen Kastens Totenort.
 Eben abgelegt,
 Hängt er unbewegt,
Klein und müde an der Türe dort.

Und ward nicht in die Küche nachmittags geblickt?
Kaffee roch winterlich und Uhr hat laut getickt.
 Atmend stand verwundert,
 Der vorher getschundert
Übers Glatteis mit den Brüderchen geschickt.

Auch hat die Frau mir heut wie immer Angst gemacht
Vor jenem Wächter Kakiz, der den Park bewacht.
 Oft zu öder Zeit
 Hör im Traum ich weit
Diesen Teufel säbelschleppen in der Nacht.

Die treue Alte, warum kommt sie denn noch nicht?
Von Schlafesnähe allzuschwer ist mein Gesicht.
 Wenn sie doch schon käme
 Und es mit sich nähme,
Das dort oben leise singt, das Licht!

The Fat Man in the Mirror

What's filling up the mirror? O, it is not I;
Hair-belly like a beaver's house? An old dog's eye?
    The forenoon was blue
    In the mad King's zoo
Nurse was swinging me so high, so high!

The bullies wrestled on the royal bowling green;
Hammers and sickles on their hoods of black sateen . . .
    Sulking on my swing
    The tobacco King
Sliced apples with a pen-knife for the Queen.

This *I*, who used to mouse about the paraffined preserves,
And jammed a finger in the coffee-grinder, serves
    Time before the mirror.
    But this pursey terror . . .
Nurse, it is a person. *It is nerves.*

Where's the Queen-Mother waltzing like a top to staunch
The blood of Lewis, King of Faerie? Hip and haunch
    Lard the royal grotto;
    Straddling Lewis' motto,
Time, the Turk, its sickle on its paunch.

Nurse, Nurse, it rises on me . . . O, it starts to roll,
My apples, O, are ashes in the meerschaum bowl . . .
    If you'd only come,
    If you'd only come,
Darling, if . . . The apples that I stole,

Ach, abendlich besänftigt tönt kein stiller Schritt.
Und Babi dreht das Licht nicht aus und nimmt es mit.
  Nur der dicke Mann
  Schaut mich hilflos an,
Bis er tieferschrocken aus dem Spiegel tritt.

FRANZ WERFEL

While Nurse and I were swinging in the Old One's eye . . .
Only a fat man with his beaver on his eye,
   Only a fat man,
   Only a fat man
Bursts the mirror. O, it is not I!

   Robert Lowell

"O die Schornsteine"

*Und wenn diese meine Haut zerschlagen sein wird, so werde ich ohne
mein Fleisch Gott schauen.* —HIOB

O die Schornsteine
Auf den sinnreich erdachten Wohnungen des Todes,
Als Israels Leib zog aufgelöst in Rauch
Durch die Luft—
Als Essenkehrer ihn ein Stern empfing
Der schwarz wurde
Oder war es ein Sonnenstrahl?

O die Schornsteine!
Freiheitswege für Jeremias und Hiobs Staub—
Wer erdachte euch und baute Stein auf Stein
Den Weg für Flüchtlinge aus Rauch?

O die Wohnungen des Todes,
Einladend hergerichtet
Für den Wirt des Hauses, der sonst Gast war—
O ihr Finger,
Die Eingangsschwelle legend
Wie ein Messer zwischen Leben und Tod—

O ihr Schornsteine,
O ihr Finger,
Und Israels Leib im Rauch durch die Luft!

"O the chimneys"

And though after my skin worms destroy this body, yet in my flesh shall I see God. —JOB 19:26

O the chimneys
On the ingeniously devised habitations of death
When Israel's body drifted as smoke
Through the air—
Was welcomed by a star, a chimney sweep,
A star that turned black
Or was it a ray of sun?

O the chimneys!
Freedomway for Jeremiah and Job's dust—
Who devised you and laid stone upon stone
The road for refugees of smoke?

O the habitations of death,
Invitingly appointed
For the host who used to be a guest—
O you fingers
Laying the threshold
Like a knife between life and death—

O you chimneys,
O you fingers
And Israel's body as smoke through the air!

Michael Roloff

"Wer aber leerte den Sand aus euren Schuhen"

Wer aber leerte den Sand aus euren Schuhen,
Als ihr zum Sterben aufstehen mußtet?
Den Sand, den Israel heimholte,
Seinen Wandersand?
Brennenden Sinaisand,
Mit den Kehlen von Nachtigallen vermischt,
Mit den Flügeln des Schmetterlings vermischt,
Mit dem Sehnsuchtsstaub der Schlangen vermischt,
Mit allem was abfiel von der Weisheit Salomos vermischt,
Mit dem Bitteren aus des Wermuts Geheimnis vermischt—

O ihr Finger,
Die ihr den Sand aus Totenschuhen leertet,
Morgen schon werdet ihr Staub sein
In den Schuhen Kommender!

NELLY SACHS

"But who emptied your shoes of sand"

But who emptied your shoes of sand
When you had to get up, to die?
The sand which Israel gathered,
Its nomad sand?
Burning Sinai sand,
Mingled with throats of nightingales,
Mingled with wings of butterflies,
Mingled with the hungry dust of serpents;
Mingled with all that fell from the wisdom of Solomon,
Mingled with what is bitter in the mystery of wormwood—

O you fingers
That emptied the deathly shoes of sand.
Tomorrow you will be dust
In the shoes of those to come.

Michael Hamburger

Chor der Geretteten

Wir Geretteten,
Aus deren hohlem Gebein der Tod schon seine Flöten schnitt,
An deren Sehnen der Tod schon seinen Bogen strich—
Unsere Leiber klagen noch nach
Mit ihrer verstümmelten Musik.
Wir Geretteten,
Immer noch hängen die Schlingen für unsere Hälse gedreht
Vor uns in der blauen Luft—
Immer noch füllen sich die Stundenuhren mit unserem tropfenden Blut.
Wir Geretteten,
Immer noch essen an uns die Würmer der Angst.
Unser Gestirn ist vergraben im Staub.
Wir Geretteten
Bitten euch:
Zeigt uns langsam eure Sonne.
Führt uns von Stern zu Stern im Schritt.
Laßt uns das Leben leise wieder lernen.
Es könnte sonst eines Vogels Lied,
Das Füllen des Eimers am Brunnen
Unseren schlecht versiegelten Schmerz aufbrechen lassen
Und uns wegschäumen—
Wir bitten euch:
Zeigt uns noch nicht einen beißenden Hund—
Es könnte sein, es könnte sein
Daß wir zu Staub zerfallen—
Vor euren Augen zerfallen in Staub.
Was hält denn unsere Webe zusammen?
Wir odemlos gewordene,
Deren Seele zu Ihm floh aus der Mitternacht
Lange bevor man unseren Leib rettete
In die Arche des Augenblicks.
Wir Geretteten,
Wir drücken eure Hand,

NELLY SACHS

Chorus of the Rescued

We, the rescued,
From whose hollow bones death had begun to whittle his flutes,
And on whose sinews he had already stroked his bow—
Our bodies continue to lament
With their mutilated music.
We, the rescued,
The nooses wound for our necks still dangle
Before us in the blue air—
Hourglasses still fill with our dripping blood.
We, the rescued,
The worms of fear still feed on us.
Our constellation is buried in dust.
We, the rescued,
Beg you:
Show us your sun, but gradually.
Lead us from star to star, step by step.
Be gentle when you teach us to live again.
Lest the song of a bird,
Or a pail being filled at the well,
Let our badly sealed pain burst forth again
And carry us away—
We beg you:
Do not show us an angry dog, not yet—
It could be, it could be
That we will dissolve into dust—
Dissolve into dust before your eyes.
For what binds our fabric together?
We whose breath vacated us,
Whose soul fled to Him out of that midnight
Long before our bodies were rescued
Into the ark of the moment.
We, the rescued,
We press your hand

Wir erkennen euer Auge—
Aber zusammen hält uns nur noch der Abschied,
Der Abschied im Staub
Hält uns mit euch zusammen.

NELLY SACHS

We look into your eye—
But all that binds us together now is leave-taking,
The leave-taking in the dust
Binds us together with you.

Michael Roloff

"Diese Kette von Rätseln"

Diese Kette von Rätseln
um den Hals der Nacht gelegt
Königswort weit fort geschrieben
unlesbar
vielleicht in Kometenfahrt
wenn die aufgerissene Wunde des Himmels
schmerzt

da
in dem Bettler der Raum hat
und auf Knieen gehend
ausgemessen hat alle Landstraßen
mit seinem Leib

denn es muß ausgelitten werden
das Lesbare
und Sterben gelernt
im Geduldigsein—

NELLY SACHS

"This chain of enigmas"

This chain of enigmas
hung on the neck of night
a king's word written far away
illegible
perhaps in comet journeys
when the torn-open wound of the sky
hurts

there
within the beggar who has room
and crawling upon his knees
has measured out the roads
with his body

for the legible
must be suffered to its end
and dying learned
in patience—

Ruth and Matthew Mead

"Auch dir, du mein Geliebter"

Auch Dir, du mein geliebter,
Haben zwei Hände, zum Darreichen geboren,
Die Schuhe abgerissen,
Bevor sie dich töteten.
Zwei Hände, die sich darreichen müssen
Wenn sie zu Staub zerfallen.
Deine Schuhe waren aus einer Kalbshaut.
Wohl waren sie gegerbt, gefärbt,
Der Pfriem hatte sie durchstochen—
Aber wer weiß, wo noch ein letzter lebendiger
Hauch wohnt?
Während der kurzen Trennung
Zwischen deinem Blut und der Erde
Haben sie Sand hineingespart wie eine Stundenuhr
Die jeden Augenblick Tod füllt.
Deine Füße!
Die Gedanken eilten ihnen voraus.
Die so schnell bei Gott waren,
So wurden deine Füße müde,
Wurden wund um dein Herz einzuholen.
Aber die Kalbshaut,
Darüber einmal die warme leckende Zunge
Des Muttertieres gestrichen war,
Ehe sie abgezogen wurde—
Wurde noch einmal abgezogen
Von deinen Füßen,
Abgezogen—
O du mein Geliebter!

NELLY SACHS

"Two hands, born to give"

Two hands, born to give,
Tore off your shoes
My beloved,
Before they killed you.
Two hands, which will have to give themselves up
When they turn to dust.
Your shoes were made of calfskin.
They were well tanned and dyed,
The awl had pierced them—
But who knows where a last living breath
Still dwells?
During the short parting
Between your blood and earth
They trickled sand like an hourglass
Which fills each moment with death.
Your feet!
The thoughts sped before them.
They came so quickly to God
That your feet grew weary,
Grew sore in trying to catch up with your heart.
But the calfskin
That the warm licking tongue
Of the mother-cow once stroked
Before the skin was stripped—
Was stripped once more
From your feet,
Torn off—
Oh my beloved

Ruth and Matthew Mead and Michael Hamburger

Gesang an die Welt

Ach knallige Welt, du Lunapark,
Du seliges Abnormitätenkabinett,
Paß auf! Hier kommt G r o ß,
Der traurigste Mensch in Europa,
"Ein Phänomen an Trauer."
Steifen Hut im Genick,
Kein schlapper Hund!!!!
Niggersongs im Schädel,
Bunt wie Hyazinthenfelder,
Oder turbulente D-Züge,
Über rasselnde Brücken knatternd—
Ragtimetänzer,
Am Staketenzaun wartend mit der Menge
Auf Rob. E. Lee.
- -

Horido!
Beim Bart des Oberlehrers Wotan—
Nachmittags verbrämte Kloaken,
Überpinselte Fäulnis,
Parfümierter Gestank—
G r o ß   w i t t e r t s.
Parbleu! Hier riecht's nach gebratenen Kindern.

*

Sammelt euch, boys!!!!!!!!!!!!
Ankurbelt den Benz—150 km (KA-EM)!
Die Straßenbänder bergab!
Knall auf Motor!
Auch dich ekelt der kalte Schweiß
In Lümmelgesicht!
- -

GEORGE GROSZ

Hymn to the World

I

O whizzbang world, you luna park,
You delicious cabinet of horrors,
Watch out! Here comes Grosz,
The saddest man in Europe,
"A phenomenon of sadness."
Hard hat pushed back,
By no means a softie!!!
A skull full of black blues,
Bright as fields of hyacinths
Or rushing express trains
Clattering over bridges—
Ragtime dancer,
Waiting with the crowds by the picket fence
For Robert E. Lee.

Horido!
By the beard of headmaster Wotan—
Afternoons of prettified sewers,
Painted over putrition,
Perfumed stench—
Grosz can sniff it.
Parbleu! I smell roast babies.

II

Get yourselves together, lads!
Crank up the Benz—150 kmh
Down the ribboning roads!
Engine, purr!
You too are disgusted by the cold sweat
On flaccid features!

Turbulenz der Welt!
Liebe Freunde!—ahoi!
Seid gegrüßt, boys, über den Atlantic!
Du *I. W. Hurban*, du *Lewis*, du *Abraham*,
Du *Theo F. Morse*
Und du *Lillian Elmore*.
Den Urwald zogt ihr auf Noten
Mit eurer Banjo Musik der Neuen Welt
Starr hochwachsende Turmhäuser.
Frei das graue Auge.
Glattrasiert und breit.

Den Hudson abwärts gleitet das Hausboot—
Und dunkle Nächte und die
Schwarzbehaupteten Nigger!

GEORGE GROSZ

Turbulence of the world!
My dear friends! Ahoy!
Greetings, y'all, boys over the water!
I. W. Hurban, Lewis, Abraham,
Theo F. Morse,
Lillian Elmore.
You converted the jungle into notes
With your New World banjo music.
Stiff standing skyscrapers.
The grey eye at liberty.
Cleanshaven and broad.

The houseboat glides down the Hudson—
With dark nights
And Negroes in black hats!

Michael Hofmann

Apfelböck, oder die Lilie auf dem Felde

1

In mildem Lichte Jakob Apfelböck
Erschlug den Vater und die Mutter sein
Und schloß sie beide in den Wäscheschrank
Und blieb im Hause übrig, er allein.

2

Es schwammen Wolken unterm Himmel hin
Und um sein Haus ging mild der Sommerwind
Und in dem Hause saß er selber drin
Vor sieben Tagen war es noch ein Kind.

3

Die Tage gingen und die Nacht ging auch
Und nichts war anders außer mancherlei
Bei seinen Eltern Jakob Apfelböck
Wartete einfach, komme was es sei.

4

Es bringt die Milchfrau noch die Milch ins Haus
Gerahmte Buttermilch, süß, fett und kühl.
Was er nicht trinkt, das schüttet Jakob aus
Denn Jakob Apfelböck trinkt nicht mehr viel.

5

Es bringt der Zeitungsmann die Zeitung noch
Mit schwerem Tritt ins Haus beim Abendlicht
Und wirft sie scheppernd in das Kastenloch
Doch Jakob Apfelböck, der liest sie nicht.

BERTOLT BRECHT

Apfelböck, or the Lily of the Field

1

Mild was the light as Jakob Apfelböck
Struck both his father and his mother down
And shut their bodies in the linen press
And hung about the house all on his own.

2

The clouds went floating past beneath the sky
Around his house the summer winds blew mild
Inside the house he passed the time away
Who just a week before was still a child.

3

The days went by, the nights went by as well
And nothing changed except a thing or two.
Beside his parents Jakob Apfelböck
Waited to see what time would find to do.

4

The woman still delivers milk each day
Sweet thick cool skim milk, left behind the door.
What Jakob doesn't drink he pours away
For Jakob's hardly drinking any more.

5

The paper man still brings the paper round
He steps up to the house with heavy tread
And stuffs the paper in the letter box
But Jakob Apfelböck leaves it unread.

6

Und als die Leichen rochen durch das Haus
Da weinte Jakob und ward krank davon.
Und Jakob Apfelböck zog weinend aus
Und schlief von nun an nur auf dem Balkon.

7

Es sprach der Zeitungsmann, der täglich kam:
Was riecht hier so? Ich rieche doch Gestank.
In mildem Licht sprach Jakob Apfelböck:
Es ist die Wäsche in dem Wäscheschrank.

8

Es sprach die Milchfrau einst, die täglich kam:
Was riecht hier so? Es riecht, als wenn man stirbt!
In mildem Licht sprach Jakob Apfelböck:
Es ist das Kalbfleisch, das im Schrank verdirbt.

9

Und als sie einstens in den Schrank ihm sahn
Stand Jakob Apfelböck in mildem Licht
Und als sie fragten, warum er's getan
Sprach Jakob Apfelböck: Ich weiß es nicht.

10

Die Milchfrau aber sprach am Tag danach:
Ob wohl das Kind einmal, früh oder spät
Ob Jakob Apfelböck wohl einmal noch
Zum Grabe seiner armen Eltern geht?

BERTOLT BRECHT

6

And when the smell of corpses filled the house
Jakob felt queasy and began to cry.
Tearfully, Jakob Apfelböck moved out
And slept henceforward on the balcony.

7

Up spoke the paper man then on his round:
What is that smell? Something gone off, I'd say.
The light was mild as Jakob Apfelböck
Said: Just some dirty clothes I shut away.

8

Up spoke the milk woman then on her round:
What is that smell? I'd say that something's died.
The light was mild as Jakob Apfelböck
Said: Just some meat that mother put aside.

9

And when they came to open the press door
Jakob stood by, the light was mild and clear
And when they asked him what he did it for
Said Jakob Apfelböck: I've no idea.

10

A few days later the milk woman said
She wondered what would happen by and by:
Would Jakob Apfelböck, the child, perhaps
Visit the grave where his poor parents lie?

John Willett

Vom Schwimmen in Seen und Flüssen

1

Im bleichen Sommer, wenn die Winde oben
Nur in dem Laub der großen Bäume sausen
Muß man in Flüssen liegen oder Teichen
Wie die Gewächse, worin Hechte hausen.
Der Leib wird leicht im Wasser. Wenn der Arm
Leicht aus dem Wasser in den Himmel fällt
Wiegt ihn der kleine Wind vergessen
Weil er ihn wohl für braunes Astwerk hält.

2

Der Himmel bietet mittags große Stille.
Man macht die Augen zu, wenn Schwalben kommen.
Der Schlamm ist warm. Wenn kühle Blasen quellen
Weiß man: ein Fisch ist jetzt durch uns geschwommen.
Mein Leib, die Schenkel und der stille Arm
Wir liegen still im Wasser, ganz geeint
Nur wenn die kühlen Fische durch uns schwimmen
Fühl ich, daß Sonne überm Tümpel scheint.

3

Wenn man am Abend von dem langen Liegen
Sehr faul wird, so, daß alle Glieder beißen
Muß man das alles, ohne Rücksicht, klatschend
In blaue Flüsse schmeißen, die sehr reißen.
Am besten ist's, man hält's bis Abend aus.
Weil dann der bleiche Haifischhimmel kommt
Bös und gefräßig über Fluß und Sträuchern
Und alle Dinge sind, wie's ihnen frommt.

BERTOLT BRECHT

Of Swimming in Lakes and Rivers

1

In the pale summer when the winds above
Only in great trees' leaves a murmur make
You ought to lie in rivers or in ponds
As do the waterweeds which harbour pike.
The body grows light in the water. When your arm
Falls easily from water into sky
The little wind rocks it absentmindedly
Taking it likely for a brownish bough.

2

The sky at noon offers ample calm.
You close your eyes when swallows pass.
The mud is warm. Cool bubbles welling up
Show that a fish has just swum through us.
My body and thighs and resting arm
We lie in the water quite at one and still
Only when the cool fish swim through us
I sense the sun shining above the pool.

3

By the evening having grown very lazy
With lying so long, each limb begins to smart
You have to dash all that with a reckless smack
Into blue streams which scatter far apart.
It's best to last out until the evening
For then the pale shark-like sky will come
Evil and greedy over bush and river
And all things will assume their aptest form.

4

Natürlich muß man auf dem Rücken liegen
So wie gewöhnlich. Und sich treiben lassen.
Man muß nicht schwimmen, nein, nur so tun, als
Gehöre man einfach zu Schottermassen.
Man soll den Himmel anschaun und so tun
Als ob einen ein Weib trägt, und es stimmt.
Ganz ohne großen Umtrieb, wie der liebe Gott tut
Wenn er am Abend noch in seinen Flüssen schwimmt.

BERTOLT BRECHT

4

Of course you must lie upon your back
As if by habit. And drift along.
You need not swim, no, only behave as if
It's just to the mass of gravel you belong.
You should look at the sky and act
As if a woman held you, which is right.
Quite without great upheaval as the good God does
When he swims in his rivers at evening light.

Lesley Lendrum

Erinnerung an die Marie A.

1

An jenem Tag im blauen Mond September
Still unter einem jungen Pflaumenbaum
Da hielt ich sie, die stille bleiche Liebe
In meinem Arm wie einen holden Traum.
Und über uns im schönen Sommerhimmel
War eine Wolke, die ich lange sah
Sie war sehr weiß und ungeheuer oben
Und als ich aufsah, war sie nimmer da.

2

Seit jenem Tag sind viele, viele Monde
Geschwommen still hinunter und vorbei
Die Pflaumenbäume sind wohl abgehauen
Und fragst du mich, was mit der Liebe sei?
So sag ich dir: Ich kann mich nicht erinnern.
Und doch, gewiß, ich weiß schon, was du meinst
Doch ihr Gesicht, das weiß ich wirklich nimmer
Ich weiß nur mehr: Ich küßte es dereinst.

3

Und auch den Kuß, ich hätt ihn längst vergessen
Wenn nicht die Wolke da gewesen wär
Die weiß ich noch und werd ich immer wissen
Sie war sehr weiß und kam von oben her.
Die Pflaumenbäume blühn vielleicht noch immer
Und jene Frau hat jetzt vielleicht das siebte Kind
Doch jene Wolke blühte nur Minuten
Und als ich aufsah, schwand sie schon im Wind.

BERTOLT BRECHT

A Cloud

One evening in the blue month of September
We lay at peace beneath an apple bough;
I took her in my arms, my gentle lover,
And held her closely like a dream come true—
While far up in the tranquil summer heaven
There was a cloud, I saw it high and clear.
It was so white and so immense above us
And, as I watched, it was no longer there.

Since then so very many different evenings
Have drifted blindly past in the general flow.
Perhaps the apple orchard has been flattened;
And if you ask me where the girl is now
I have to admit I really don't remember.
I can imagine what you're going to say
But even her face I truly can't recapture;
I only know I kissed it there that day.

Even the kiss I would have long forgotten
If that one cloud had not been up there too—
I see it and will always see it plainly,
So white and unexpected in the blue.
Perhaps the apple boughs are back in blossom,
Maybe she holds a fourth child on her knees;
The cloud, though, hung there for a moment only
And, as I watched, it broke up in the breeze.

Derek Mahon

Die Ballade vom Liebestod

1

Von schwarzem Regen siebenfach zerfressen
Ein schmieriger Gaumen, der die Liebe frißt
Mit Mullstors, die wie Totenlaken nässen:
Das ist die Kammer, die die letzte ist.

2

Aussätzig die Tapeten, weiß vom Schimmel!
In Hölzer sie gepfercht, verschweißt und hart:
Wie lieblich scheinet der verschlissne Himmel
Dem weißen Paare, das sich himmlisch paart.

3

Im Anfang sitzt er oft in nassen Tüchern
Und lutscht Virginias, schwarz, die sie ihm gibt
Und nützt die Zeit, ihr nickend zu versichern
Mit halbgeschlossenem Lid, daß er sie liebt.

4

Sie fühlt, wie er behaart ist und so weise!
Er sieht im Schlitz des Lids den Tag verschwemmt
Und grün wie Seife wölkt sich das Gehäuse
Des Himmels und ihm schwant: jetzt fault mein Hemd.

5

Sie gießen Kognak in die trocknen Leichen
Er füttert sie mit grünem Abendlicht
Und es entzünden sich schon ihre Weichen
Und es verblaßt schon mählich ihr Gesicht.

BERTOLT BRECHT

Ballad of the Love-Death

1

Eaten away by black rain seven times over
A sordid mouth which gollops down their love
With muslin curtains damp as shrouds for cover:
Such is the attic which they'll never leave.

2

Leprous the wallpaper, mildewed and crumbling!
Shut in by wooden boards they're welded, tight:
To this white couple in its heavenly coupling
The threadbare heaven seems a sheer delight.

3

To start with he'll sit there in damp towels, chewing
The black cheroots she gives him. Mouth askew
He'll kill the time nodding his head, and cooing
With drooping eyelid that he loves her true.

4

Such hairiness, she feels, and oh, such wisdom!
He sees the day dissolve, his eyes a slot
While, green as soap, the clouds shut off the sky's dome
And all he thinks is: how my shirt will rot.

5

They're pouring brandy down their dried-up bodies
He's feeding her on evening's pale green light
And now her things are covered with red blotches
And now her face is slowly going white.

6

Sie ist wie eine halbersoffne Wiese
(Sie sind verwaist und taub, im Fleische matt!)
Er will gern schlafen, wenn sie ihn nur ließe!
Ein grüner Himmel, der geregnet hat!

7

Am zweiten Tage hüllen sie die Leichen
In steife Tücher, den verschweißten Stor
Und nehmen schmierige Laken in die Weichen
Weil sie jetzt wissen, daß es sie oft fror.

8

Und ach, die Liebe ging durch sie so schneidend
Wie wenn Gott Hageleis durch Wasser schmiß!
Und tief in ihnen quoll, sie ganz ausweidend
Und dick wie Hefe grüne Bitternis.

9

Von Schweiß, Urin, Geruch in ihren Haaren
Sie wittern ferner nicht mehr Morgenluft.
Es kommt der Morgen wahrlich noch nach Jahren
Vertiert und grau in die Tapetengruft.

10

Ach, ihr zarter Kinderleib perlmuttern!
Holz und Liebe schlugen ihn so rauh
Schmilzt wie Holz salzflutzerschlagner Kutter
Unter Sturmflut! Gras in zuviel Tau!

BERTOLT BRECHT

6

She's like some waterlogged field by the river
(They're deaf, they're orphaned, all their flesh is drained!)
He wants his sleep, but will she let him leave her?
Green sky above, that recently has rained!

7

The second day they used the sweat-stained curtains
As stiffened sheets to wrap their corpses in
And packed their thighs with greasy strips of shirting
Because they've learned that's where the chills begin.

8

And, oh, love stabbed them through and through, so neatly
As when God's hailstones through the water hiss.
And deep within them, gutting them completely
And thick as yeast, welled up green bitterness.

9

Their hair filled with the smells of sweat and urine
They'll never see again the break of day.
Yet, years from now, the day will come and pour in
To that wallpaper vault, bestial and grey.

10

Oh, her young pearly body, soft as butter!
Beaten so raw by wood and love right through
Dissolves like wood in some old battered cutter
Beneath a storm. Like grass soggy with dew.

11

Ach, die Hand an ihrer Brust wie gräsern!
In den Beinen schwarzer Pestgestank!
Milde Luft floß ab an Fenstergläsern
Und sie staken im verfaulten Schrank!

12

Wie Spülicht floß der Abend an die Scheiben
Und die Gardinen räudig von Tabak.
In grünen Wassern zwei Geliebte treiben
Von Liebe ganz durchregnet, wie ein Wrack

13

Am Meergrund, das, geborsten, in den Tropen
Zwischen Algen und weißlichen Fischen hängt
Und von einem Salzwind über die Fläche oben
Tief in den Wassern unten zu schaukeln anfängt.

14

Am vierten Tage, in der Früh, mit Streichen
Knirschender Äxte brachen Nachbarn ein
Und hörten Stille dort und sahen Leichen
(Und munkelten von einem grünen Schein

15

Der von Gesichtern ausgehn kann), auch roch noch
Verliebt das Bett, das Fenster barst vor Frost:
Ein Leichnam ist was Kaltes! Ach, es kroch noch
Ein schwarzer Faden Kälte aus der Brust.

BERTOLT BRECHT

11

Oh, but the hand that holds her breast is grassy!
And black the stench of plague in every limb!
Mild air rinsed down the window, hard and glassy
While still the rotten cupboard sheltered them.

12

Like dishwater the evening rinsed the skylight
Its curtains mangy with tobacco smoke.
Across green seas two lovers in the twilight
Drift, soaked in love, like some rain-sodden hulk

13

Which, breaking up deep in the tropic oceans
Hangs there between seaweed and the pallid fish
And, far below, starts gentle rocking motions
Caught from the surface where the salt winds swish.

14

On the fourth morning neighbours got up, fetched their
Thundering sledgehammers and smashed down the door
They heard the silence, saw the corpses stretched there
(And murmured saying what a greenish glare

15

Can come from faces); what is more, the bed kept
Its smell of love, the window burst with frost:
A corpse is such a cold thing! And a thread crept
Thin, cold and black, towards them from its breast.

John Willett

Vom armen B.B.

1

Ich, Bertolt Brecht, bin aus den schwarzen Wäldern.
Meine Mutter trug mich in die Städte hinein
Als ich in ihrem Leibe lag. Und die Kälte der Wälder
Wird in mir bis zu meinem Absterben sein.

2

In der Asphaltstadt bin ich daheim. Von allem Anfang
Versehen mit jedem Sterbsakrament:
Mit Zeitungen. Und Tabak. Und Branntwein.
Mißtrauisch und faul und zufrieden am End.

3

Ich bin zu den Leuten freundlich. Ich setze
Einen steifen Hut auf nach ihrem Brauch.
Ich sage: es sind ganz besonders riechende Tiere
Und ich sage: es macht nichts, ich bin es auch.

4

In meine leeren Schaukelstühle vormittags
Setze ich mir mitunter ein paar Frauen
Und ich betrachte sie sorglos und sage ihnen:
In mir habt ihr einen, auf den könnt ihr nicht bauen.

5

Gegen abends versammle ich um mich Männer
Wir reden uns da mit "Gentlemen" an
Sie haben ihre Füße auf meinen Tischen
Und sagen: es wird besser mit uns. Und ich frage nicht: wann.

BERTOLT BRECHT

Of Poor B.B.

1

I, Bertolt Brecht, come from the black forests.
My mother carried me into the cities
When I was in her belly. And the chill of the forests
Will be in me till my dying day.

2

The asphalt city is my home. Furnished
From the outset with every sacramental perquisite:
With newspapers. And tobacco. And brandy.
Distrustful and idle and contented to the end.

3

I am friendly to people. I put on
A top hat because that's what they do.
I tell myself: They are animals with a particular smell.
And I tell myself: What of it, so am I.

4

In the morning I like to set a woman or two
In my empty rocking chairs
And I look at them insouciantly and I say to them:
In me you have someone on whom there is no relying.

5

Towards evening it's men I gather round about me
And we address our company as "gentlemen."
They park their feet on my table
And say: Things are looking up. And I don't ask: When?

6

Gegen Morgen in der grauen Frühe pissen die Tannen
Und ihr Ungeziefer, die Vögel, fängt an zu schrein.
Um die Stunde trink ich mein Glas in der Stadt aus und schmeiße
Den Tabakstummel weg und schlafe beunruhigt ein.

7

Wir sind gesessen ein leichtes Geschlechte
In Häusern, die für unzerstörbare galten
(So haben wir gebaut die langen Gehäuse des Eilands Manhattan
Und die dünnen Antennen, die das Atlantische Meer unterhalten).

8

Von diesen Städten wird bleiben: der durch sie hindurchging, der Wind!
Fröhlich machet das Haus den Esser: er leert es.
Wir wissen, daß wir Vorläufige sind
Und nach uns wird kommen: nichts Nennenswertes.

9

Bei den Erdbeben, die kommen werden, werde ich hoffentlich
Meine Virginia nicht ausgehen lassen durch Bitterkeit
Ich, Bertolt Brecht, in die Asphaltstädte verschlagen
Aus den schwarzen Wäldern in meiner Mutter in früher Zeit.

BERTOLT BRECHT

6

In the grey pre-dawn the pine trees micturate
And their parasites, the birds, start to bawl.
At that hour I empty my glass in the city and throw away
My cigar end and worriedly go to sleep.

7

We have settled, a whimsical tribe,
In dwellings it pleased us to think of as indestructible
(In the same spirit we built the tall constructions on the island of
    Manhattan
And the thin antennae that underwire the Atlantic Ocean).

8

Of these cities there will remain only what passed through them, the
    wind.
The house makes glad the eater: he polishes it off.
We know we are provisional,
And that after us will come: really nothing worth mentioning.

9

In the coming earthquakes I trust
I will not let my Virginia go bitter on me,
I, Bertolt Brecht, removed to the asphalt cities
From the black forests in my mother in the early times.

Michael Hofmann

Gedanken über die Dauer des Exils

I

Schlage keinen Nagel in die Wand
Wirf den Rock auf den Stuhl!
Warum vorsorgen für vier Tage?
Du kehrst morgen zurück.

Laß den kleinen Baum ohne Wasser!
Wozu noch einen Baum pflanzen?
Bevor er so hoch wie eine Stufe ist
Gehst du froh weg von hier.

Zieh die Mütze ins Gesicht, wenn Leute vorbeigehn!
Wozu in einer fremden Grammatik blättern?
Die Nachricht, die dich heimruft
Ist in bekannter Sprache geschrieben.

So wie der Kalk vom Gebälk blättert
(Tue nichts dagegen!)
Wird der Zaun der Gewalt zermorschen
Der an der Grenze aufgerichtet ist
Gegen die Gerechtigkeit.

II

Sieh den Nagel in der Wand, den du eingeschlagen hast:
Wann, glaubst du, wirst du zurückkehren?
Willst du wissen, was du im Innersten glaubst?
Tag um Tag
Arbeitest du an der Befreiung
Sitzend in der Kammer schreibst du.
Willst du wissen, was du von deiner Arbeit hältst?
Sieh den kleinen Kastanienbaum im Eck des Hofes
Zu dem du die Kanne voll Wasser schlepptest!

BERTOLT BRECHT

Thoughts on the Duration of Exile

I

Don't knock any nails in the wall
Just throw your coat on the chair.
Why plan for four days?
Tomorrow you'll go back home.

Leave the little tree without water.
Why plant a tree now?
You'll pack your bags and be away
Before it's as high as a doorstep.

Pull your cap over your eyes when people pass.
What use thumbing through a foreign grammar?
The message that calls you home
Is written in a language you know.

As whitewash peels from the ceiling
(Do nothing to stop it!)
So the block of force will crumble
That has been set up at the frontier
To keep out justice.

II

Look at the nail you knocked into the wall:
When do you think you will go back?
Do you want to know what your heart of hearts is saying?
Day after day
You work for the liberation.
You sit in your room, writing.
Do you want to know what you think of your work?
Look at the little chestnut tree in the corner of the yard—
You carried a full can of water to it.

Christopher Middleton

Zufluchtsstätte

Ein Ruder liegt auf dem Dach. Ein mittlerer Wind
Wird das Stroh nicht wegtragen.
Im Hof für die Schaukel der Kinder sind
Pfähle eingeschlagen.
Die Post kommt zweimal hin
Wo die Briefe willkommen wären.
Den Sund herunter kommen die Fähren.
Das Haus hat vier Türen, daraus zu fliehn.

BERTOLT BRECHT

Place of Refuge

An oar lies on the roof. A moderate wind
Will not carry away the thatch.
In the yard posts are set for
The children's swing.
The mail comes twice a day
Where letters would be welcome.
Down the Sound come the ferries.
The house has four doors to escape by.

John Willett

An die Nachgeborenen

I

Wirklich, ich lebe in finsteren Zeiten!
Das arglose Wort ist töricht. Eine glatte Stirn
Deutet auf Unempfindlichkeit hin. Der Lachende
Hat die furchtbare Nachricht
Nur noch nicht empfangen.

Was sind das für Zeiten, wo
Ein Gespräch über Bäume fast ein Verbrechen ist
Weil es ein Schweigen über so viele Untaten einschließt!
Der dort ruhig über die Straße geht
Ist wohl nicht mehr erreichbar für seine Freunde
Die in Not sind?

Es ist wahr: ich verdiene noch meinen Unterhalt
Aber glaubt mir: das ist nur ein Zufall. Nichts
Von dem, was ich tue, berechtigt mich dazu, mich satt zu essen.
Zufällig bin ich verschont. (Wenn mein Glück aussetzt
Bin ich verloren.)

Man sagt mir: iß und trink du! Sei froh, daß du hast!
Aber wie kann ich essen und trinken, wenn
Ich es dem Hungernden entreiße, was ich esse, und
Mein Glas Wasser einem Verdurstenden fehlt?
Und doch esse und trinke ich.

Ich wäre gerne auch weise.
In den alten Büchern steht, was weise ist:
Sich aus dem Streit der Welt halten und die kurze Zeit
Ohne Furcht verbringen
Auch ohne Gewalt auskommen
Böses mit Gutem vergelten
Seine Wünsche nicht erfüllen, sondern vergessen

BERTOLT BRECHT

To Those Born Later

I

Truly, I live in dark times!
The guileless word is folly. A smooth forehead
Suggests insensitivity. The man who laughs
Has simply not yet had
The terrible news.

What kind of times are they, when
A talk about trees is almost a crime
Because it implies silence about so many horrors?
That man there calmly crossing the street
Is already perhaps beyond the reach of his friends
Who are in need?

It is true I still earn my keep
But, believe me, that is only an accident. Nothing
I do gives me the right to eat my fill.
By chance I've been spared. (If my luck breaks, I am lost.)

They say to me: Eat and drink! Be glad you have it!
But how can I eat and drink if I snatch what I eat
From the starving, and
My glass of water belongs to one dying of thirst?
And yet I eat and drink.

I would also like to be wise.
In the old books it says what wisdom is:
To shun the strife of the world and to live out
Your brief time without fear
Also to get along without violence
To return good for evil
Not to fulfil your desires but to forget them

Gilt für weise.
Alles das kann ich nicht:
Wirklich, ich lebe in finsteren Zeiten!

2

In die Städte kam ich zu der Zeit der Unordnung
Als da Hunger herrschte.
Unter die Menschen kam ich zu der Zeit des Aufruhrs
Und ich empörte mich mit ihnen.
So verging meine Zeit
Die auf Erden mir gegeben war.

Mein Essen aß ich zwischen den Schlachten
Schlafen legte ich mich unter die Mörder
Der Liebe pflegte ich achtlos
Und die Natur sah ich ohne Geduld.
So verging meine Zeit
Die auf Erden mir gegeben war.

Die Straßen führten in den Sumpf zu meiner Zeit.
Die Sprache verriet mich dem Schlächter.
Ich vermochte nur wenig. Aber die Herrschenden
Saßen ohne mich sicherer, das hoffte ich.
So verging meine Zeit
Die auf Erden mir gegeben war.

Die Kräfte waren gering. Das Ziel
Lag in großer Ferne
Es war deutlich sichtbar, wenn auch für mich
Kaum zu erreichen.
So verging meine Zeit
Die auf Erden mir gegeben war.

BERTOLT BRECHT

Is accounted wise.
All this I cannot do:
Truly, I live in dark times.

 11

I came to the cities in a time of disorder
When hunger reigned there.
I came among men in a time of revolt
And I rebelled with them.
So passed my time
Which had been given to me on earth.

My food I ate between battles
To sleep I lay down among murderers
Love I practised carelessly
And nature I looked at without patience.
So passed my time
Which had been given to me on earth.

All roads led into the mire in my time.
My tongue betrayed me to the butchers.
There was little I could do. But those in power
Sat safer without me: that was my hope.
So passed my time
Which had been given to me on earth.

Our forces were slight. Our goal
Lay far in the distance
It was clearly visible, though I myself
Was unlikely to reach it.
So passed my time
Which had been given to me on earth.

3

Ihr, die ihr auftauchen werdet aus der Flut
In der wir untergegangen sind
Gedenkt
Wenn ihr von unsern Schwächen sprecht
Auch der finsteren Zeit
Der ihr entronnen seid.

Gingen wir doch, öfter als die Schuhe die Länder wechselnd
Durch die Kriege der Klassen, verzweifelt
Wenn da nur Unrecht war und keine Empörung.

Dabei wissen wir ja:
Auch der Haß gegen die Niedrigkeit
Verzerrt die Züge.
Auch der Zorn über das Unrecht
Macht die Stimme heiser. Ach, wir
Die wir den Boden bereiten wollten für Freundlichkeit
Konnten selber nicht freundlich sein.

Ihr aber, wenn es soweit sein wird
Daß der Mensch dem Menschen ein Helfer ist
Gedenkt unsrer
Mit Nachsicht.

BERTOLT BRECHT

III

You who will emerge from the flood
In which we have gone under
Remember
When you speak of our failings
The dark time too
Which you have escaped.

For we went, changing countries oftener than our shoes
Through the wars of the classes, despairing
When there was injustice only, and no rebellion.

And yet we know:
Hatred, even of meanness
Contorts the features.
Anger, even against injustice
Makes the voice hoarse. Oh, we
Who wanted to prepare the ground for friendliness
Could not ourselves be friendly.

But you, when the time comes at last
And man is a helper to man
Think of us
With forbearance.

John Willett

Motto

Dies ist nun alles und ist nicht genug.
Doch sagt es euch vielleicht, ich bin noch da.
Dem gleich ich, der den Backstein mit sich trug
Der Welt zu zeigen, wie sein Haus aussah.

BERTOLT BRECHT

Motto

This is all there is, and it's not enough.
It might do to let you know I'm hanging on.
I'm like that man who carried a brick around with him
To show the world what his house used to look like.

Michael Hofmann

1940

1

Das Frühjahr kommt. Die linden Winde
Befreien die Schären vom Wintereis.
Die Völker des Nordens erwarten zitternd
Die Schlachtflotten des Anstreichers.

2

Aus den Bücherhallen
Treten die Schlächter.
Die Kinder an sich drückend
Stehen die Mütter und durchforschen entgeistert
Den Himmel nach den Erfindungen der Gelehrten.

3

Die Konstrukteure hocken
Gekrümmt in den Zeichensälen:
Eine falsche Ziffer und die Städte des Feindes
Bleiben unzerstört.

4

Nebel verhüllt
Die Straße
Die Pappeln
Die Gehöfte und
Die Artillerie.

5

Ich befinde mich auf dem Inselchen Lidingö.
Aber neulich nachts
Träumte ich schwer und träumte, ich war in einer Stadt

BERTOLT BRECHT

1940

I

Spring is coming. The gentle winds
Are freeing the cliffs of their winter ice.
Trembling, the peoples of the north await
The battle fleets of the house-painter.

II

Out of the libraries
Emerge the butchers.
Pressing their children closer
Mothers stand and humbly search
The skies for the inventions of learned men.

III

The designers sit
Hunched in the drawing offices:
One wrong figure, and the enemy's cities
Will remain undestroyed.

IV

Fog envelops
The road
The poplars
The farms and
The artillery.

V

I am now living on the small island of Lidingö.
But one night recently
I had heavy dreams and I dreamed I was in a city

Und entdeckte, die Beschriftungen der Straßen
Waren deutsch. In Schweiß gebadet
Erwachte ich und mit Erleichterung
Sah ich die nachtschwarze Föhre vor dem Fenster und wußte:
Ich war in der Fremde.

6

Mein junger Sohn fragt mich: Soll ich Mathematik lernen?
Wozu, möchte ich sagen. Daß zwei Stück Brot mehr ist als eines
Das wirst du auch so merken.
Mein junger Sohn fragt mich: Soll ich Englisch lernen?
Wozu, möchte ich sagen. Dieses Reich geht unter. Und
Reibe du nur mit der flachen Hand den Bauch und stöhne
Und man wird dich schon verstehen.
Mein junger Sohn fragt mich: Soll ich Geschichte lernen?
Wozu, möchte ich sagen. Lerne du deinen Kopf in die Erde stecken
Da wirst du vielleicht übrigbleiben.
Ja, lerne Mathematik, sage ich
Lerne Englisch, lerne Geschichte!

7

Vor der weißgetünchten Wand
Steht der schwarze Soldatenkoffer mit den Manuskripten.
Darauf liegt das Rauchzeug mit den kupfernen Aschbechern.
Die chinesische Leinwand, zeigend den Zweifler
Hängt darüber. Auch die Masken sind da. Und neben der Bettstelle
Steht der kleine sechslampige Lautsprecher.
In der Früh
Drehe ich den Schalter um und höre
Die Siegesmeldungen meiner Feinde.

BERTOLT BRECHT

And discovered that its street signs
Were in German, I awoke
Bathed in sweat, saw the fir tree
Black as night before my window, and realised with relief:
I was in a foreign land.

VI

My young son asks me: Should I learn mathematics?
What for, I'm inclined to say. That two bits of bread are more than one
You'll notice anyway.
My young son asks me: Should I learn French?
What for, I'm inclined to say. That empire is going under.
Just rub your hand across your belly and groan
And you'll be understood all right.
My young son asks me: Should I learn history?
What for, I'm inclined to say. Learn to stick your head in the ground
Then maybe you'll come through.
Yes, learn mathematics, I tell him
Learn French, learn history!

VII

In front of the whitewashed wall
Stands the black military case with the manuscripts.
On it lie the smoking things with the copper ashtrays.
The Chinese scroll depicting the Doubter
Hangs above it. The masks are there too. And by the bedstead
Stands the little six-valve radio.
Mornings
I turn it on and hear
The victory bulletins of my enemies.

8

Auf der Flucht vor meinen Landsleuten
Bin ich nun nach Finnland gelangt. Freunde
Die ich gestern nicht kannte, stellten ein paar Betten
In saubere Zimmer. Im Lautsprecher
Höre ich die Siegesmeldungen des Abschaums. Neugierig
Betrachte ich die Karte des Erdteils. Hoch oben in Lappland
Nach dem Nördlichen Eismeer zu
Sehe ich noch eine kleine Tür.

BERTOLT BRECHT

VIII

Fleeing from my fellow-countrymen
I have now reached Finland. Friends
Whom yesterday I didn't know, put up some beds
In clean rooms. Over the radio
I hear the victory bulletins of the scum of the earth. Curiously
I examine a map of the continent. High up in Lapland
Towards the Arctic Ocean
I can still see a small door.

Sammy McLean

Nachdenkend über die Hölle

Nachdenkend, wie ich höre, über die Hölle
Fand mein Bruder Shelley, sie sei ein Ort
Gleichend ungefähr der Stadt London. Ich
Der ich nicht in London lebe, sondern in Los Angeles
Finde, nachdenkend über die Hölle, sie muß
Noch mehr Los Angeles gleichen.

Auch in der Hölle
Gibt es, ich zweifle nicht, diese üppigen Gärten
Mit den Blumen, so groß wie Bäume, freilich verwelkend
Ohne Aufschub, wenn nicht gewässert mit sehr teurem Wasser. Und
    Obstmärkte
Mit ganzen Haufen von Früchten, die allerdings
Weder riechen noch schmecken. Und endlose Züge von Autos
Leichter als ihr eigener Schatten, schneller als
Törichte Gedanken, schimmernde Fahrzeuge, in denen
Rosige Leute, von nirgendher kommend, nirgendhin fahren.
Und Häuser, für Glückliche gebaut, daher leerstehend
Auch wenn bewohnt.

Auch die Häuser in der Hölle sind nicht alle häßlich.
Aber die Sorge, auf die Straße geworfen zu werden
Verzehrt die Bewohner der Villen nicht weniger als
Die Bewohner der Baracken.

BERTOLT BRECHT

On Thinking About Hell

On thinking about Hell, I gather
My brother Shelley found it was a place
Much like the city of London. I
Who live in Los Angeles and not in London
Find, on thinking about Hell, that it must be
Still more like Los Angeles.

In Hell too
There are, I've no doubt, these luxuriant gardens
With flowers as big as trees, which of course wither
Unhesitantly if not nourished with very expensive water. And fruit
    markets
With great heaps of fruit, albeit having
Neither smell nor taste. And endless processions of cars
Lighter than their own shadows, faster than
Mad thoughts, gleaming vehicles in which
Jolly-looking people come from nowhere and are nowhere bound.
And houses, built for happy people, therefore standing empty
Even when lived in.

The houses in Hell, too, are not all ugly.
But the fear of being thrown on the street
Wears down the inhabitants of the villas no less than
The inhabitants of the shanty towns.

Nicholas Jacobs

Hollywood-Elegien

I

Das Dorf Hollywood ist entworfen nach den Vorstellungen
Die man hierorts vom Himmel hat. Hierorts
Hat man ausgerechnet, daß Gott
Himmel und Hölle benötigend, nicht zwei
Etablissements zu entwerfen brauchte, sondern
Nur ein einziges, nämlich den Himmel. Dieser
Dient für die Unbemittelten, Erfolglosen
Als Hölle.

II

Am Meer stehen die Öltürme. In den Schluchten
Bleichen die Gebeine der Goldwäscher. Ihre Söhne
Haben die Traumfabriken von Hollywood gebaut.
Die vier Städte
Sind erfüllt von dem Ölgeruch
Der Filme.

III

Die Stadt ist nach den Engeln genannt
Und man begegnet allenthalben Engeln.
Sie riechen nach Öl und tragen goldene Pessare
Und mit blauen Ringen um die Augen
Füttern sie allmorgendlich die Schreiber in ihren Schwimmpfühlen.

IV

Unter den grünen Pfefferbäumen
Gehen die Musiker auf den Strich, zwei und zwei
Mit den Schreibern. Bach
Hat ein Strichquartett im Täschchen. Dante schwenkt
Den dürren Hintern.

BERTOLT BRECHT

Hollywood Elegies

I

The village of Hollywood was planned according to the notion
People in these parts have of heaven. In these parts
They have come to the conclusion that God
Requiring a heaven and a hell, didn't need to
Plan two establishments but
Just the one: heaven. It
Serves the unprosperous, unsuccessful
As hell.

II

By the sea stand the oil derricks. Up the canyons
The gold prospectors' bones lie bleaching. Their sons
Built the dream factories of Hollywood.
The four cities
Are filled with the oily smell
Of films.

III

The city is named after the angels
And you meet angels on every hand.
They smell of oil and wear golden pessaries
And, with blue rings round their eyes
Feed the writers in their swimming pools every morning.

IV

Beneath the green pepper trees
The musicians play the whore, two by two
With the writers. Bach
Has written a Strumpet Voluntary. Dante wriggles
His shrivelled bottom.

V

Die Engel von Los Angeles
Sind müde vom Lächeln. Am Abend
Kaufen sie hinter den Obstmärkten
Verzweifelt kleine Fläschchen
Mit Geschlechtsgeruch.

VI

Über den vier Städten kreisen die Jagdflieger
Der Verteidigung in großer Höhe
Damit der Gestank der Gier und des Elends
Nicht bis zu ihnen heraufdringt.

BERTOLT BRECHT

V

The angels of Los Angeles
Are tired out with smiling. Desperately
Behind the fruit stalls of an evening
They buy little bottles
Containing sex odours.

VI

Above the four cities the fighter planes
Of the Defense Department circle at a great height
So that the stink of greed and poverty
Shall not reach them.

John Willett

Vom Sprengen des Gartens

O Sprengen des Gartens, das Grün zu ermutigen!
Wässern der durstigen Bäume! Gib mehr als genug. Und
Vergiß nicht das Strauchwerk, auch
Das beerenlose nicht, das ermattete
Geizige! Und übersieh mir nicht
Zwischen den Blumen das Unkraut, das auch
Durst hat. Noch gieße nur
Den frischen Rasen oder den versengten nur:
Auch den nackten Boden erfrische du.

BERTOLT BRECHT

Of Sprinkling the Garden

O sprinkling the garden, to enliven the green!
Watering the thirsty trees. Give them more than enough
And do not forget the shrubs
Even those without berries, the exhausted
Niggardly ones. And do not neglect
The weeds growing between the flowers, they too
Are thirsty. Nor water only
The fresh grass or only the scorched.
Even the naked soil you must refresh.

Patrick Bridgwater

aus **Buckower Elegien**

DER RADWECHSEL

Ich sitze am Straßenhang.
Der Fahrer wechselt das Rad.
Ich bin nicht gern, wo ich herkomme.
Ich bin nicht gern, wo ich hinfahre.
Warum sehe ich den Radwechsel
Mit Ungeduld?

DIE LÖSUNG

Nach dem Aufstand des 17. Juni
Ließ der Sekretär des Schriftstellerverbands
In der Stalinallee Flugblätter verteilen
Auf denen zu lesen war, daß das Volk
Das Vertrauen der Regierung verscherzt habe
Und es nur durch verdoppelte Arbeit
Zurückerobern könne. Wäre es da
Nicht doch einfacher, die Regierung
Löste das Volk auf und
Wählte ein anderes?

BERTOLT BRECHT

from **Buckow Elegies**

CHANGING THE WHEEL

I sit by the roadside
The driver changes the wheel.
I do not like the place I have come from.
I do not like the place I am going to.
Why with impatience do I
Watch him changing the wheel?

Michael Hamburger

THE SOLUTION

After the uprising of the 17th June
The Secretary of the Writers' Union
Had leaflets distributed in the Stalinallee
Stating that the people
Had forfeited the confidence of the government
And could win it back only
By redoubled efforts. Would it not be easier
In that case for the government
To dissolve the people
And elect another?

Derek Bowman

VOR ACHT JAHREN

Da war eine Zeit
Da war alles hier anders.
Die Metzgerfrau weiß es.
Der Postbote hat einen zu aufrechten Gang.
Und was war der Elektriker?

BEI DER LEKTÜRE EINES SPÄTGRIECHISCHEN DICHTERS

In den Tagen, als ihr Fall gewiß war
Auf den Mauern begann schon die Totenklage
Richteten die Troer Stückchen grade, Stückchen
In den dreifachen Holztoren, Stückchen.
Und begannen Mut zu haben und gute Hoffnung.

Auch die Troer also . . .

"UND ICH DACHTE IMMER"

Und ich dachte immer: die allereinfachsten Worte
Müssen genügen. Wenn ich sage, was ist
Muß jedem das Herz zerfleischt sein.
Daß du untergehst, wenn du dich nicht wehrst
Das wirst du doch einsehen.

BERTOLT BRECHT

EIGHT YEARS AGO

There was a time
When all was different here.
The butcher's wife knows.
The postman has too erect a gait.
And what was the electrician?

Derek Bowman

READING A LATE GREEK POET

At the time when their fall was certain—
On the ramparts the lament for the dead had begun—
The Trojans adjusted small pieces, small pieces
In the triple wooden gates, small pieces.
And began to take courage, to hope.

The Trojans too, then.

Michael Hamburger

"AND I ALWAYS THOUGHT"

And I always thought: the very simplest words
Must be enough. When I say what things are like
Everyone's heart must be torn to shreds.
That you'll go down if you don't stand up for yourself.
Surely you see that.

Michael Hamburger

Landschaft hinter Warschau

Spitzhackig schlägt der März
Das Eis des Himmels auf.
Es stürzt das Licht aus rissigem Spalt,
Niederbrandend
Auf Telegrafendrähte und kahle Chausseen.
Am Mittag nistet es weiß im Röhricht,
Ein großer Vogel.
Spreizt er die Zehen, glänzt hell
Die Schwimmhaut aus dünnem Nebel.

Schnell wird es dunkel.
Flacher als ein Hundegaumen
Ist dann der Himmel gewölbt.
Ein Hügel raucht,
Als säßen dort noch immer
Die Jäger am nassen Winterfeuer.
Wohin sie gingen?
Die Spur des Hasen im Schnee
Erzählte es einst.

Landscape Beyond Warsaw

March with its sharp pick
Splits the ice of the sky.
From the cracks light pours
Billowing down
On to telegraph wires and bare main roads.
At noon white it roosts in the reeds,
A great bird.
When it spreads its claws, brightly
The webs gleam out of thin mist.

Nightfall is brief.
Then more shallow than a dog's palate
The sky arches.
A hill smokes
As though still the huntsmen
Were sitting there by the damp winter fire.
Where have they gone?
The hare's tracks in the snow
Once told us where.

Michael Hamburger

Chausseen

Erwürgte Abendröte
Stürzender Zeit!
Chausseen. Chausseen.
Kreuzwege der Flucht.
Wagenspuren über den Acker,
Der mit den Augen
Erschlagener Pferde
Den brennenden Himmel sah.

Nächte mit Lungen voll Rauch,
Mit hartem Atem der Fliehenden,
Wenn Schüsse
Auf die Dämmerung schlugen.
Aus zerbrochenem Tor
Trat lautlos Asche und Wind,
Ein Feuer,
Das mürrisch das Dunkel kaute.

Tote,
Über die Gleise geschleudert,
Den erstickten Schrei
Wie einen Stein am Gaumen.
Ein schwarzes
Summendes Tuch aus Fliegen
Schloß ihre Wunden.

PETER HUCHEL

Roads

Choked sunset glow
Of crashing time.
Roads. Roads.
Intersections of flight.
Cart tracks across the ploughed field
That with the eyes
Of killed horses
Saw the sky in flames.

Nights with lungs full of smoke,
With the hard breath of the fleeing
When shots
Struck the dusk.
Out of a broken gate
Ash and wind came without a sound,
A fire
That sullenly chewed the darkness.

Corpses,
Flung over the rail tracks,
Their stifled cry
Like a stone on the palate.
A black
Humming cloth of flies
Closed their wounds.

   Michael Hamburger

Die Pappeln

Zeit mit rostiger Sense,
Spät erst zogest du fort,
Den Hohlweg hinauf
Und an den beiden Pappeln vorbei.
Sie schwammen
Im dünnen Wasser des Himmels.
Ein weißer Stein ertrank.
War es der Mond, das Auge der Ödnis?

Am Gräbergebüsch die Dämmerung.
Sie hüllte ihr Tuch,
Aus Gras und Nebel grob gewebt,
Um Helme und Knochen.
Die erste Frühe, umkrustet von Eis,
Warf blinkende Scherben ins Schilf.
Schweigend schob der Fischer
Den Kahn in den Fluß. Es klagte
Die frierende Stimme des Wassers,
Das Tote um Tote flößte hinunter.

Wer aber begrub sie, im frostigen Lehm,
In Asche und Schlamm,
Die alte Fußspur der Not?
Im Kahlschlag des Kriegs glänzt Ackererde,
Es drängt die quellende Kraft des Halms.
Und wo der Schälpflug wendet,
Die Stoppel stürzt,
Stehn auf dem Hang die beiden Pappeln.
Sie ragen ins Licht
Als Fühler der Erde.

Schön ist die Heimat,
Wenn über der grünen Messingscheibe
Des Teichs der Kranich schreit

PETER HUCHEL

The Poplars

Time with your rusty scythe,
Late you went on your way,
Up the narrow path
And past the two poplars.
They swam
In the sky's thin water.
A white stone drowned.
Was it the moon, desolation's eye?

Dusk on the graveside bushes.
It wound its cloth
Coarsely woven of grass and mist
Around helmets and bones.
The dawn light, encrusted with ice,
Threw glinting shards into rushes.
In silence the fisherman pushed
His boat into the river. The water's
Freezing voice complained,
Bearing corpse after corpse downstream.

But who buried them in the frosty clay,
In ashes and mud,
Disaster's old footprints?
Amid the razing impact of war
The ploughed field glistens, the corn blade's power wells up.
And where the paring plough turns,
Where stubble falls,
On the slope the two poplars remain.
They loom into light
As the antennae of Earth.

Lovely our homeland is
When over the green brass disc
Of the pond a crane cries

Und das Gold sich häuft
Im blauen Oktobergewölbe;
Wenn Korn und Milch in der Kammer schlafen,
Sprühen die Funken
Vom Amboß der Nacht.
Die rußige Schmiede des Alls
Beginnt ihr Feuer zu schüren.
Sie schmiedet
Das glühende Eisen der Morgenröte.
Und Asche fällt
Auf den Schatten der Fledermäuse.

PETER HUCHEL

And gold gathers
In October's blue vault;
When corn and milk sleep in the store-room
The sparks fly up
From night's anvil.
The world's sooty forge
Begins to fan its fire.
It beats out
The glowing iron of dawn.
And ash falls
On the shadows of bats.

Michael Hamburger

Der Garten des Theophrast

Meinem Sohn

Wenn mittags das weiße Feuer
Der Verse über den Urnen tanzt,
Gedenke, mein Sohn. Gedenke derer,
Die einst Gespräche wie Bäume gepflanzt.
Tot ist der Garten, mein Atem wird schwerer,
Bewahre die Stunde, hier ging Theophrast,
Mit Eichenlohe zu düngen den Boden,
Die wunde Rinde zu binden mit Bast.
Ein Ölbaum spaltet das mürbe Gemäuer
Und ist noch Stimme im heißen Staub.
Sie gaben Befehl, die Wurzel zu roden.
Es sinkt dein Licht, schutzloses Laub.

PETER HUCHEL

The Garden of Theophrastus

To my son

When at noon the white fire of verses
Flickering dances above the urns,
Remember, my son. Remember the vanished
Who planted their conversations like trees.
The garden is dead, more heavy my breathing,
Preserve the hour, here Theophrastus walked,
With oak bark to feed the soil and enrich it,
To bandage with fiber the wounded bole.
An olive tree splits the brickwork grown brittle
And still is a voice in the mote-laden heat.
Their order was to fell and uproot it.
Your light is fading, defenceless leaves.

Michael Hamburger

Psalm

Daß aus dem Samen des Menschen
Kein Mensch
Und aus dem Samen des Ölbaums
Kein Ölbaum
Werde,
Es ist zu messen
Mit der Elle des Todes.

Die da wohnen
Unter der Erde
In einer Kugel aus Zement,
Ihre Stärke gleicht
Dem Halm
Im peitschenden Schnee.

Die Öde wird Geschichte.
Termiten schreiben sie
Mit ihren Zangen
In den Sand.

Und nicht erforscht wird werden
Ein Geschlecht,
Eifrig bemüht,
Sich zu vernichten.

PETER HUCHEL

Psalm

That from the seed of men
No man
And from the seed of the olive tree
No olive tree
Shall grow,
This you must measure
With the yardstick of death.

Those who live
Under the earth
In a capsule of cement,
Their strength is like
A blade of grass
Lashed by snow in a blizzard.

The desert now will be history.
Termites with their pincers
Write it
On sand.

And no one will enquire
Into a species
Eagerly bent
On self-extinction.

    Michael Hamburger

Der Schlammfang

Eines Abends kamen
aus einem Loch im Asphalt
Männer mit Masken.
Sie rochen nach seifigem Schlamm,
im Netzwerk trug einer
tote Fische
und grüne Wasserratten.
Abwässer liefen von ihren Stiefeln.
Niemand wollte sie sehen
in der Stadt,
jeder schloß die Tür.
Sie zogen über den Markt und schwanden
im Gebüsch verkohlter Schrebergärten.
Eine schillernde Muschel
hing einem im Haar.
Noch lange glomm sie
im öligen Spiegel der Straße.

PETER HUCHEL

The Mudcatchers

One night from a hole in the asphalt
masked men arrived.
They smelled of soapy mud.
In his net
one of them carried
dead fish
and green water rats.
Effluent oozed from their boots.
No one wanted to see them
in the town,
everyone locked his door.
They crossed the market square and vanished
in the shrubs of the small allotments.
A glittering mussel shell
clung to the hair of one.
For a long time it glimmered
in the street's oily mirror.

Michael Hamburger

Inventur

Dies ist meine Mütze,
dies ist mein Mantel,
hier mein Rasierzeug
im Beutel aus Leinen.

Konservenbüchse:
Mein Teller, mein Becher,
ich hab in das Weißblech
den Namen geritzt.

Geritzt hier mit diesem
kostbaren Nagel,
den vor begehrlichen
Augen ich berge.

Im Brotbeutel sind
ein Paar wollene Socken
und einiges, was ich
niemand verrate,

so dient es als Kissen
nachts meinem Kopf.
Die Pappe hier liegt
zwischen mir und der Erde.

Die Bleistiftmine
lieb ich am meisten:
Tags schreibt sie mir Verse,
die nachts ich erdacht.

GÜNTER EICH, 1907–1972

Inventory

This is my cap,
this is my coat,
here is my shaving set
in a linen bag.

A tin can:
my plate, my cup,
in the metal
I have scratched my name.

Scratched it with this
precious nail,
which I hide
from greedy eyes.

In my haversack are
a pair of woolen socks
and some things I don't
tell anyone about,

it serves as a pillow
at night for my head.
The cardboard lies here
between me and the earth.

The pencil lead
I love the most:
by day it writes verses for me
that I have thought up by night.

Dies ist mein Notizbuch,
dies meine Zeltbahn,
dies ist mein Handtuch,
dies ist mein Zwirn.

GÜNTER EICH

This is my notebook,
this is my canvas,
this is my towel,
this is my thread.

   Charlotte Melin

Bericht aus einem Kurort

Ich habe das Wasser noch nicht getrunken,
halte auch nichts davon.
Aber der Bahnhofsumbau
läßt an Zukunft denken,
das macht mich störrisch.

Mein Blutbild und Koniferenozon,
das Mißtrauen der Badeärzte.
Natur
ist eine Form der Verneinung.
Die Gedichte in der Kurzeitung
sind besser.

GÜNTER EICH

Report from a Spa

I haven't tried the water yet,
that can wait.
But the redecorated station
implies future,
which makes me mulish.

Corpuscle count and forest ozone,
suspicion of the spa doctors.
Nature
is a form of negation.
Better to stick to
the ditties in the spa newsletter.

Michael Hofmann

Brüder Grimm

Brennesselbusch.
Die gebrannten Kinder
warten hinter den Kellerfenstern.
Die Eltern sind fortgegangen,
sagten, sie kämen bald.

Erst kam der Wolf,
der die Semmeln brachte,
die Hyäne borgte sich den Spaten aus,
der Skorpion das Fernsehprogramm.

Ohne Flammen
brennt draußen der Brennesselbusch.
Lange
bleiben die Eltern aus.

GÜNTER EICH

Brothers Grimm

Nettlebush.
The burnt children
wait behind the cellar windows.
Their parents have gone out,
saying they will be back soon.

First came the wolf,
bringing rolls,
the hyena wanted to borrow a garden-fork,
the scorpion came for the TV guide.

Without flames
the nettlebush burns outside.
Their parents
are gone a long time.

   Michael Hofmann

Aussicht vom Spezial-Keller

Kulissen vor meiner Trunksucht
und Rauch in den Etüden für Julia,
keine Erbschaft,
die mich anziehend machte,
und meine Freunde
sind mir noch nicht begegnet.

GÜNTER EICH

Perspective from the Spezial-Keller

A backdrop for my bibulousness
and smoke towards Julia's sketches,
no fortune
to make me attractive to anyone,
and my friends
have yet to show.

Michael Hofmann

Auskünfte aus dem Nachlaß

Nach dem Kalkofen befragt:
Iltisse wohnen dort
und freundliche Mädchen.

In den Schutthaufen
Anfänge von grauem Star,
die Schöpfung
nah vor der Lesebrille.

Ich höre wenig:
Die Gänge im Motor,
Hilferufe, wenn niemand ruft.

Immer habe ich Brennesseln geliebt,
und jetzt erfahren,
daß sie nützlich sind.

GÜNTER EICH

Tips from the Posthumous Papers

Asked after the lime-kiln:
pole-cats live there
and kindly girls.

To the scrapheap
the onset of cataracts,
creation right up against
my reading-glasses.

I don't hear much:
gear changes,
screams for help in silence.

I have always loved nettles,
and only now learned
of their usefulness.

Michael Hofmann

Bett hüten

Anginatage, blauer Schnee,
die Zeit versteckt
in Ausschnittbögen,
die Zeit ist blau, die Zeit ist Schnee,
und rote Ärmel, schwarzer Hut,
die Zeit ist eine gelbe Frau.

Anginatage, schweizerisch,
ist blau Devon,
schwarz Cambrium,
Commedia dell'arte Zeit,
Pantoffeln rot und rot Silur,
ein Plan von England gelb und Zeit.

Anginatage, blaues Kent,
die Zeit so gelb,
daß keiner sie erkennt,
ein schwarzer Zeigefinger
aus einem blauen Handschuh zeigt
die rote Mauer lang nachhause.

GÜNTER EICH

Confined to Bed

Angina days, blue snow,
time tucked away
in cut-out arches,
time is blue, time is snow,
red sleeves, black hat,
time is a yellow woman.

Angina days, Swiss,
blue Devon,
black Cambrium,
commedia dell'arte time,
slipper red and Silurian red,
wall map of England yellow and time.

Angina days, blue Kent,
time so yellow that none
can tell it, a black index finger
protrudes from a blue glove
and points you the way home
along the red wall.

Michael Hofmann

Monolog der Menschen

Wir sind die Welt gewöhnt.
Wir haben die Welt lieb wie uns.
Würde Welt plötzlich anders,
wir weinten.

Im Nichts hausen die Fragen.
Im Nichts sind die Pupillen groß.
Wenn Nichts wäre,
o wir schliefen jetzt nicht,
und der kommende Traum
sänke zu Tode unter blöden Riesenstein.

Human Monologue

We are used to the world.
We love the world as we love ourselves.
Were the world suddenly changed
we would weep.

In nothingness questions dwell.
In nothingness the pupils are large.
If there was no nothingness
we would not sleep now
and the coming dream
would sink among giant bashful stones.

Georg M. Gugelberger

Kindheit

Da hab ich
den Pirol geliebt—
das Glockenklingen, droben
aufscholls, niedersanks
durch das Laubgehäus,

wenn wir hockten am Waldrand,
auf einen Grashalm reihten
rote Beeren; mit seinem
Wägelchen zog der graue
Jude vorbei.

Mittags dann in der Erlen
Schwarzschatten standen die Tiere,
peitschten zornigen Schwanzschlags
die Fliegen davon.

Dann fiel die strömende, breite
Regenflut aus dem offenen
Himmel; nach allem Dunkel
schmeckten die Tropfen
wie Erde.

Oder die Burschen kamen
den Uferpfad her mit den Pferden,
auf den glänzenden braunen
Rücken ritten sie lachend
über die Tiefe.

Hinter dem Zaun
wölkte Bienengetön.
Später, durchs Dornicht am Schilfsee,
fuhr die Silberrassel

JOHANNES BOBROWSKI

Childhood

Then I loved
the oriole—
the toll of bells sounded
above, sank low
through the greenwood,

when we squatted at the edge of the wood,
threaded red berries
on a grass-blade; the grey Jew
went by
with his cart.

At noon then the cattle stood
in the alders' black shadows
flicking away the flies
with angry tails.

Then the streaming rain-flood
fell from the open
sky; after all that darkness
the drops tasted
like earth.

Or the lads came
along the towpath with the horses,
on the shining brown
backs they rode laughing
across the deep.

Behind the fence
hummed clouds of bees.
Later the silver rattle of fear
ran through the thorn thicket

der Angst.
Es verwuchs, eine Hecke,
Düsternis Fenster und Tür.

Da sang die Alte in ihrer
duftenden Kammer. Die Lampe
summte. Es traten die Männer
herein, sie riefen den Hunden
über die Schulter zu.

Nacht, lang verzweigt im Schweigen—
Zeit, entgleitender, bittrer
von Vers zu Vers während:
Kindheit—
da hab ich den Pirol geliebt—

JOHANNES BOBROWSKI

by the reedy lake.
It grew wild, a hedge,
darkening window and door.

Then the old woman sang in her
fragrant chamber. The lamp
hummed. The men
entered calling over their shoulders
to the dogs.

Night, long interlocked with silence—
time, slipping away, bitterer,
lasting from verse to verse:
childhood—
then I loved the oriole.

    Ruth and Matthew Mead

Lettische Lieder

Mein Vater der Habicht.
Großvater der Wolf.
Und der Ältervater der räubrische Fisch im Meer.

Ich, unbärtig, ein Narr,
an den Zäunen taumelnd,
mit schwarzen Händen
würgend ein Lamm um das Frühlicht. Ich,

der die Tiere schlug
statt des weißen
Herrn, ich folg auf zerspülten
Wegen dem Rasselzug,

durch der Zigeunerweiber
Blicke geh ich. Dann
am baltischen Ufer treff ich den Uexküll, den Herrn.
Er geht unterm Mond.

Ihm redet die Finsternis nach.

JOHANNES BOBROWSKI

Latvian Songs

My father the hawk.
Grandfather the wolf.
And my forefather the rapacious fish in the sea.

I, unbearded, a fool,
lurching against the fences,
my black hands strangling a lamb
in the early light. I,

who beat the animals
instead of the white
master, I follow the rattling caravans
on washed-out roads,

I pass through the glances
of the gipsy women. Then
on the Baltic shore I meet Uexküll, the master.
He walks beneath the moon.

Behind him, the darkness speaks.

Ruth and Matthew Mead

Ungesagt

Schwer,
ich wachse hinab,
Wurzeln
breite ich in den Grund,
die Wasser der Erde
finden mich, steigen,
Bitternis schmeck ich—du
bist ohne Erde,
ein Vogel den Lüften, leichter
immer im Licht,
nur meine Angst noch
hält dich
im irdischen Wind.

JOHANNES BOBROWSKI

Unsaid

Heavy,
I grow down,
I spread roots
in the ground,
the waters of earth
find me, rise,
I taste bitterness—you
are without earth,
a bird of the air, lighter
always in light,
only my fear still
holds you
in the earthly wind.

Ruth and Matthew Mead

Bericht

Bajla Gelblung,
entflohen in Warschau
einem Transport aus dem Ghetto,
das Mädchen
ist gegangen durch Wälder,
bewaffnet, die Partisanin
wurde ergriffen
in Brest-Litowsk,
trug einen Militärmantel (polnisch),
wurde verhört von deutschen
Offizieren, es gibt
ein Foto, die Offiziere sind junge
Leute, tadellos uniformiert,
mit tadellosen Gesichtern,
ihre Haltung
ist einwandfrei.

JOHANNES BOBROWSKI

Report

Bajla Gelblung,
escaped in Warsaw
from a transport from the Ghetto,
the girl took to the woods,
armed, was picked up
as partisan
in Brest-Litovsk,
wore a military coat (Polish),
was interrogated by German
officers, there is
a photo, the officers are young
chaps, faultlessly uniformed,
with faultless faces,
their bearing
is unexceptionable.

Ruth and Matthew Mead

Mozart

Am Schuh die Schnalle
ist lose, ein silberner Knopf
hat hier gesessen, mich schmerzt
der Hals, die Augen,
wenn ich sie schlösse—

Damals fiel mir auf
die neue Falte
in Colloredos Gesicht—
in Prag das Häuschen,
schwimmend über den Hang,
Gesträuch, eine weiße Woge,
vor sich her—als der endlose
Regen vorüber war, eines
Abends das Licht
auf dem Stainschen Clavier.

Es gab noch zu schreiben
eine Musik,
Holz, ein Dröhnen, irdisch,
unter den Füßen, im Haus
schlägt eine Tür, ich frag nicht,
ich hör sie allein,
ich hab es nicht gern, wenn Constanze
mit dem gläsernen Munde
lacht.

JOHANNES BOBROWSKI

Mozart

The buckle is loose
on my shoe, there was
a silver button there,
my throat hurts me, my eyes,
if I closed them—

Then I noticed
the new wrinkle
in Colloredo's face . . .
the little house in Prague
floating down the slope,
bushes, a white wave,
in front of it—when the endless
rain was over, the light
one evening
on Stein's piano.

There was still a music
to be written,
wood, a thudding, earthly,
beneath the feet, a door
bangs in the house, I do not question,
I alone hear it,
I do not like it when Constanze
laughs
with her glassy mouth.

Ruth and Matthew Mead

Trakl

Stirn.
Der braune Balken.
Dielenbretter. Die Schritte
zum Fenster.
Das Grün großer Blätter. Zeichen,
geschrieben über den Tisch.

Die splitternde Schwelle. Und
verlassen. Langsam
hinter dem Fremdling her
unter Flügeln der Dohlen
in Gras und Staub
die Straße ohne Namen.

JOHANNES BOBROWSKI

Trakl

Brow.
The brown beam.
Floorboards. The steps
to the window.
The green of large leaves. Signs,
written over the table.

The splintering threshold. And
deserted. Slowly
pursuing the stranger
under the jackdaws' wings
in grass and dust
the road with no name.

> *Michael Hamburger*

Vormittag

Immer um sechs kommt der Milchmann
Nach sieben hinkt die Zeitungsfrau heran
Gegen acht komme ich zu mir selber
Auf dem Tisch steht noch die Weinflasche
von gestern abend und das Glas, leer.
Und da liegen auch die Briefe
immer mit freundlichen Grüßen—
Aufstehen, umhergehen, lesen
Prediger elf
Süß ist dem Auge das Licht
und köstlich ist es, die Sonne zu schauen . . .

Morning

Each day the milkman comes at six
A little after seven the newspaper lady limps along
At eight I start coming round
On the table there's still the wine bottle
from last night and the glass, empty.
And there too are the letters
all of them sincerely mine—
Get up, walk around, read
Ecclesiastes eleven
truly the light is sweet
and a pleasant thing it is for the eyes to behold the sun . . .

    Michael Hofmann

Alleinstehende Männer

Einer sammelt Steine.
Einer erwirbt Briefmarken.
Ein dritter spielt Fernschach
und einer steht lauernd am Abend im Park.
Einer lernt Russisch.
Einer liest Shakespeare.
Einer schreibt Brief um Brief
und einer trinkt Rotwein am Abend,
sonst geschieht nichts.
Sie trinken, lesen, lauern, erwerben,
die Männer allein am Abend.
Sie schreiben, lernen, spielen, sammeln,
ein jeder für sich nach Feierabend.
Einer besucht eine Operette.
Einer hört Bach.
Einer hütet ein Geheimnis.
Wie ein Hund an der Kette
läuft er Abend für Abend entlang den Alleen.

RAINER BRAMBACH

Single Men

One collects stones.
One acquires stamps.
A third plays chess by mail
and one stands and lurks in the park in the evenings.
One studies Russian.
One reads Shakespeare.
One writes one letter after another,
and one drinks wine in the evening,
otherwise nothing to report.
They drink, read, lurk, acquire,
these men alone in their evening.
They write, study, play, collect,
each for himself after the close of work.
One visits the operetta.
One listens to Bach.
One keeps a secret.
Like a dog on a chain,
he runs down the avenues, night after night.

Michael Hofmann

Erinnerung an Frankreich

Du denk mit mir: der Himmel von Paris, die große Herbstzeitlose ...
Wir kauften Herzen bei den Blumenmädchen:
sie waren blau und blühten auf im Wasser.
Es fing zu regnen an in unserer Stube,
und unser Nachbar kam, Monsieur Le Songe, ein hager Männlein.
Wir spielten Karten, ich verlor die Augensterne;
du liehst dein Haar mir, ich verlors, er schlug uns nieder.
Er trat zur Tür hinaus, der Regen folgt' ihm.
Wir waren tot und konnten atmen.

Memory of France

Together with me recall: the sky of Paris, that giant autumn crocus . . .
We went shopping for hearts at the flower girl's booth:
they were blue and they opened up in the water.
It began to rain in our room,
and our neighbour came in, Monsieur Le Songe, a lean little man.
We played cards, I lost the irises of my eyes;
you lent me your hair, I lost it, he struck us down.
He left by the door, the rain followed him out.
We were dead and were able to breathe.

Michael Hamburger

Corona

Aus der Hand frißt der Herbst mir sein Blatt: wir sind Freunde.
Wir schälen die Zeit aus den Nüssen und lehren sie gehn:
die Zeit kehrt zurück in die Schale.

Im Spiegel ist Sonntag,
im Traum wird geschlafen,
der Mund redet wahr.

Mein Aug steigt hinab zum Geschlecht der Geliebten:
wir sehen uns an,
wir sagen uns Dunkles,
wir lieben einander wie Mohn und Gedächtnis,
wir schlafen wie Wein in den Muscheln,
wie das Meer im Blutstrahl des Mondes.

Wir stehen umschlungen im Fenster, sie sehen uns zu von der Straße:
es ist Zeit, daß man weiß!
Es ist Zeit, daß der Stein sich zu blühen bequemt,
daß der Unrast ein Herz schlägt.
Es ist Zeit, daß es Zeit wird.

Es ist Zeit.

PAUL CELAN

Corona

Autumn eats its leaf out of my hand: we are friends.
From the nuts we shell time and we teach it to walk:
then time returns to the shell.

In the mirror it's Sunday,
in dream there is room for sleeping,
our mouths speak the truth.

My eye moves down to the sex of my loved one:
we look at each other,
we exchange dark words,
we love each other like poppy and recollection,
we sleep like wine in the conches,
like the sea in the moon's blood ray.

We stand by the window embracing, and people look up from the street:
it is time they knew!
It is time the stone made an effort to flower,
time unrest had a beating heart.
It is time it were time.

It is time.

Michael Hamburger

Todesfuge

Schwarze Milch der Frühe wir trinken sie abends
wir trinken sie mittags und morgens wir trinken sie nachts
wir trinken und trinken
wir schaufeln ein Grab in den Lüften da liegt man nicht eng
Ein Mann wohnt im Haus der spielt mit den Schlangen der schreibt
der schreibt wenn es dunkelt nach Deutschland dein goldenes Haar
    Margarete
er schreibt es und tritt vor das Haus und es blitzen die Sterne er pfeift
    seine Rüden herbei
er pfeift seine Juden hervor läßt schaufeln ein Grab in der Erde
er befiehlt uns spielt auf nun zum Tanz

Schwarze Milch der Frühe wir trinken dich nachts
wir trinken dich morgens und mittags wir trinken dich abends
wir trinken und trinken
Ein Mann wohnt im Haus der spielt mit den Schlangen der schreibt
der schreibt wenn es dunkelt nach Deutschland dein goldenes Haar
    Margarete
Dein aschenes Haar Sulamith wir schaufeln ein Grab in den Lüften da
    liegt man nicht eng

Er ruft stecht tiefer ins Erdreich ihr einen ihr andern singet und spielt
er greift nach dem Eisen im Gurt er schwingts seine Augen sind blau
stecht tiefer die Spaten ihr einen ihr andern spielt weiter zum Tanz auf

Schwarze Milch der Frühe wir trinken dich nachts
wir trinken dich mittags und morgens wir trinken dich abends
wir trinken und trinken
ein Mann wohnt im Haus dein goldenes Haar Margarete
dein aschenes Haar Sulamith er spielt mit den Schlangen

Er ruft spielt süßer den Tod der Tod ist ein Meister aus Deutschland
er ruft streicht dunkler die Geigen dann steigt ihr als Rauch in die Luft
dann habt ihr ein Grab in den Wolken da liegt man nicht eng

PAUL CELAN

Deathfugue

Black milk of daybreak we drink it at evening
we drink it at midday and morning we drink it at night
we drink and we drink
we shovel a grave in the air where you won't lie too cramped
A man lives in the house he plays with his vipers he writes
he writes when it grows dark to Deutschland your golden hair Margareta
he writes it and steps out of doors and the stars are all sparkling he
    whistles his hounds to stay close
he whistles his Jews into rows has them shovel a grave in the ground
he commands us play up for the dance

Black milk of daybreak we drink you at night
we drink you at morning and midday we drink you at evening
we drink and we drink
A man lives in the house he plays with his vipers he writes
he writes when it grows dark to Deutschland your golden hair Margareta
Your ashen hair Shulamith we shovel a grave in the air where you won't
    lie too cramped

He shouts dig this earth deeper you lot there you others sing up and play
he grabs for the rod in his belt he swings it his eyes are so blue
stick your spades deeper you lot there you others play on for the dancing

Black milk of daybreak we drink you at night
we drink you at midday and morning we drink you at evening
we drink and we drink
a man lives in the house your goldenes Haar Margareta
your aschenes Haar Shulamith he plays with his vipers

He shouts play death more sweetly this Death is a master from
    Deutschland
he shouts scrape your strings darker you'll rise up as smoke to the sky
you'll then have a grave in the clouds where you won't lie too cramped

Schwarze Milch der Frühe wir trinken dich nachts
wir trinken dich mittags der Tod ist ein Meister aus Deutschland
wir trinken dich abends und morgens wir trinken und trinken
der Tod ist ein Meister aus Deutschland sein Auge ist blau
er trifft dich mit bleierner Kugel er trifft dich genau
ein Mann wohnt im Haus dein goldenes Haar Margarete
er hetzt seine Rüden auf uns er schenkt uns ein Grab in der Luft
er spielt mit den Schlangen und träumet der Tod ist ein Meister aus
    Deutschland

dein goldenes Haar Margarete
dein aschenes Haar Sulamith

PAUL CELAN

Black milk of daybreak we drink you at night
we drink you at midday Death is a master aus Deutschland
we drink you at evening and morning we drink and we drink
this Death is ein Meister aus Deutschland his eye it is blue
he shoots you with shot made of lead shoots you level and true
a man lives in the house your goldenes Haar Margarete
he looses his hounds on us grants us a grave in the air
he plays with his vipers and daydreams der Tod ist ein Meister aus
    Deutschland

dein goldenes Haar Margarete
dein aschenes Haar Sulamith

John Felstiner

"Zähle die Mandeln"

Zähle die Mandeln,
zähle, was bitter war und dich wachhielt,
zähl mich dazu:

Ich suchte dein Aug, als du's aufschlugst und niemand dich ansah,
ich spann jenen heimlichen Faden,
an dem der Tau, den du dachtest,
hinunterglitt zu den Krügen,
die ein Spruch, der zu niemandes Herz fand, behütet.

Dort erst tratest du ganz in den Namen, der dein ist,
schrittest du sicheren Fußes zu dir,
schwangen die Hämmer frei im Glockenstuhl deines Schweigens,
stieß das Erlauschte zu dir,
legte das Tote den Arm auch um dich,
und ihr ginget selbdritt durch den Abend.

Mache mich bitter.
Zähle mich zu den Mandeln.

PAUL CELAN

"Count the almonds"

Count the almonds,
count what was bitter and kept you awake,
count me in:

I looked for your eye when you opened it, no one was looking at you,
I spun that secret thread
on which the dew you were thinking
slid down to the jugs
guarded by words that to no one's heart found their way.

Only there did you wholly enter the name that is yours,
sure-footed stepped into yourself,
freely the hammers swung in the bell frame of your silence,
the listened for reached you,
what is dead put its arm round you also
and the three of you walked through the evening.

Make me bitter.
Count me among the almonds.

Michael Hamburger

Tenebrae

Nah sind wir, Herr,
nahe und greifbar.

Gegriffen schon, Herr,
ineinander verkrallt, als wär
der Leib eines jeden von uns
dein Leib, Herr.

Bete, Herr,
bete zu uns,
wir sind nah.

Windschief gingen wir hin,
gingen wir hin, uns zu bücken
nach Mulde und Maar.

Zur Tränke gingen wir, Herr.

Es war Blut, es war,
was du vergossen, Herr.

Es glänzte.

Es warf uns dein Bild in die Augen, Herr.
Augen und Mund stehn so offen und leer, Herr.
Wir haben getrunken, Herr.
Das Blut und das Bild, das im Blut war, Herr.

Bete, Herr.
Wir sind nah.

PAUL CELAN

Tenebrae

Near are we, Lord,
near and graspable.

Grasped already, Lord,
clawed into each other, as if
each of our bodies were
your body, Lord.

Pray, Lord,
pray to us,
we are near.

Wind-skewed we went there,
went there to bend
over pit and crater.

Went to the water-trough, Lord.

It was blood, it was
what you shed, Lord.

It shined.

It cast your image into our eyes, Lord.
Eyes and mouth stand so open and void, Lord.
We have drunk, Lord.
The blood and the image that was in the blood, Lord.

Pray, Lord.
We are near.

    John Felstiner

Matière de Bretagne

Ginsterlicht, gelb, die Hänge
eitern gen Himmel, der Dorn
wirbt um die Wunde, es läutet
darin, es ist Abend, das Nichts
rollt seine Meere zur Andacht,
das Blutsegel hält auf dich zu.

Trocken, verlandet
das Bett hinter dir, verschilft
seine Stunde, oben,
beim Stern, die milchigen
Priele schwatzen im Schlamm, Steindattel,
unten, gebuscht, klafft ins Gebläu, eine Staude
Vergänglichkeit, schön,
grüßt dein Gedächtnis.

(Kanntet ihr mich,
Hände? Ich ging
den gegabelten Weg, den ihr wiest, mein Mund
spie seinen Schotter, ich ging, meine Zeit,
wandernde Wächte, warf ihren Schatten—kanntet ihr mich?)

Hände, die dorn—
umworbene Wunde, es läutet,
Hände, das Nichts, seine Meere,
Hände, im Ginsterlicht, das
Blutsegel
hält auf dich zu.

PAUL CELAN

Matière de Bretagne

Gorselight, yellow, the slopes
suppurate heavenward, the thorn
woos the wound, bells ring
within, it is evening. Nothing
rolls its seas to the service,
the blood sail makes for you.

Dry, the bed behind you
fills with silt, its hour
clogs with rushes, above,
by the star, the milky
tideways jabber through mud, date shell,
below, bunched, yawns into blueness, a shrub
of transience, beautiful,
meets your memory, greets it.

(Did you know me,
hands? I went
the forked way you showed me, my mouth
spewed out its chippings, I went, my time,
a shifting snow-wall, cast its shadow—did you know me?)

Hands, the thorn—
wooed wound, hands,
Nothing is ringing its seas.
Hands, in the gorselight, the
blood sail
makes for you.

Du
du lehrst
du lehrst deine Hände
du lehrst deine Hände du lehrst
du lehrst deine Hände
                    schlafen

PAUL CELAN

You
you teach
you teach your hands
you teach your hands you teach
you teach your hands
                    how to sleep

Michael Hamburger

"Es war Erde in ihnen"

Es war Erde in ihnen, und
sie gruben.

Sie gruben und gruben, so ging
ihr Tag dahin, ihre Nacht. Und sie lobten nicht Gott,
der, so hörten sie, alles dies wollte,
der, so hörten sie, alles dies wußte.

Sie gruben und hörten nichts mehr;
sie wurden nicht weise, erfanden kein Lied,
erdachten sich keinerlei Sprache.
Sie gruben.

Es kam eine Stille, es kam auch ein Sturm,
es kamen die Meere alle.
Ich grabe, du gräbst, und es gräbt auch der Wurm,
und das Singende dort sagt: Sie graben.

O einer, o keiner, o niemand, o du:
Wohin gings, da's nirgendhin ging?
O du gräbst und ich grab, und ich grab mich dir zu,
und am Finger erwacht uns der Ring.

PAUL CELAN

"There was earth inside them"

There was earth inside them, and
they dug.

They dug and dug, and so
their day went past, their night. And they did not praise God,
who, so they heard, wanted all this,
who, so they heard, witnessed all this.

They dug and heard nothing more;
they did not grow wise, invented no song,
devised for themselves no sort of language.
They dug.

There came a stillness then, came also storm,
all of the oceans came.
I dig, you dig, and it digs too, the worm,
and the singing there says: They dig.

O one, o none, o no one, o you:
Where did it go then, making for nowhere?
O you dig and I dig, and I dig through to you,
and the ring on our finger awakens.

John Felstiner

Tübingen, Jänner

Zur Blindheit über–
redete Augen.
Ihre—"ein
Rätsel ist Rein-
entsprungenes"—, ihre
Erinnerung an
schwimmende Hölderlintürme, möwen–
umschwirrt.

Besuche ertrunkener Schreiner bei
diesen
tauchenden Worten:

Käme,
käme ein Mensch,
käme ein Mensch zur Welt, heute, mit
dem Lichtbart der
Patriarchen: er dürfte,
spräch er von dieser
Zeit, er
dürfte
nur lallen und lallen,
immer-, immer-
zuzu.

("Pallaksch. Pallaksch.")

PAUL CELAN

Tübingen, January

Eyes talked in–
to blindness.
Their—"a
riddle, what is purely
arisen"—their
memory of
floating Hölderlintowers, gullenswirled.

Visits of drowned joiners to
these
plunging words:

Came, if there
came a man,
came a man to the world, today, with
the patriarchs'
light-beard: he could,
if he spoke of this
time, he
could
only babble and babble,
ever- ever-
moremore.

("Pallaksch. Pallaksch.")

John Felstiner

"Schläfenzange"

Schläfenzange,
von deinem Jochbein beäugt.
Ihr Silberglanz da,
wo sie sich festbiss:
du und der Rest deines Schlafs—
bald
habt ihr Geburtstag.

PAUL CELAN

"Temple-pincers"

Temple-pincers
eyed by your cheekbone.
Their silver gleam
where they bit in:
you and the rest of your sleep—
soon
it's your birthday.

John Felstiner

"Schreib dich nicht"

Schreib dich nicht
zwischen die Welten,

komm auf gegen
der Bedeutungen Vielfalt,

vertrau der Tränenspur
und lerne leben.

PAUL CELAN

"Don't write yourself"

Don't write yourself
in between worlds,

rise up against
multiple meanings,

trust the trail of tears
and learn to live.

John Felstiner

Ostia wird dich empfangen

ich werde in Ostia sein
ich werde dich dort erwarten
ich werde dich dort umarmen
ich werde deine Hände halten in Ostia
ich werde dort sein
in Ostia
ist die Mündung des Tiber
des alten Flusses

ich werde in Ostia nicht sein
ich werde dich dort nicht erwarten
ich werde dich dort nicht umarmen
ich werde deine Hände nicht halten in Ostia
ich werde nicht dort sein
in Ostia
ist die Mündung des alten Flusses
des Tiber

FRIEDERIKE MAYRÖCKER, 1924–

Ostia Will Receive You

I'll be in Ostia
I'll be there waiting for you
I'll be there embracing you
I shall be holding your hands in Ostia
I'll be there
in Ostia
there's the mouth of the Tiber
that age-old river

I shall not be in Ostia
I shall not be there waiting for you
I shall not be there embracing you
I shan't be holding your hands in Ostia
I shall not be there
in Ostia
there's the mouth of that age-old river
the Tiber

Reinhold Grimm

Verlust und Nähe

Ich weiß nicht
warum aber plötzlich
zwischen Lastenstraße und Ring
überfiel es mich wieder:
ich wollte
dir noch einmal begegnen—
jemand
der mir entgegenkam sah
dir ähnlich, ich suchte nach
weiteren Zeichen, die weiße und blaue
Daune, die scharfen
Kringel im Eis, in einer Fotokabine
blitzte es auf, der Mond
wurde blasser, rückte
in den Zenit, die
Dohlen kreuzten und schrien, es roch
nach gebratenen Äpfeln, etwas
federte in meinem Kopf, die
Augen brannten, im hellen
Winkel der Mauerkrone
deine mit Efeu umwachsenen
Glieder, deine nach oben gestreckte
geschwärzte Hand . . .

FRIEDERIKE MAYRÖCKER

Lost and Near

Don't know why but
suddenly between
Lastenstrasse and the Ring the feeling
came over me again I'd like
once more to see you
Someone
walking toward me looked
like you, I sought
more signs, the white and blue quilt,
the sharp
crusts in ice, a flash
came from a photo automat, the moon
went dimmer, shifted
into the zenith, jackdaws
crisscrossed and called, there was a smell
of baked apples, in my head
something swam, my
eyes were hot, in the illuminated top
angle of the wall your
limbs in a tangle of ivy,
and stretching up and up
your blackened hand . . .

Christopher Middleton

aus **das große e**

e) gegen sechs gehen mehrere mehreren entgegen
   gegen zehn stehen mehrere neben mehreren
   gegen elf sehen mehrere mehrere stehen
   gegen sechs sprechen mehrere gegen mehrere
   gegen zehn helfen mehrere mehreren gegen mehrere
   gegen elf helfen mehrere mehreren weg
   gegen sechs gehen mehrere mehreren entgegen

e) erregendes erregt erregendes
   erregtes erregendes erregt erregendes
   erregtes erregendes steht erregtem erregenden entgegen
   erregtes geht gegen erregtes
   versteckendes erregtes bettet steckendes bewegtes erregtes
   klebendes wechselt versteckende steckende erregte bewegte gebettete

e) jeder kennt ehen
   neben ehen kennt jeder ehen
   neben ehen kennt jeder ehen neben ehen
   ehen entstehen eben
   ehen entstehen neben ehen
   ehen neben ehen entstehen eben neben ehen
   ehen geben leben
   leben entsteht
   leben entsteht nebenher
   leben entsteht neben ehen
   leben entsteht eben

e) schweres hebt schweres schwerem entgegen
   wege legen wege neben wegen weg
   lebendes dreht lebendes lebendem entgegen
   gestrecktes streckt gestrecktes gestrecktem entgegen

ERNST JANDL

from **the big e**

e) even sex-hexed men mend nets
   even zen-spent men need mend
   even elf-seen men bend necks
   even sex-flecked men's seeds fend
   even zen-helped men breed sex seeds
   even elf-helped men tend wrecks
   even sex-hexed men mend nets

e) errers err re errers
   e'en ere errers err errers erst err'd
   e'en ere errers stretch erect extended
   fete genteel genes effete
   vexed errers better stet bedwetters err'r
   lest vexed errers kept stetted ere bedwetters get better

e) ever seek ether
   needles even seek ether-seekers
   needles even seek ether needle-seekers seek
   ether evens eden
   ether evens needle-eden
   ether needles ethers even eden-needles seek
   ether greets lechers
   lechers enter
   lechers enter needles even
   lechers enter needle-ether
   lechers enter eden

e) sweet herbs sweeten sweeter elements
   wet stems whet nettles' wetter welt
   tethers tethered tetherers' tenderer elements
   effected stretches reflect defect tenements

quellen entquellen quellen neben quellen
stellen stellen stellen neben stellen weg
helles bellt hell hellem entgegen
festes preßt festes neben festem fest

ERNST JANDL

quellers squelch quellers' nerve-swell
sellers sell cells' nerve-swelled whey
hell's belt held helen's element
feller's press'd-festered neck festers best

Guy Bennett

"1944/1945"

1944	1945
krieg	krieg
krieg	krieg
krieg	krieg
krieg	krieg
krieg	mai
krieg	
krieg	
krieg	
krieg	
krieg	
krieg	
krieg	

ERNST JANDL

marking a turn

1944	1945
war	war
war	war
war	war
war	war
war	may
war	
war	
war	
war	
war	
war	
war	

Rosmarie Waldrop

oberflächenübersetzung

mai hart lieb zapfen eibe hold
er renn bohr in sees kai
so was sieht wenn mai lauft begehen
so es sieht nahe emma mahen
so biet wenn arschel grollt
ohr leck mit ei!
seht steil dies fader rosse mahen
in teig kurt wisch mai desto bier
baum deutsche deutsch bajonett schur alp eiertier

Ernst Jandl

(surface translation — after William Wordsworth)

Ernst Jandl's poem is a surface translation, or transliteration, of Wordsworth's famous original, like Louis Zukovsky's versions from Catullus, say; to give a sense of it, I offer a transliteration of it back, as it were: may hard dear cone yew fair / he run drill in lake's quay / so something sees when may runs walk / so it sees near emma mow / so offer when little arse scolds / ear lick with egg! / see steep this dull horses mow / in dough kurt wipe may the more beer / tree german german bayonet stir alp ballbeast

My heart leaps up when I behold
   A rainbow in the sky:
So was it when my life began;
So it is now I am a man;
So be it when I shall grow old,
   Or let me die!
The child is father of the man;
   And I could wish my days to be
   Bound each to each by natural piety

William Wordsworth

Um 1800

Zierlich der Kratzfuß
der Landeskinder,

während wer fürstlich
aufstampft.

Gedichtzeilen.
Stockschläge.

Viele träumen,
daß man sie verkauft.

Die Tinte leuchtet.

Deutschlands
klassische Zeit.

Circa 1800

The natives'
shy heel-click

while some blueblood
clumps around.

Lines of verse.
Blows with a stick.

Many have a dream
of being sold.

Wet ink glistens.

Classicism
in Germany.

Michael Hofmann

Unterm Schutt III

Als ich Wasser holte fiel ein Haus auf mich
Wir haben das Haus getragen
Der vergessene Hund und ich.
Fragt mich nicht wie
Ich erinnere mich nicht.
Fragt den Hund wie.

Under the Rubble III

When I went to fetch water
The house collapsed on top of me
We supported the house
The abandoned dog and me.
Don't ask me how we did it
I don't remember.
Ask the dog.

Michael Hofmann

Der schwarze Wagen

Da kommt der schwarze Wagen
Das Pferd, das geht im Schritt
Und wer allein nicht laufen kann
Den nimmt der Wagen mit.

INGE MÜLLER

The Black Cart

Here comes the black cart
The horse walks at a trot
And whoever can't keep up
Gets to go in the black cart.

Michael Hofmann

"Du hast versprochen mit mir"

Du hast versprochen mit mir
In die Sonne zu gehn
Und an den Fluß, wo die Bäume
Noch grün sind
. . .
Die Bäume waren grün seitdem
Zum vierten Mal
Die freien Tage selten
Wie Sonne im Spätherbst—
Blätter rascheln
Auf unsern Schreibtischen

INGE MÜLLER

"You promised you would walk with me"

You promised you would walk with me
In the sun
And by the river, where the trees
Are still in leaf
. . .
The trees have been in leaf
Four times since then
Days off are as rare
As sun in late fall—
Leaves rustle
On our desks.

Michael Hofmann

"Ich habe dich heute Nacht verlassen"

Ich habe dich heute Nacht verlassen
Für lange Zeit, mir ist: für immer.
Der Morgen war ein graues Zimmer
Und als du gingst war Rauch in den Straßen.

INGE MÜLLER

"I left you last night"

I left you last night
For a long time—I have a feeling, for good.
The morning was a grey room
And when you went out the streets were full of smoke.

Michael Hofmann

Die gestundete Zeit

Es kommen härtere Tage.
Die auf Widerruf gestundete Zeit
wird sichtbar am Horizont.
Bald mußt du den Schuh schnüren
und die Hunde zurückjagen in die Marschhöfe.
Denn die Eingeweide der Fische
sind kalt geworden im Wind.
Ärmlich brennt das Licht der Lupinen.
Dein Blick spurt im Nebel:
die auf Widerruf gestundete Zeit
wird sichtbar am Horizont.

Drüben versinkt dir die Geliebte im Sand,
er steigt um ihr wehendes Haar,
er fällt ihr ins Wort,
er befiehlt ihr zu schweigen,
er findet sie sterblich
und willig dem Abschied
nach jeder Umarmung.

Sieh dich nicht um.
Schnür deinen Schuh.
Jag die Hunde zurück.
Wirf die Fische ins Meer.
Lösch die Lupinen!

Es kommen härtere Tage.

The Time Allotted

Worse days are coming.
The time allotted for disavowals
Comes due on the skyline.
Soon you will lace up your shoes
And drive the dogs back to the marshes.

For the intestines of fish
Have frozen up in the wind.
The lupines burn with a feeble light.
Your glance cuts through the fog:
The time allotted for disavowals
Comes due on the skyline.

In the distance your mistress sinks under the sand,
It pours through her wind-loosened hair,
It covers her words,
It turns her to silence,
It finds her mortal
And ready to part
With every embrace.

Don't look around.
Lace up your shoes.
Drive the dogs back.
Throw the fish in the sea.
Smother the lupines!

Worse days are coming.

Jerome Rothenberg

Abschied von England

Ich habe deinen Boden kaum betreten,
schweigsames Land, kaum einen Stein berührt,
ich war von deinem Himmel so hoch gehoben,
so in Wolken, Dunst und in noch Ferneres gestellt,
daß ich dich schon verließ,
als ich vor Anker ging.

Du hast meine Augen geschlossen
mit Meerhauch und Eichenblatt,
von meinen Tränen begossen,
hieltst du die Gräser satt;
aus meinen Träumen gelöst,
wagten sich Sonnen heran,
doch alles war wieder fort,
wenn dein Tag begann.
Alles blieb ungesagt.

Durch die Straßen flatterten die großen grauen Vögel
und wiesen mich aus.
War ich je hier?

Ich wollte nicht gesehen werden.

Meine Augen sind offen.
Meerhauch und Eichenblatt?
Unter den Schlangen des Meers
seh ich, an deiner Statt,
das Land meiner Seele erliegen.

Ich habe seinen Boden nie betreten.

INGEBORG BACHMANN

Departure from England

I have barely set foot upon your land,
silent country, barely disturbed a stone.
I was lifted so high by your sky,
placed so in clouds, mist, and remoteness,
that I had already left you
the moment I set anchor.

You have closed my eyes
with sea breeze and oak leaf,
upon the tears I cried
you let the grasses feed;
out of my dreams, suns dared
to venture across the land,
yet everything disappeared
as soon as your day began.
Everything remained unspoken.

Through streets flapped the great gray birds
that singled me out for expulsion.
Was I ever here?

I didn't want to be seen.

My eyes are open.
Sea breeze and oak leaf?
Under the serpentine sea
in place of you I see
the country of my soul succumb.

I have never set foot on its land.

Peter Filkins

Herbstmanöver

Ich sage nicht: das war gestern. Mit wertlosem
Sommergeld in den Taschen liegen wir wieder
auf der Spreu des Hohns, im Herbstmanöver der Zeit.
Und der Fluchtweg nach Süden kommt uns nicht,
wie den Vögeln, zustatten. Vorüber, am Abend,
ziehen Fischkutter und Gondeln, und manchmal
trifft mich ein Splitter traumsatten Marmors,
wo ich verwundbar bin, durch Schönheit, im Aug.

In den Zeitungen lese ich viel von der Kälte
und ihren Folgen, von Törichten und Toten,
von Vertriebenen, Mördern und Myriaden
von Eisschollen, aber wenig, was mir behagt.
Warum auch? Vor dem Bettler, der mittags kommt,
schlag ich die Tür zu, denn es ist Frieden
und man kann sich den Anblick ersparen, aber nicht
im Regen das freudlose Sterben der Blätter.

Laßt uns eine Reise tun! Laßt uns unter Zypressen
oder auch unter Palmen oder in den Orangenhainen
zu verbilligten Preisen Sonnenuntergänge sehen,
die nicht ihresgleichen haben! Laßt uns die
unbeantworteten Briefe an das Gestern vergessen!
Die Zeit tut Wunder. Kommt sie uns aber unrecht,
mit dem Pochen der Schuld: wir sind nicht zu Hause.
Im Keller des Herzens, schlaflos, find ich mich wieder
auf der Spreu des Hohns, im Herbstmanöver der Zeit.

INGEBORG BACHMANN

Autumn Maneuver

I don't say: ah, yesterday. With worthless
summer money pocketed, we lie again
on the chaff of scorn, in time's autumn maneuver.
And the escape southward isn't feasible for us
as it is for the birds. In the evening
trawlers and gondolas pass, and sometimes
a splinter of dream-filled marble pierces me
in the eye, where I am most vulnerable to beauty.

In the papers I read about the cold
and its effects, about fools and dead men,
about exiles, murderers and myriads
of ice floes, but little that comforts me.
Why should it be otherwise? In the face of the beggar
who comes at noon I slam the door, for we live in peacetime
and one can spare oneself such a sight, but not
the joyless dying of leaves in the rain.

Let's take a trip! Let us stroll under cypresses
or even under palms or in the orange groves
to see at reduced rates sunsets
that are beyond compare! Let us forget
the unanswered letters to yesterday!
Time works wonders. But if it arrives inconveniently
with the knocking of guilt: we're not at home.
In the heart's cellar, sleepless, I find myself again
on the chaff of scorn, in time's autumn maneuver.

Peter Filkins

Salz und Brot

Nun schickt der Wind die Schienen voraus,
wir werden folgen in langsamen Zügen
und diese Inseln bewohnen,
Vertrauen gegen Vertrauen.

In die Hand meines ältesten Freunds leg ich
mein Amt zurück; es verwaltet der Regenmann
jetzt mein finsteres Haus und ergänzt
im Schuldbuch die Linien, die ich zog,
seit ich seltener blieb.

Du, im fieberweißen Ornat,
holst die Verbannten ein und reißt
aus dem Fleisch der Kakteen einen Stachel
—das Zeichen der Ohnmacht,
dem wir uns willenlos beugen.

Wir wissen,
daß wir des Kontinentes Gefangene bleiben
und seinen Kränkungen wieder verfallen,
und die Gezeiten der Wahrheit
werden nicht seltener sein.

Schläft doch im Felsen
der wenig erleuchtete Schädel,
die Kralle hängt in der Kralle
im dunklen Gestein, und verheilt
sind die Stigmen am Violett des Vulkans.

Von den großen Gewittern des Lichts
hat keines die Leben erreicht.

INGEBORG BACHMANN

Salt and Bread

Now the wind sends its rails ahead;
we will follow in slow trains
and inhabit these islands,
intimacy exchanged for intimacy.

Into the hand of my oldest friend
I place the key to my post: the rain man will now manage
my darkened house and complete
the lines of the ledger which I drew up
after I was seldom around.

You, in fever-white vestments,
gather the exiled and tear,
from the flesh of cactus, a thorn
—symbol of impotence
to which we meekly bow.

We know
that we'll remain the continent's captives,
and again we'll succumb to its troubled ills,
and the tides of truth
will be no rarer.

For sleeping in the cliff
is the barely lit skull,
the claw hangs in the claw
in the dark stone, and the stigmata
are healed in the violet of the volcano.

Of the great storms of light,
none has come to life.

So nehm ich vom Salz,
wenn uns das Meer übersteigt,
und kehre zurück
und legs auf die Schwelle
und trete ins Haus.

Wir teilen ein Brot mit dem Regen,
ein Brot, eine Schuld und ein Haus.

INGEBORG BACHMANN

So I gather the salt
when the sea overcomes us,
and turn back
and lay it on the threshold
and step into the house.

We share bread with the rain;
bread, a debt, and a house.

    Peter Filkins

Tage in Weiß

In diesen Tagen steh ich auf mit den Birken
und kämm mir das Weizenhaar aus der Stirn
vor einem Spiegel aus Eis.

Mit meinem Atem vermengt,
flockt die Milch.
So früh schäumt sie leicht.
Und wo ich die Scheibe behauch, erscheint,
von einem kindlichen Finger gemalt,
wieder dein Name: Unschuld!
Nach so langer Zeit.

In diesen Tagen schmerzt mich nicht,
daß ich vergessen kann
und mich erinnern muß.

Ich liebe. Bis zur Weißglut
lieb ich und danke mit englischen Grüßen.
Ich hab sie im Fluge erlernt.

In diesen Tagen denk ich des Albatros',
mit dem ich mich auf–
und herüberschwang
in ein unbeschriebenes Land.

Am Horizont ahne ich,
glanzvoll im Untergang,
meinen fabelhaften Kontinent
dort drüben, der mich entließ
im Totenhemd.

Ich lebe und höre von fern seinen Schwanengesang!

INGEBORG BACHMANN

Days in White

These days I rise with the birches
and brush the corn hair from my brow
before a mirror of ice.

Blended with my breath,
milk is beaten.
This early it foams easily.
And where I fog the pane there appears,
traced by a child-like finger,
again your name: Innocence!
After all these years.

These days I feel no pain
that I can forget
or that I must remember.

I love. Incandescently
I love and give thanks with Ave Marias.
I learned them with ease.

These days I think of the albatross
with whom I swung
up and over
into an uncharted land.

On the horizon I ascertain,
splendid in the sunset,
my marvelous continent
just over there, releasing me
wrapped in a shroud.

I live, and from afar, I hear its swan song!

Peter Filkins

dominotaurus

dominotaurusbekistandaradeilandrogynstigmagmasto-
donauberginereidentaluminiumsatzungenitalmini-
strantepenultimathulethargiebelcantopascalibertina-
geleebenslangmuterintestikularborealsozusagenhaf-
tungeheuerlköniginsterlingeniöresundsoweiterminde-
stensionenklavemariasklepiadäischemathematischä-
deltabulaturmalinsengerichtschnurzegaliziengramma-
tikasteroideenzephalokratiegelsemiorganisatorgau-
mentoraxialgeneröseleneandertalsperresistancestral-
sundsofortepianostradamuskellochsensecamusikanten-
takelhorreurichtungsramadanterrinebukadnezarathu-
strapezunterosmarinternationaledamaszenergygestisch-
beinhartmankolibrisedankefirmakulaturtele-
kompotipharaokarinavigareedemiurgesteintrachten-
ballustradebilsenillustrepanationdulatwerglaubtesat-
mosphärebustaminaturbinekrologarhythmusketeflon-
donquijotemporatatouilleriennevaplusquamperfidel-
katakombinärrischkatalanselmodernierekapitulatent-
schiedenkendloszillomorphemphasekundsoweiterbeu-
leandergleichendeheparlando

Dominotaurus

dominotaurusbekistandrogynecologistigmamasto
donauberginereidentaluminumbergenitalentrante
penultimathulethargypsychodramabelcantopicto
graphicalibertinagelatincanuterintesticularboreal
penstockmarkettlesterlinguanomenclavemariascle
piusageoldtimermaidenheadstarterrinebuchadnez
zarathustrapezebrandishwasherballustradebility
cooneandertalmudslidemiteflondonquixotempo
ratatouillerriennevapluperfectodermatitisepiano
stradamuscletterpressuresistancestralepharpoti
pharaocarinavigatoreador

Rosmarie Waldrop

Klappstühle

Wie traurig sind diese Veränderungen.
Die Leute schrauben ihre Namensschilder ab,
nehmen den Topf mit dem Rotkohl,
wärmen ihn auf, anderen Ortes.

Was sind das für Möbel,
die für den Aufbruch werben?
Die Leute nehmen ihre Klappstühle
und wandern aus.

Mit Heimweh und Brechreiz beladene Schiffe
tragen patentierte Sitzgelegenheiten
und patentlose Besitzer
hin und her.

Auf beiden Seiten des großen Wassers
stehen nun Klappstühle;
wie traurig sind diese Veränderungen.

Folding Chairs

How sad these changes are.
People unscrew the nameplates from the doors,
take the saucepan of cabbage
and heat it up again, in a different place.

What sort of furniture is this
that advertises departure?
People take up their folding chairs
and emigrate.

Ships laden with homesickness and seasickness
carry patented seating contraptions
and their unpatented owners
to and fro.

Now on both sides of the great ocean
there are folding chairs;
how sad these changes are.

Michael Hamburger

Im Ei

Wir leben im Ei.
Die Innenseite der Schale
haben wir mit unanständigen Zeichnungen
und den Vornamen unserer Feinde bekritzelt.
Wir werden gebrütet.

Wer uns auch brütet,
unseren Bleistift brütet er mit.
Ausgeschlüpft eines Tages,
werden wir uns sofort
ein Bildnis des Brütenden machen.

Wir nehmen an, daß wir gebrütet werden.
Wir stellen uns ein gutmütiges Geflügel vor
und schreiben Schulaufsätze
über Farbe und Rasse
der uns brütenden Henne.

Wann schlüpfen wir aus?
Unsere Propheten im Ei
streiten sich für mittelmäßige Bezahlung
über die Dauer der Brutzeit.
Sie nehmen einen Tag X an.

Aus Langeweile und echtem Bedürfnis
haben wir Brutkästen erfunden.
Wir sorgen uns sehr um unseren Nachwuchs im Ei.
Gerne würden wir jener, die über uns wacht
unser Patent empfehlen.

Wir aber haben ein Dach überm Kopf.
Senile Küken,

GÜNTER GRASS

In the Egg

We live in the egg.
We have covered the inside wall
of the shell with dirty drawings
and the Christian names of our enemies.
We are being hatched.

Whoever is hatching us
is hatching our pencils as well.
Set free from the egg one day
at once we shall draw a picture
of whoever is hatching us.

We assume that we're being hatched.
We imagine some good-natured fowl
and write school essays
about the colour and breed
of the hen that is hatching us.

When shall we break the shell?
Our prophets inside the egg
for a middling salary argue
about the period of incubation.
They posit a day called X.

Out of boredom and genuine need
we have invented incubators.
We are much concerned about our offspring inside the egg.
We should be glad to recommend our patent
to her who looks after us.

But we have a roof over our heads.
Senile chicks,

Embryos mit Sprachkenntnissen
reden den ganzen Tag
und besprechen noch ihre Träume.

Und wenn wir nun nicht gebrütet werden?
Wenn diese Schale niemals ein Loch bekommt?
Wenn unser Horizont nur der Horizont
unserer Kritzeleien ist und auch bleiben wird?
Wir hoffen, daß wir gebrütet werden.

Wenn wir auch nur noch vom Brüten reden,
bleibt doch zu befürchten, daß jemand,
außerhalb unserer Schale, Hunger verspürt,
uns in die Pfanne haut und mit Salz bestreut.
Was machen wir dann, ihr Brüder im Ei?

GÜNTER GRASS

polyglot embryos
chatter all day
and even discuss their dreams.

And what if we're not being hatched?
If this shell will never break?
If our horizon is only that
of our scribbles, and always will be?
We hope that we're being hatched.

Even if we only talk of hatching
there remains the fear that someone
outside our shell will feel hungry
and crack us into the frying pan with a pinch of salt.
What shall we do then, my brethren inside the egg?

Michael Hamburger

Dreht euch nicht um

Geh nicht in den Wald,
im Wald ist der Wald.
Wer im Wald geht,
Bäume sucht,
wird im Wald nicht mehr gesucht.

Hab keine Angst,
die Angst riecht nach Angst.
Wer nach Angst riecht,
den riechen
Helden, die wie Helden riechen.

Trink nicht vom Meer,
das Meer schmeckt nach mehr.
Wer vom Meer trinkt,
hat fortan
nur noch Durst auf Ozean.

Bau dir kein Haus,
sonst bist du zuhaus.
Wer zuhaus ist,
wartet auf
späten Besuch und macht auf.

Schreib keinen Brief,
Brief kommt ins Archiv.
Wer den Brief schreibt,
unterschreibt,
was von ihm einst überbleibt.

GÜNTER GRASS

Don't Turn Round

Don't go into the wood,
in the wood is the wood.
Whoever walks in the wood,
looks for trees,
will not be looked for later in the wood.

Have no fear,
fear smells of fear.
Whoever smells of fear
will be smelled out
by heroes who smell like heroes.

Don't drink from the sea,
the sea tastes of more sea.
Whoever drinks from the sea
henceforth feels
a thirst only for oceans.

Don't build a home,
or you'll be at home.
Whoever is at home
waits for
late callers and opens the door.

Don't write a letter,
archives will boast of letters you post.
Whoever writes the letter
lends his name
to the posthumous paper game.

    Michael Hamburger

Die Festung wächst

Liegt brach das Land zum Fraß der Krähenschar.
Der Maulwurf mehrt sich, und verdächtig häufig
sind längs den Zäunen fremde Hunde läufig.
Wir sollen zahlen: auf die Hand und bar.

Weil in der Mitte liegend, reich und ungeschützt,
hat planend Furcht ein Bauwerk ausgeschwitzt:
als Festung will Novemberland sich sicher machen
vor Roma, Schwarzen, Juden und Fellachen.

Nach Osten hin soll Polen Grenzmark sein;
so schnell fällt nützlich uns Geschichte ein.
Das Burgenbauen war schon immer unsre Lust,
den Wall zu ziehn, die Mauer zu errichten,
und gegen Festungskoller, Stumpfsinn, Lagerfrust
half stets ein Hölderlin im Brotsack mit Gedichten.

GÜNTER GRASS

The Fortress Grows

The land lies fallow, food now for rooks and crows.
The moles proliferate and, as they'd never done,
suspect, along the fences strange dogs run.
We are to pay: in cash, and through the nose.

Because mid-European, wealthy and vulnerable,
fear sweated out its draughts for a defensive wall:
now as a fortress Novemberland seeks to be
safe from Black, Fellah, Jew, Turk, Romany.

As eastern border Poland will serve again:
so fast we think of history, to our gain.
Building of castles has always been our special joy,
to raise the rampart, excavate the moat;
and against fortress, megrims, dullness, gloom attacks
always a Hölderlin helped with poems in our packs.

Michael Hamburger

Auf den Tod eines Dichters

Mein Freund, der Dichter, ist gestorben.
Wir haben ihn unter einer Akazie begraben.
Seine Lebensgefährtin—ein böses Weib—
putzte die Gasthaussuppe aus seinem Smoking
(er trug ihn zum Begräbnis),
denn er hatte sich, sagte sie,
zeit seines Lebens nach Reinheit gesehnt.
Im übrigen fand sie, die Akazie dufte zu sehr,
er habe schon immer
über ihr schweres Parfum heimlich geklagt.
Sie aber habe gelitten, ach, gelitten
unter seinem Geruch
nach Tintenentferner und Bühnenstaub
und aufgeschnittnem Papier und manchmal
—leider—manchmal nach einer Sorte von Puder,
die sie niemals benützte.
Das sagte die Lebensgefährtin
auf dem Heimweg vom Grab,
und mehr war über sein Leben auch nicht zu sagen.

Indessen lag er still unter der süßen Akazie.
Hätt' ers gewußt, er hätte nächtelang nicht geschlafen
und sich um Verse gequält,
um Verse von weißen Akaziendolden
und graufeuchten Morgen
und bleichenden Knochen unter dem Gras.

HERTHA KRÄFTNER

On the Death of a Poet

My friend the poet is dead.
We buried him under an acacia tree.
His companion—a real shrew—
scrubbed the restaurant soup out of his tuxedo
(he wore it for the funeral)
because all his life, she said,
he had longed for purity.
She also thought the acacia smelled too strong,
he had always complained privately
about her heavy perfume.
She in turn had suffered, o, suffered she had
from his smell
of ink remover and stage dust
and cut-open paper and sometimes
—unfortunately—sometimes of a kind of powder
that she never used.
That's what his companion said
on the way home from the grave,
and that was all that could be said about his life.

Meanwhile he lay quietly under the sweet acacia tree.
If he had known it, he would have stayed up for nights
and tortured himself over some verses,
verses about white acacia blossoms
and a gray, moist morning
and bones bleaching under the grass.

Charlotte Melin

Über einige davongekommene

Als der Mensch
unter den Trümmern
seines
bombardierten Hauses
hervorgezogen wurde,
schüttelte er sich
und sagte:
Nie wieder

Jedenfalls nicht gleich.

About Some Who Survived

When the man
was pulled out
from
under the debris
of his bombed house,
he shook himself
and said:
Never again

At least not right away.

Charlotte Melin

Film — Verkehrt eingespannt

Als ich erwachte
Erwachte ich im atemlosen Schwarz
Der Kiste. Ich hörte: Die Erde tat sich
Auf zu meinen Häupten. Erdschollen
Flogen flatternd zur Schaufel zurück.
Die teure Schachtel mit mir dem teuren
Verblichenen stieg schnell empor.
Der Deckel klappte hoch und ich
Erhob mich und fühlte gleich: Drei
Geschosse fuhren aus meiner Brust
In die Gewehre der Soldaten die
Abmarschierten schnappend
Aus der Luft ein Lied
Im ruhig festen Tritt
Rückwärts.

GÜNTER KUNERT

Film Put in Backwards

When I woke
I woke in the breathless black
Of the box.
        I heard: the earth
Was opening over me. Clods
Fluttered back
        To the shovel. The
Dear box, with me the dear
        Departed, gently rose.
The lid flew up and I
Stood, feeling:
        Three bullets travel
Out of my chest
Into the rifles of soldiers, who
        Marched off, gasping
Out of the air a song
With calm firm steps
        Backwards.

Christopher Middleton

Vor seinem Angesicht

für Wolfgang Koeppen

Deus absconditus wohnt gegenüber
dem Englischen Garten himmelsnah
unterm Dach. Seine Tür unverriegelt. Tritt ein
Wallfahrer von Ferne. Auf einem Sperrmüllsofa
im Flur Zerberus, Erbstück gezähmten Heidentums
mit schwarzem Fell und sanfter Lefze.
Sodann er selber und unverhüllt
in Gestalt eines schlecht rasierten Patriarchen
mit blindem verwirrten Lächeln
dem untrüglichen Erkennungszeichen.
Eine starke Brille anstelle der Augen
um uns besser übersehen zu können.
Schwache begrüßende Geste. Tremor der Rechten,
Folge einsamer Abende, vieler Getränke.
Kaum daß er unser gewahr ward, erklang
ein telefonisches De Profundis,
verzweifelter Menschheitsappell aus dem Ortsnetz.
Gott legte den Hörer auf
um so zu tun, als wären wir alle
gleichgeschaffen nach seiner regelfrommen
Willkür
mit Macht und Beharrlichkeit.

GÜNTER KUNERT

Shelley Plain

for Wolfgang Koeppen

Deus absconditus lives opposite
the Englischer Garten, under the eaves
and close to heaven. His door on the latch. A pilgrim
comes from afar. On a sofa (salvaged from a skip)
in the hallway lounges Cerberus, a tamed heathen
with black pelt and soft muzzle.
Then himself, barely concealed
in the guise of a badly shaved patriarch
with bewildered blinking smile
as his unmistakeable sign.
Powerful spectacles for eyes,
the better to disregard us with.
Vague gesture of welcome. Shakes in the right hand.
A consequence of lonely evenings and much drinking.
No sooner had he caught sight of us than
a telephonic De Profundis rang out,
a frantic human appeal from the local exchange.
God put down the receiver,
in the stern pretence that we are all
created alike, in accordance with his inflexible
capriciousness
towards power and tenacity.

Michael Hofmann

Brecht

Wirklich, er lebte in finsteren Zeiten.
Die Zeiten sind heller geworden.
Die Zeiten sind finstrer geworden.
Wenn die Helle sagt, ich bin die Finsternis
Hat sie die Wahrheit gesagt.
Wenn die Finsternis sagt, ich bin
Die Helle, lügt sie nicht.

Brecht

Truly, he lived in dark times.
The times have brightened.
The times have darkened.
When brightness says, I am darkness,
It has told the truth.
When darkness says, I am
Brightness, it does not lie.

Reinhold Grimm

Die Hyäne

Die Hyäne liebt die Panzer, die in der Wüste stehen bleiben, weil die Besatzung stirbt. Sie kann warten. Sie wartet, bis der tausendunderste Sandsturm den Stahl zerfrißt. Dann kommt ihre Stunde. Die Hyäne ist das Wappentier der Mathematik, sie weiß, daß kein Rest bleiben darf. Ihr Gott ist die Null.

HEINER MÜLLER

The Hyena

The hyena loves the tanks stranded in the desert, because the crews are dying. She can wait. She waits until the thousand-and-first sandstorm has gnawed through the steel. Then her hour has come. The hyena is the heraldic beast of mathematics, she knows there must be nothing left over. Her god is zero.

Michael Hofmann

Herz aus Finsternis nach Joseph Conrad

für Gregor Gysi

Schaurige Welt, kapitalistische Welt   (GOTTFRIED BENN
in einem Radiogespräch mit Johannes R. Becher, 1930)

In der Valuta-Bar des Hotels METROPOL
Berlin Hauptstadt der DDR bemüht sich
Eine polnische Hure Gastarbeiterin
Um einen Greis mit Schnupfen
Zwischen den Kapiteln seines Vortrags
Über die Freiheit in den USA
Rotzt er ins Taschentuch und schreit nach dem Abfalleimer
Noch im Griff des Mitleids mit ihrem schweren Beruf
Höre ich zwei Geschäftsreisende
Bayern dem Geräusch nach
Asien verteilen: ALSO MALAYSIA TÄT MIR GFALLN
THAILAND AUCH KOREA GHÖRT DAZU
ALSO DAS KREUZSCHIENENSYSTEM FÜR DEN JEMEN
TÄT ICH NOCH PLANEN DANN
HAT SICH DIE SACHE
                    CHINA GHÖRT AUCH DAZU
CHINA IST ALS EINZIGES PROJEKT VERKAUFT WORDN
In der S-Bahn ZOOLOGISCHER GARTEN
    FRIEDRICHSTRASSE
Habe ich zwei DDR-Bürger kennengelernt
Einer erzählt Mein Sohn drei Wochen alt
Wurde geboren mit einem Schild vor der Brust
ICH WAR AM NEUNTEN NOVEMBER IM WESTEN
Meine Tochter gleichaltrig Ich habe Zwillinge
Trägt die Aufschrift ICH AUCH
THE HORROR THE HORROR THE HORROR

HEINER MÜLLER

Heart of Darkness adapted from Joseph Conrad

for Gregor Gysi

Gruesome world, capitalist world — GOTTFRIED BENN,
in a radio interview with Johannes R. Becher, 1930

In the hard-currency-bar of the Hotel METROPOL
Berlin Capital of the **GDR** a Polish whore
A foreign worker is hitting
Up a very old man with a cold
Between the chapters of his lecture
About freedom in the **USA**
He snorts into a snot-rag and yells for the trash can
Still feeling pity for her difficult profession
I hear two travelling salesmen
Bavarian from the sound of it
Dividing up Asia: WELL I WOULD LIKE MALAYSIA
THAILAND KOREA TOO IS PART OF IT
WELL I WOULD ALSO PLAN THE CROSS-TRACK SYSTEM
FOR YEMEN THEN
THAT WOULD TAKE CARE OF IT
                         CHINA IS PART OF IT TOO
CHINA IS THE ONLY PROJECT THAT'S BEEN SOLD
In the elevated train ZOOLOGISCHER GARTEN
  FRIEDRICHSTRASSE
I came to know two citizens of the GDR
One of them says My son three weeks old
Was born with a sign in front of his chest
I WAS IN THE WEST ON THE NINTH OF NOVEMBER
My daughter same age I have twins
Carries the inscription ME TOO
THE HORROR THE HORROR THE HORROR

Margitt Lehbert

Das Ende der Eulen

Ich spreche von euerm nicht,
ich spreche vom Ende der Eulen.
Ich spreche von Butt und Wal
in ihrem dunkeln Haus,
dem siebenfältigen Meer,
von den Gletschern,
sie werden kalben zu früh,
Rab und Taube, gefiederten Zeugen,
von allem was lebt in Lüften
und Wäldern, und den Flechten im Kies,
vom Weglosen selbst, und vom grauen Moor
und den leeren Gebirgen:

Auf Radarschirmen leuchtend
zum letzten Mal, ausgewertet
auf Meldetischen, von Antennen
tödlich befingert Floridas Sümpfe
und das sibirische Eis, Tier
und Schilf und Schiefer erwürgt
von Warnketten, umzingelt
vom letzten Manöver, arglos
unter schwebenden Feuerglocken,
im Ticken des Ernstfalls.

Wir sind schon vergessen.
Sorgt euch nicht um die Waisen,
aus dem Sinn schlagt euch
die mündelsichern Gefühle,
den Ruhm, die rostfreien Psalmen.

HANS MAGNUS ENZENSBERGER

HANS MAGNUS ENZENSBERGER, 1929–

the end of the owls

i speak for none of your kind,
i speak of the end of the owls.
i speak for the flounder and whale
in their unlighted house,
the seven-cornered sea,
for the glaciers
they will have calved too soon,
raven and dove, feathery witnesses,
for all those that dwell in the sky
and the woods, and the lichen in gravel,
for those without paths, for the colorless bog
and the desolate mountains.

glaring on radar screens,
interpreted one final time
around the briefing table, fingered
to death by antennas, floridas swamps
and the siberian ice, beast
and bush and basalt strangled
by earlybird, ringed
by the latest maneuvers, helpless
under the hovering firebells,
in the ticking of crises.

we're as good as forgotten.
don't fuss with the orphans,
just empty your mind
of its longing for nest eggs,
glory or psalms that won't rust.

Ich spreche nicht mehr von euch,
Planern der spurlosen Tat,
und von mir nicht, und Keinem.
Ich spreche von dem was nicht spricht,
von den sprachlosen Zeugen,
von Ottern und Robben,
von den alten Eulen der Erde.

HANS MAGNUS ENZENSBERGER

i speak for none of you now,
all you plotters of perfect crimes,
nor for me, nor for anyone.
i speak for those who can't speak,
for the deaf and dumb witnesses,
for otters and seals,
for the ancient owls of the earth.

Jerome Rothenberg

Karl Heinrich Marx

Riesiger Großvater
jahvebärtig
auf braunen Daguerreotypien
ich seh dein Gesicht
in der schlohweißen Aura
selbstherrlich   streitbar
und die Papiere im Vertiko:
Metzgersrechnungen
Inauguraladressen
Steckbriefe

Deinen massigen Leib
seh ich im Fahndungsbuch
riesiger Hochverräter
displaced person
in Bratenrock und Plastron
schwindsüchtig   schlaflos
die Galle verbrannt
von schweren Zigarren
Salzgurken   Laudanum
und Likör

Ich seh dein Haus
in der rue d'Alliance
Dean Street   Grafton Terrace
riesiger Bourgeois
Haustyrann
in zerschlissnen Pantoffeln:
Ruß und "ökonomische Scheiße"
Pfandleihen "wie gewöhnlich"
Kindersärge
Hintertreppengeschichten

HANS MAGNUS ENZENSBERGER

Karl Heinrich Marx

gigantic grandfather
jehovah-bearded
on brown daguerreotypes
i see your face
in the snow-white aura
despotic quarrelsome
and your papers in the linen press:
butcher's bills
inaugural addresses
warrants for your arrest

your massive body
i see in the "wanted" book
gigantic traitor
displaced person
in tail coat and plastron
consumptive sleepless
your gall-bladder scorched
by heavy cigars
salted gherkins laudanum
and liqueur

i see your house
in the rue d'alliance
dean street grafton terrace
gigantic bourgeois
domestic tyrant
in worn-out slippers:
soot and "economic shit"*
usury "as usual"
children's coffins
rumours of sordid affairs

*Quotations from Marx's letters to Engels in the 1850s and 1860s. *H.M.E.*

Keine Mitrailleuse
in deiner Prophetenhand:
ich seh sie ruhig
im British Museum
unter der grünen Lampe
mit fürchterlicher Geduld
dein eigenes Haus zerbrechen
riesiger Gründer
andern Häusern zuliebe
in denen du nimmer erwacht bist

Riesiger Zaddik
ich seh dich verraten
von deinen Anhängern:
nur deine Feinde
sind dir geblieben:
ich seh dein Gesicht
auf dem letzten Bild
vom April zweiundachtzig:
eine eiserne Maske:
die eiserne Maske der Freiheit

HANS MAGNUS ENZENSBERGER

no machine-gun
in your prophet's hand:
i see it calmly
in the british museum
under the green lamp
break up your own house
with a terrible patience
gigantic founder
for the sake of other houses
in which you never woke up

gigantic zaddik
i see you betrayed
by your disciples:
only your enemies
remained what they were:
i see your face
on the last picture
of april eighty-two:
an iron mask:
the iron mask of freedom

Michael Hamburger

Schaum

Ich bin geblendet geboren, Schaum in den Augen,
brüllend vor Wehmut, ohne den Himmel zu sehen,
am schwarzen Freitag, heute vor dreißig Jahren.

Schaum vor dem Mund des Jahrhunderts! Schaum
in den Kassenschränken! Jaulender Schaum
in den Gebärmüttern und den Luxusbunkern!
Schaum in den rosa Bidets!

Dagegen hilft kein himmlischer Blitz! Das blüht,
das überzieht die Erde an Haupt und Gliedern
mit rasendem Rotz! Das reutet kein Feuer,
kein Schwert! Das endet nicht! Dagegen gibt es,
ehrlich gesagt, keinen Rat, kein Beil, kein Geheimnis.
Das ist zu süß! Das steigt aus dem Abgrund auf
und schäumt! und schmunzelt! und schäumt!

Reicht mir die Bruderhand, ihr Verräter,
übersät mit Warzen, Flaksplittern und Brillanten,
Bewohner schmutziger Nebensätze,
reicht mir den Adamsapfel zum Judasbiß,
das schäumende Seifenherz und den Kontoauszug,
rosig von Hämoglobin! Zieht mich zu Grund,
tiefer zu euch, zu den anderen Quallen,
in den freiberuflichen Schaum!

Hier stehe ich täglich, ein Feuerschlucker wie ihr,
wie alle andern, an meiner Straßenecke, von neun
bis fünf, und schlucke mühsam für zwanzig Mark
mein eigenes Feuer, knietief im schäumenden Status quo,
unter Vergasern und Ampeln.
                    Horch!

HANS MAGNUS ENZENSBERGER

foam

at the hour of birth i was blinded with foam in my eyes
crying with grief unable to look at the sky
on a black friday thirty years in the past

foam hangs from the century's mouth foam
in the bank vaults foam howling
in the wombs of mothers in the lead-lined bunkers
foam in the pink-tinged bidets

no bolt from the blue can undo it: it flowers
it covers the length and breadth of the earth
with its maddening snot: no fire no sword
can stop it it's endless no fooling there's nothing
that does it no plan no hatchet no secret device
it's too sweet it rises up from the depths
and it foams it smirks and it foams

slip me a brotherly handshake you sellouts
your fingers flecked with warts shrapnel diamonds
subsisting on obscene subordinate clauses
deliver your adams apples to my judasbite
your foaming soap hearts and your bank accounts
stained red with haemoglobin: pull me down to the ground
as far down as you as the other gobs of phlegm
in that professional muck.

i'm here any day of the week a fire-eater like you
like everyone else: standing on my corner from nine
to five taking painful shots of my own fire
for ten bucks a day kneedeep in foaming status quo
between carburettors and street lights
hear o hear

Wer ruft Grüßgott aus dem Schaum?
Wer heißt mich hoffen? Und warum hoffen?
Wer reicht mir die klebrige Bruderhand?

Loslassen! Loslassen! Ich bin keiner von euch
und keiner von uns: ich bin zufällig geboren
unter schäumenden Wasserwerfern, zufällig brüllend,
ehrlich gesagt, allein, ohne Brüder, geblendet,
am schwarzen Freitag, in einem rosa Bidet.

Und warum allein? und warum rosa? und warum
nicht? und warum ehrlich gesagt?

Wer schluckt nicht sein eigenes Feuer? Wer
watet nicht durch abgemähte Fingernägel fürbaß?
Wer hat keine schmierige Klausel in seinem Vertrag?
Wer will erlöst werden und von wem? und wovon?
Wer frißt nicht unaufhörlich mit vorzüglicher Hochachtung?
Wer ist nicht veranlagt? Wer hat die Angstschreie
auf den Hauptversammlungen nicht vernommen?

Wer hat keine Bronchien aus Plastik? Na also!
Wer war schon in einer Fabrik? Wer
riecht nicht aus dem Hals? Wer
ist nicht geschieden, und warum nicht?
Wer schreibt keine Ansichtskarten aus Capri?
Wer hurt nicht mit der Geschichte herum?
Wen reut sein Leben nicht? und warum nicht?
und warum nicht? Wer sagt nicht: und so weiter?
und warum so weiter? Wer schreit Hilfe?
und warum Hilfe? und warum warum?

Wer weiß nicht, daß er verreckt? Aber woher denn,
daran stirbt man nicht! Wer ist nicht Tachist?

HANS MAGNUS ENZENSBERGER

who hollers god bless you out of the foam?
who tells me to hope? and what should i hope for?
who slips me a clammy brotherly handshake?

all right get off it i'm not one of you
i'm not one of us: i somehow got to be born
when the riot squads turned on the hoses: i somehow
started to howl no fooling alone without brothers blinded
on a black friday in a pink-tinged bidet

and why alone and why pink-tinged and why
not and why no fooling

who doesn't schluck his own fire? who
doesn't wade through piles of clipped fingernails?
who doesn't leave an oily loophole in his contracts?
who waits to be saved? and by whom? and from what?
who doesn't bolt endless food with sincerest best wishes?
who doesn't get taxed? who hasn't caught
the cry of fear at the stockholders meeting?

who doesn't have a lung made of plastic? okay then
who's ever been through a factory? who
hasn't got that smell in his throat? who
isn't divorced? and why not?
who's never sent a picture postcard from capri?
who doesn't fuck around with history?
who isn't sorry he's living? and why not?
and why not? who doesn't say and so forth?
and why and so forth? who hollers for help?
and why help? and why why?

who doesn't know that he's croaking? but why all the sweat
if nobody dies from it? who isn't a walking tachistoscope?

Wer hat keine Handschellen vor dem Mund,
und kein desinfiziertes Gehirn? Aber woher,
aber woher denn die Honorare, und warum nicht?
Woher die Müllhaufen, aus denen Pfauen brechen
und mystische Rosen? und, ehrlich gesagt: woher,
woher dieser Schaum?

Gebt mir die Hand, erloschene Feuerschlucker!
Mumien, vermummt in rosigen Schaum, Grüßgott!
Reicht mir die schaumige Speiseröhre zum Gruß,
siehe, ich bin einer von euch,
ich will euch ersticken im eigenen Schaum!
Denn zufällig lebe ich noch!
Zufällig bin ich stark wie ein Krüppel,
der Niemand heißt, ehrlich gesagt,
daran stirbt man nicht, stark
und ohne Adresse und kalt wie der Himmel.

So geht doch! Geht! Worauf wartet ihr noch?
Auf die Hochbahn, auf die Niewiedergutmachung,
auf die steuerbegünstigte Sintflut?

Das Jüngste Gericht ist bestochen,
Leihwagen fahren die Päpste
in ihrer Tiara aus Schaum.

An glühenden Telefonen baumeln die Makler
im Schweiß ihrer schweinsledernen Gesichter:
Der Klassenkampf ist zu Ende, am Boden liegt
die Beute in ihrem Fett, liquide,
Schaum in den rosigen Augen. Verschimmelt
in den Vitrinen ruhn, unter Cellophan,

HANS MAGNUS ENZENSBERGER

who doesn't have handcuffs on his mouth
and a saniflushed brain? but why all the sweat?
why all the sweat about royalty checks? and why not?
why all the sweat if the garbage cans blossom with peacocks
and mystical roses? no fooling why all the sweat?
why all the sweat with this foam?

o fire-eater with the heat turned off slip me some skin
o mummy in your mummy-cloth of pink-tinged foam
    god bless you
deliver your bubbling gullet to my kow-tow
for behold i am one of you
i'd like to strangle you in your own foam
because i somehow still happen to be living
somehow i'm tough as some old cripple
who calls himself no man who somehow
gets by and won't die from it: tough
and without an address and cold as the sky

so get going get moving what are you waiting here for?
for the el-train maybe? for the non-reparations?
for the tax-deductible deluge?

the fix is on the last judgment
company cars deliver the popes
in their foam-flecked tiaras

over red-hot telephone wires brokers are bobbing their heads
in the sweat of their pig-leather faces:
the class struggle's ended the victim's
sprawled on the floor in his fat:
liquid holdings: foam in the rose-colored eyes
moldy banners and barricades wrapped in cellophane

Banner und Barrikaden. Aus einer antiken Jukebox dröhnt
die Internationale, ein müder Rock.

Die Generalstäbe spielen Weltraumgolf.
Hinter der Schallmauer nimmt der Fortschritt
eine Parade von lenkbaren Lehrstühlen ab.
In den Staatsbanken singen kastrierte Kassierer
schaumige Arien, bis die begeisterten Damen
ihr Gefrierfleisch aus dem Chinchilla schälen.

Tränengas, Cadillacs und Baracken
für die Afrikaner! Rabattmarken her
für die Hungerödeme der Freien Welt!

Und warum nicht diese prämierten Euter?
Filmhintern in rosigem Schaum, Striptease
des Abendlandes von Bottrop bis San Diego?

Ehrlich gesagt: warum nicht? und warum
keine Rampen? Sollen es unsere Kinder vielleicht
besser haben als wir? Aber woher denn!

Woher die möblierten Herren, die unter die Teppiche kriechen
und das geflammte Furnier und die Stellenangebote zerbeißen?
Woher? und wohin mit ihnen? Wohin mit den Witwen?
Wohin mit den Kommunisten? Wohin mit dem,
was da Hölderlin sagt und meint Himmler, mit dem,
was da Raketen und Raten abstottert, was da filmt
und vögelt und fusioniert? Wohin mit den Erzbischöfen?

Wohin mit den abgeschabten Genies, die vor Angst
aus dem Fenster fallen? Hinaus, hinaus in den Regen!
In den tiefen ranzigen Schaum, in die Irrenhäuser,

HANS MAGNUS ENZENSBERGER

propped in the showcase: while from an antique jukebox
the internationale drones: a beat rock and roll

the chiefs of staff play golf out in space
beyond the sound barrier progress
reviews the ranks of its housebroken scientists
castrated cashiers in the federal reserve sing
arias dripping with foam: till the rapturous clubwomen
peel the chinchilla wraps from their deep-frozen bosoms

cadillacs tear gas and barracks
for africa s & h stamps
for the free world's waterlogged bellies

and why not give prizes for tits? hollywood
ass in the rose-colored foam: striptease
of the western world from dortmund to san diego

no fooling why not? and why not build
launching pads? should our kids maybe
have things better than us? why all the sweat?

why all the sweat when the prize lodgers crawl under the rugs
and take bites out of the woodwork and chew up the want ads?
why all the sweat? and what can we do with them? what can we do with
    the widows?
what can we do with the communists? what can we do with everyone
who says hölderlin and means himmler with everyone
who pays off rockets and cops in installments who makes movies
and fucks and connects? what can we do with the archbishops?

what can we do with the unemployed geniuses who fall
whimpering out of their windows? get them out get them out in the rain
in the deep rancid foam in the madhouses

in die Gefängnisse, in die Kongreßhallen,
wo der Speichel der Lügner von den Wänden rinnt,
wohin denn sonst? In die gußeisernen Krematorien,
und in die hundertfältig verfluchten Zollämter,
Hauptzollämter und Zollaufsichtsbehörden!

Und wohin mit uns? Wohin mit dem,
was die Fußballstadien schäumend füllt
und schreit nach Coca-Cola und Blut?
Wohin mit dem lieben Gott? Wohin
mit seinem glasscherbenfressenden Ebenbild?
Freiwillig in die Bundeswehr! in den Schaum!

in den rasenden schwarzen rosigen Schaum!
in den wiehernden schäumenden Schaum!

Loslassen! Finger weg! Zufällig lebe ich noch!
Zufällig bin ich geboren!

Und ich kenne diesen Geschmack nach Chlor und Blei:
schmeckt ihr es nicht im Sahnebaiser,
ihr unaufhörlichen fressenden Leichen bei Kranzler?
Heil Hitler! Vergelts Gott! diesen Geschmack
nach Auschwitz im Café Flore, im Doney,
nach Budapest, im Savoy, und nach Johannesburg?

Und warum so weiter? und warum dieses Gebären
alberner Fünflinge aus bloßem Zeitungspapier,
diese Ausbrüche rührender alter Vulkane,
diese Krönungen und Krawalle? Schluß damit!
Aufhören! Ehrlich gesagt, diese Springfluten,
daran stirbt man nicht! Man stirbt auf dem Stuhl,
wenn man bedenkt, daß sich die Menschen essen,
ein Mensch, ehrlich gesagt, den andern!

HANS MAGNUS ENZENSBERGER

in the prisons in the lobbies of congress
where the spit of liars runs down the walls
and where else? in the cast iron crematoria maybe
or just let them rot down at customs: at the
goddamn bureau the goddamn bureau the goddamn bureau of customs

and what can we do with ourselves? and the crowds
that fill up the football stadiums crying
for coca-colas and bloodbaths: what can we do with them?
what can we do with god? what can we do with his
holy likeness sitting there gobbling up glass splinters?
volunteer him into the army: into the foam

into the maddening black and pink foam
into the whinnying foam-sloshing foam

let go get your hands off: i'm somehow still living
i somehow got to be born

and i know this taste of chlorine and lead
can't you sniff it under the whipped cream?
you stiffs that keep lapping it up in your coffins
heil hitler god bless you: this taste
of auschwitz in the cafe flore in doney's:
of budapest in the savoy: of johannesburg where?

and why and so forth? and why the birth
of some bloody quintuplets right there in the papers?
the eruptions of turbulent ancient volcanoes?
these coronations and riots? the hell with it
ditch it no fooling: these spring floods
that none of you die from: you die on the can
when you realize that men eat each other
no fooling: that each man gobbles his neighbour

Und warum nicht? und warum kein Lebkuchenherz
und keine Gratisaktien für den Kultusminister?
Na und? und warum keinen Mokka? Warum kein Koma?
Warum kein Amok? Daran stirbt man nicht!
Man stirbt in der Nato, an Herzverseifung,
ehrlich gesagt, in einem Knäuel von Ministranten,
in einem Schaumgummihochhaus in Düsseldorf,
man stirbt auf dem Stuhl, ehrlich gesagt,
wenn man bedenkt, wer man ist!

Kauft euch Särge mit Klimaanlage und Wasserspülung,
wahrlich, wahrlich, die Preise steigen, ade!
Bald habt ihr Schmirgel im Hals.
Worauf wartet ihr noch? Stopft euch den Schmuck
in die Busen, den Büchsenöffner, das Cembalo,
bietet der Nemesis eine Pauschale an
und packt! Packt die Vergütungen ein,
die Gasmaske und den Unterleib!
Kauft Geigerzähler und alte Meister!
Kauft Knaben auf und verrichtet an ihnen,
solange Vorrat, euer Gesabber!
Kauft euch den Montag, das Meer!
Kauft euch Porridge und Bomben, kauft
vom Flugplatz weg das Genie!
Kauft euch das Gift, das ich euch
auf die käuflichen Zungen lege,
um euch zu töten, um euch zu erfrischen!
Kauft euch Kultur und wälzt sie wie einen Kaugummi
zwischen den Kiefern! Gründet euch schnöde Schweizen!
Stockt auf! Warum nicht? Setzt um! Stellt glatt!
Macht flüssig! Schreibt ab! Schüttet aus!

HANS MAGNUS ENZENSBERGER

and why not? why no gingerbread hearts?
and no free market tips for the council of churches?
so okay why no mocha? why no coma?
why no amuck? nobody dies from it
you die in nato no fooling from too much fat
in your hearts: in a cabal of acolytes
in a foam-rubber skyscraper in düsseldorf
you die on the can no fooling
when you realize just who you are

so buy your air-conditioned coffins with the built-in toilets
verily verily price going up whoops
you wind up with a throat full of steel wool
what are you waiting for? stuff the diamonds in
under your shirt: shove the can opener in and the harpsichord
shake your nemesis down for a lump sum payment
and pack your bags pack the securities in
pack in your gasmasks pack in your bellies
buy geiger counters and old masters
buy little boys and bequeath them
your juice while it lasts
buy up monday buy up the ocean
buy up branflakes and bombs buy
the geniuses out at the airport
buy poison and wait till i
smear it over your affluent tongues
(it'll kill you or give you a charge)
buy up some kulcher and roll it around on your gums
like a life-saver: play the crummy swiss market
sit tight why not? sell out stand pat
cash in sign over pay off

Und warum nicht? Warum keine Kopfjäger
in kessen Kabriolets? Warum keine Kübel
voll Affenhormon in der Nervenklinik?
Wer wirft da, ehrlich gesagt, den ersten Stein?

Wer lebt nicht von Spritzen? Wer knackt,
auf den Kreuzungen, keine Schädel? Na also!
Wer ist nicht am Schleimhauthandel beteiligt?
Wer weiß nicht was Waschzwang ist? Wer heißt nicht Pilatus?

Aufmachen! Schluß! Die Steuerfahndung ist da! Die Trauzeugen!
Das Bundesverdienstkreuz! Der gemischte Chor! Die Statistik!
Der himmlische Bräutigam und der Generalstreik!
Die Gashähne auf! Stoßgebet! Furcht und Zittern!

Grüß Gott! An die Barren! Zur Riesenkippe! Ein Lied!
Bis dat qui cito dat! Vergelts Gott! Die Fahne hoch!
Si vis pacem para bellum! Ausziehen! Hinlegen!
In saecula saeculorum!

Das hört nicht auf! Das stirbt, ununterbrochen,
aber nicht ganz, das faselt geschmeichelt
von Apokalypse, das frißt am Nullpunkt noch Kaviar
und spritzt sein Eiweiß gegen die Zuchthauswand!
Lebewohl, lebewohl, interkontinentales Rülpsen,
das krault durch Ströme von Gin und Chanel,
und riecht nach Schaum und Kloake! Das hört nicht auf!

Das hat keinen Zweck! Da hilft kein himmlischer Blitz!
Da hilft kein Rilke und kein Dior! Das stinkt
auf den automatischen Bachwochen zum Himmel!
Das sind Gesichter aus Mayonnaise und Kitt!

HANS MAGNUS ENZENSBERGER

and why not? why no headhunters
in furlined convertibles? why no vats
full of monkey glands for the fancy clinics?
who here should throw the first stone?

who doesn't live through the mainline? who hasn't cracked
open a skull at the crossroads? so okay
who isn't mixed up with the international mucous membrane cartel?
who doesn't know what waschzwang is? who isn't called pilate?

open up ditch it enter the federal fuzz the marriage guest cometh
the congressional medal of honor steps forth: the mixed chorus the latest
      statistics
the heavenly bridegroom and the general strike
open the gas-jets amen fear and tremble

god bless you: head for the bars for the brink start singing
bis dat qui cito dat gold help you: flags up
si vis pacem para bellum strip down sprawl out
in saecula saeculorum

they won't stop they die a little bit more every minute
but never completely they talk dumb they go on and on
about doomsday: with the pointer at zero
they still slop their caviar still splatter
egg white over the walls of their cell
faretheewell my honey my intercontinental fart faretheewell
they breaststroke up rivers of gin and chanel
smelling of foam and clogged pipes it's too much!

it's mad: no bolt from the blue can undo them
no rilkes can save them no diors they stink
to high heaven while bach weeks screech from the jukebox
they wear masks made of mayonnaise and putty

337

Das schlägt in der Stunde seines Absterbens zu
mit Schaumlöscher, Gasrohr und Aktennotiz!

Loslassen! Schluß! Davon weiß ich nichts!
Ich bin keiner von uns! Ich bin niemand!
Finger weg! Ich bin allein! Laßt mich los!

Ich will euch nicht ändern! Vergelts Gott!
Das läßt mich kalt! Das hat keinen Zweck!

Brüder im Schaum, Prälaten und Feuerschlucker,
schaumgeborene Aufsichtsräte, ich sehe euch zu,
gleichgültig, ehrlich gesagt, und frage mich:
Wahrlich, wahrlich, wohin mit euch,
geblendete Seifenherzen, wohin? und warum
zur Hölle, und warum nicht? und warum
liebt ihr Johann Sebastian Bach? und warum
habt ihr Nasen wie ich? und warum schäumt süß
wie ein fernes Blutgerinnsel die Zukunft
am rosigen Himmel?

Ja, hieße ich Niemand, wäre ich niemands Bruder
im Niemandsland, wäre ich weggerissen, so,
daß ich ruhen könnte, von den Lebendigen!
Wäre ich, zufällig, keiner von euch und von uns,
wäre ich frei davon, von uns, von diesem Schaum,

diesem triefenden schmunzelnden süßen Schaum
vor dem Mund des Jahrhunderts, der steigt
und steigt und bläht sich in den Tresoren,
in den Brautbetten, in den Gedichten, und,
warum nicht? in meinem schaumigen Herzen,
das schwimmt, geblendet, im kochenden Schaum

HANS MAGNUS ENZENSBERGER

they stand in the shadow of death still killing each other
with fire extinguishers gas pipes and inter-office reports

let go! ditch it! from this i know nothing
i'm not one of us i'm not one of anyone
keep off with your hands i'm alone let go

i don't want to change you god help you
it leaves me cold it's really too mad
o brothers in foam o prelates o eaters of fire
o boards of directors sprung from the waves i'm watching you
cooling it thinking it out for myself asking
verily verily where will it end with you?
foam-blinded soap hearts where will it end? and why
down in hell? and why not? and what makes you
scream for johann sebastian? and what
gives you noses like mine? and why should the future
be foaming so sweetly? a blood clot away out
in the rose-colored sky

okay call me no man: say that i'm no man's kid brother
from no man's land let me break loose so at least
i can rest from all these live people:
let's make out that i'm not one of you that i'm not one of us
that i'm free from all that, from us, from this foam,

this snivelling smirking sweet-tasting foam
that hangs from the century's mouth that rises
higher and higher and swells in the bank vaults
that smells in the honeymoon beds in your poems and
why not? in my own foam-flecked heart
while it swims around blinded in boiling foam

und rostet, und schwimmt,
unsterblich wie eine Büroklammer,

wohin wohin

in die rosige Zukunft

HANS MAGNUS ENZENSBERGER

and gets rusty and swims
immortal as a paper clip

further and further

into the rose-colored future

Jerome Rothenberg

Zum Andenken an William Carlos Williams

In seinem letzten Jahr war er fast blind,
heiter und sonderbar,
vertrat keine Ansichten, sah
nicht in die Röhre, las
keine Rezensionen,
weder *Look* noch *Life*.

Keine "repräsentative Figur":
Landarzt in Rutherford, New Jersey.
Keine Galadiners chez Kennedy:
eine Holzveranda,
"mit einem Blaugrün bemalt, das mir,
verwaschen, vergilbt, besser gefällt
als alle anderen Farben."

Für die Stockholmer Akademie
nicht ganz das Richtige,
für die Reporter unergiebig,
für *Look* nicht blind genug,
für *Life* zu lebendig
mit seinen achtzig Jahren,
sah er in seinem Hinterhof mehr
als ganz New York über zwölf Kanäle:

Hühner und kranke Leute,
das Licht und die Finsternis.

Nahm die Brille ab:
"Die Pflaumen im Eisschrank so süß und kalt" und
"Der Schritt des Alten, der Dünger sammelt,
ist majestätischer
als der von Hochwürden am Sonntag."

HANS MAGNUS ENZENSBERGER

In Memory of William Carlos Williams

In his last year, he was all but blind,
cheerful and peculiar,
expressed no opinions, didn't watch
the tube, didn't read
any reviews,
neither *Look* nor *Life*.

No "representative figure,"
country doctor in Rutherford, N.J.
No gala dinners *chez* Kennedy:
a wooden veranda,
"smeared a bluish green that,
weathered, faded, pleases me better
than all other colors."

For the Stockholm Academy
not quite right,
for the reporters unprofitable,
not blind enough for *Look*,
too alive for *Life*
with his eighty years
he perceived more in his backyard
than all of New York over twelve channels:

chickens and sick people,
the light and the darkness.

Took off his glasses:
"The plums in the icebox so sweet and cold" and
"The tread of the old man gathering dog-lime
is more majestic
than that of the Episcopal minister on Sunday."

Sah die Finsternis und das Licht,
vergaß die Hühner nicht,
war genau
und sonderbar heiter.

HANS MAGNUS ENZENSBERGER

Saw the darkness and the light,
did not forget the chickens,
was precise
and peculiarly cheerful.

   Reinhold Grimm and Felix Pollak

Erkennungsdienstliche Behandlung

Das ist nicht Dante.
Das ist eine Photographie von Dante.
Das ist ein Film, in dem ein Schauspieler auftritt, der vorgibt, Dante zu
    sein.
Das ist ein Film, in dem Dante Dante spielt.
Das ist ein Mann, der von Dante träumt.
Das ist ein Mann, der Dante heißt, aber nicht Dante ist.
Das ist ein Mann, der Dante nachäfft.
Das ist ein Mann, der sich für Dante ausgibt.
Das ist ein Mann, der träumt, er sei Dante.
Das ist ein Mann, der Dante zum Verwechseln ähnlich sieht.
Das ist eine Wachsfigur von Dante.
Das ist ein Wechselbalg, ein Zwilling, ein Doppelgänger.
Das ist ein Mann, der sich für Dante hält.
Das ist ein Mann, den alle, außer Dante, für Dante halten.
Das ist ein Mann, den alle für Dante halten, nur er selber glaubt nicht
    daran.
Das ist ein Mann, den niemand für Dante hält außer Dante.
Das ist Dante.

HANS MAGNUS ENZENSBERGER

Identity Check

This is not Dante.
This is a photograph of Dante.
This is a film showing an actor who pretends to be Dante.
This is a film with Dante in the role of Dante.
This is a man who dreams of Dante.
This is a man called Dante who is not Dante.
This is a man who apes Dante.
This is a man who passes himself off as Dante.
This is a man who dreams that he is Dante.
This is a man who is the very spit and image of Dante.
This is a wax figure of Dante.
This is a changeling, a double, an identical twin.
This is a man who believes he is Dante.
This is a man everybody, except Dante, believes to be Dante.
This is a man everybody believes to be Dante, only he himself does not
    fall for it.
This is a man nobody believes to be Dante, except Dante.
This is Dante.

Hans Magnus Enzensberger

Die Dreiunddreißigjährige

Sie hat sich das alles ganz anders vorgestellt.
Immer diese verrosteten Volkswagen.
Einmal hätte sie fast einen Bäcker geheiratet.
Erst hat sie Hesse gelesen, dann Handke.
Jetzt löst sie öfter Silbenrätsel im Bett.
Von Männern läßt sie sich nichts gefallen.
Jahrelang war sie Trotzkistin, aber auf ihre Art.
Sie hat nie eine Brotmarke in der Hand gehabt.
Wenn sie an Kambodscha denkt, wird ihr ganz schlecht.
Ihr letzter Freund, der Professor, wollte immer verhaut werden.
Grünliche Batik-Kleider, die ihr zu weit sind.
Blattläuse auf der Zimmerlinde.
Eigentlich wollte sie malen, oder auswandern.
Ihre Dissertation, *Klassenkämpfe in Ulm, 1500*
bis 1512, und ihre Spuren im Volkslied:
Stipendien, Anfänge und ein Koffer voller Notizen.
Manchmal schickt ihr die Großmutter Geld.
Zaghafte Tänze im Badezimmer, kleine Grimassen,
stundenlang Gurkenmilch vor dem Spiegel.
Sie sagt: Ich werde schon nicht verhungern.
Wenn sie weint, sieht sie aus wie neunzehn.

HANS MAGNUS ENZENSBERGER

At Thirty-three

It was all so different from what she'd expected.
Always those rusting Volkswagens.
At one time she'd almost married a baker.
First she read Hesse, then Handke.
Now often she does crosswords in bed.
With her, men take no liberties.
For years she was a Trotskyist, but in her own way.
She's never handled a ration card.
When she thinks of Kampuchea she feels quite sick.
Her last lover, the professor, always wanted her to beat him.
Greenish batik dresses, always too wide for her.
Greenflies on her *Sparmannia*.
Really she wanted to paint, or emigrate.
Her thesis, *Class Struggles in Ulm 1500*
to 1512 and References to them in Folksong:
Grants, beginnings and a suitcase full of notes.
Sometimes her grandmother sends her money.
Tentative dances in her bathroom, little grimaces,
cucumber juice for hours in front of the mirror.
She says, whatever happens I shan't starve.
When she weeps she looks nineteen.

Michael Hamburger

Der Urlaub

Jetzt, wo er frei hat, verhältnismäßig, schlurft er
oft um die Tennisplätze, läßt sich rasieren, liest.
Schwarzhändler wispern, Turnschuhe hecheln vorbei.
Starrend vor Palmen dehnt sich die Welt
am Sonntag. Im Palace brüten die ersten Huren
über dem Frühstück. Alles klar, alles fusselt.
Menschenskind, Mecki, ruft es vom Nebentisch.
Heulendes Elend am Strand. Umständehalber
schmelzen Peseten. Zufallsbekanntschaften,
sehnsüchtig eingekremt. "Was sagst du dazu, José,
wenn ich heut nacht mit dir geh? Olé, olé, olé."
Ekelhaft, dieser Tintenfisch auf dem Teller.
Das gähnende Zimmer. Sand in den Handtüchern.
Ein helles Insekt, das sich gegen die Birne wirft.
Siebzehn senkrecht: Griechische Fruchtbarkeitsgöttin.
Die Dusche riecht muffig. Auf der Straße kichert es.
Motorräder starten. Dann ist nur noch das Meer da,
das in der Ferne ächzt. Nein, nebenan ist es,
nebenenan stirbt eine Frau oder liebt sich selbst.
Olé, olé, was sagst du dazu, José? Er horcht.
Weiß im Zahnputzglas wimmeln die Schlaftabletten.

HANS MAGNUS ENZENSBERGER

The Holiday

Now that he's free, relatively, often he shuffles
round the tennis courts, pays for a shave, reads.
Black marketeers whisper, plimsolls pant past him.
Stiff with palm trees, the world expands
on Sundays. Here, in the Palace, the first whores
brood over their breakfast. All is clear, all fuzzes.
Well, if it isn't Nick! comes from the next table.
On the beach, howling misery. Complications
melt away pesetas. Chance acquaintances,
longingly primed with lotion. "What do you say, José,
if tonight we go and play? Olé, olé, olé."
Disgusting, this platter of octopus.
The yawning bedroom. Sand in the towels.
A brilliant insect that collides with the lightbulb.
Seventeen across: Greek fertility goddess.
The shower smells musty. In the street someone titters.
Motorbikes rev. Then there's only the sea
that sighs away into the distance. No, it's the next room,
in the next room a woman is dying or loving herself.
Olé, olé what do you say, José? He listens.
White in his tooth-glass the sleeping tablets teem.

Michael Hamburger

Besuch bei Ingres

Heute hätte er für das ZK gemalt, oder für die Paramount,
je nachdem. Aber damals schwitzten die Gangster noch
unter dem Hermelin, und die Hochstapler ließen sich krönen.
Also her mit Insignien, Perlen und Pfauenfedern.

Wir treffen den Künstler sinnend an. Er hat sich ausgestopft
mit "gewählten Gedanken und edlen Leidenschaften."
Eine mühsame Sache. Teure Sesselchen, Erstes Empire oder Zweites,
je nachdem. Weiches Kinn, weiche Hände, "Griechentum in der Seele."

Sechzig Jahre lang diese kalte Gier, jeder Zoll ein Könner,
bis es erreicht war: die Rosette im Knopfloch, der Ruhm.

Diese Frauen, die sich vor ihm auf dem Marmor winden
wie Robben aus Hefeteig: zwischen Daumen und Zeigefinger
die Brüste gemessen, die Oberfläche studiert wie Plüsch,
Tüll, Spiegeltaft, die Feuchtigkeit in den Augenwinkeln
zwölfmal lasiert wie Gelatine, das Inkarnat glatt
und narkotisch, besser als Kodak: ausgestellt
in der École des Beaux-Arts, eine käufliche Ewigkeit.

Wozu das Ganze? Wozu das Blech der Orden,
der fanatische Fleiß, die vergoldeten Adler aus Gips?

Merkwürdig schwammig sieht er mit achtzig aus,
erschöpft, den Zylinderhut in der linken Hand.
"Es war alles umsonst." Aber aber, verehrter Meister!
Was soll denn der Rahmenmacher, der Glaser von Ihnen denken,
die treue Köchin, der Leichenwäscher? Einzige Antwort:

HANS MAGNUS ENZENSBERGER

Visiting Ingres

Today he'd be painting for the Central Committee, or Paramount,
it all depends. But at that time a gangster still sweated
under his ermine, and the con-men had themselves crowned.
So let's have them, the insignia, pearls, the peacock feathers.

We find the artist pensive. He has stuffed himself
with "choice ideas and noble passions."
A laborious business. Expensive small armchairs, First or Second Empire,
it all depends. Soft chin, soft hands, "Hellas in his soul."

For sixty years this cold greed, every inch a craftsman,
till he's achieved it: fame, the rosette in his buttonhole.

These women, writhing in front of him on the marble
like seals made of risen dough: between thumb and forefinger
the breasts measured, the surface studied like plush,
tulle, glossy taffeta, the moisture in the corner of their eyes
glazed twelve times over like gelatine, the flesh colour smooth
and narcotic, better than Kodak: exhibited
in the École des Beaux-Arts, a venal eternity.

What's it all for? What for the tin of his decorations,
the fanatical industry, the gilt plaster eagles?

Curiously bloated he looks at eighty,
worn out, with that top hat in his left hand.
"It was all for nothing." How can you say that, most honoured Maître!
What will the frame-maker think of you, the glazier?
your faithful cook, the undertaker? His only answer:

Er seufzt. Hoch über den Wolken, onirisch, die Finger der Thetis,
die sich wie Würmer ringeln auf Jupiters schwarzem Bart.
Widerwillig werfen wir einen letzten Blick
auf den Künstler—wie kurz seine Beine sind!—
und verlassen auf Zehenspitzen das Atelier.

HANS MAGNUS ENZENSBERGER

A sigh. Far above the clouds, oniric, the fingers of Thetis
that squirm like worms on Jupiter's black beard.
Reluctantly we take a last brief look
at the artist—how short his legs are!—
and tiptoe out of the studio.

Michael Hamburger

Valse triste et sentimentale

Ja, früher, früher!
Und was ist jetzt?
Mach was du willst,
aber sei so lieb:
Keine Rechtfertigungen.

Mit oder ohne,
du hast jedenfalls.
Beziehungsweise
du hast nicht.
Das genügt.

"Was soll ich *denn* machen?
Was soll ich *denn* machen?"
Natürlich. Das kennt man.
Das fragen sie immer,
wenn es zu spät ist.

Eigentlich schade.
Manchmal vermiß ich dich schon
mit deinen ewigen Dramen,
deinen blöden Ausreden,
deinem faulen Zauber.

Ich, schlechtes Gewissen?
Da kann ich nur lachen.
Mach die Tür zu
und laß dich nie wieder
blicken!

HANS MAGNUS ENZENSBERGER

Valse triste et sentimentale

Blast the old days.
What about now?
Do as you like,
but please,
no apologies.

You did, didn't you?
With or without it.
Or else
you didn't.
That's all there is to it.

"What do you want me to do?
What do you want me to do?"
Of course. I know.
That's what they all ask
when it's too late.

A pity, really.
Sometimes I begin to miss you
with your eternal scenes,
your foggy excuses,
your hocus pocus.

Me, feeling guilty?
You make me laugh.
Get out of here
and don't show your face again,
ever.

Hans Magnus Enzensberger

Fetisch

Immer nur
an diesen Flaum
denkt er nachts
kleiner
als eine Hand
und weiter
denkt er
an nichts
Nichts anderes
ist da
als dieses Büschel
das nicht da ist
Er stellt es sich
dunkel vor
dieses Gewölle
wie es sich bauscht
hell
Er hört förmlich
wie es knistert
unter dem Druck
der Hand
Er sieht
wie es sich kräuselt
im Licht
blond schwarz
wie es glitzert
wahnsinnig
weich und widerspenstig
und nicht weiter
nennenswert

HANS MAGNUS ENZENSBERGER

Fetish

All night
he is thinking of it
a wisp of down
smaller
than the hand of a man
There is nothing else
he can think of
there is nothing
but this tuft of hair
which is not here
He imagines it
dark
a woolly mass
curling
brightly
He can almost hear it
rustle
at the touch of his hand
He sees it
bristling
in the light
blonde black
soft and unruly
glittering madly
and scarcely worth
further notice

    Hans Magnus Enzensberger

Zur Erinnerung an Sir Hiram Maxim (1840–1916)

I

Auf dem Schulweg, im Straßengraben,
das Heulen des Tieffliegers, dann
Staubwölkchen links, vorne, rechts,
lautlos, und erst hinterher
das Hämmern der Bordkanone.
Die Bewunderung hielt sich in Grenzen.

II

Später, viel später, taucht er auf
aus dem alten Lexikon. Ein Bauernjunge.
Die Farm in der Wildnis, heimgesucht
von den Bären. Das ist sehr lange her.
Mit vierzehn die Stellmacherlehre:
16 Stunden am Tag, vier Dollar Monatslohn.
Schlug sich durch als Gelbgießer,
Boxer, Instrumentenmacher, schrie:
Ein chronischer Erfinder bin ich!,
verbesserte Mausefallen, Lockenwickler
und baute ein pneumatisches Karussell.
Sein Dampfflugzeug, Kesselgewicht
1200 Pfund, drei Tonnen Speisewasser,
zerschellte am Eigengewicht.
Auch sein Kaffeersatz war kein Erfolg.
Erst die große Ausstellung in Paris,
eine Feerie aus Glühfäden und Bogenlampen,
brachte die Ehrenlegion und die Erleuchtung.

HANS MAGNUS ENZENSBERGER

In Memory of Sir Hiram Maxim (1840–1916)

I (1945)

On the way to school in the ditch,
the roar of the fighter-plane swooping down,
little clouds of dust to the left, in front of us,
to the right, soundless, and only a moment later
the aircraft gun's hammering.
We did not appreciate his invention.

II (1854–1878)

Later, much later did he emerge
from an old encyclopaedia. A country boy.
Their farm in the wilderness, harassed
by bears, a long time ago. At fourteen,
a cartwright's apprentice. Sixteen hours a day
at four dollars a month. Scraped along
as a brass-founder, boxer, instrument maker,
shouting: A chronic inventor, that's me!
Improved mousetraps and curlers
and built a pneumatic merry-go-round.
His steam aeroplane, with a boiler
of 1200 pounds, three tons water-supply,
broke down under its own dead weight.
Neither did his ersatz coffee take off.
He had to wait for the Great Paris Exhibition,
a fairy-world of arc-lamps and filaments,
for the Legion of Honour and for his illumination.

III

Drei Jahre später konnte der Prince of Wales
in den Kellergängen von Hatton Garden
ein präzises Wunder besichtigen:
es lud, spannte, verriegelte, zog ab,
öffnete den Verschluß, warf die Hülse aus,
lud und spannte, immer wieder, von selbst,
und die Kadenz—fabelhaft! Die Kadenz:
zehn Schuß pro Sekunde, Dauerfeuer.
Der Rückstoßlader! Das ist genial,
rief der Duke of Cambridge, nie wieder
wird der Krieg sein, was er gewesen ist!
Eine Waffe von unerhörter Eleganz.
Der Ritterschlag folgte postwendend.

IV

Heute natürlich, wo diese Errungenschaft
auf jedem Schulhof zu haben ist,
fällt es schwer zu empfinden,
was er empfunden hat: die triebhafte Freude
eines bärtigen Säugetiers mit 270 Patenten.
Wir jedenfalls, hundert Jahre jünger als er,
lagen wie tot da am Straßenrand.

HANS MAGNUS ENZENSBERGER

III (1881–1901)

Three years later the Prince of Wales
could inspect in the vaults of Hatton Garden
a miracle of precision:
it loaded, cocked, bolted and triggered,
opened the breech-lock, ejected the shell,
reloaded, cocked, again and again, by itself,
and the cadence was fabulous: ten rounds
per second, continuous firing.
The recoil barrel, a stroke of genius!
cried the Duke of Cambridge. Never again
will war be what it used to be!
A weapon of unprecedented elegance!
The knighthood was not long in coming.

IV (1994)

Nowadays of course, with his masterpiece
being available in any school playground,
we fail to feel what he must have felt:
the compulsive joy of a bearded mammal
with 270 patents to his credit.
As to us, his juniors by a hundred years,
we lay low as if dead in the ditch.

Hans Magnus Enzensberger

Herbst 1944

Zwar dem, der im Gras lag,
kamen sie herrlich vor,
wie sie hoch oben glitzerten
am wolkenlosen Oktoberhimmel,
die Bomberströme, und schade
war es nicht um die Andenken,
die in der Ferne verbrannten
auf dem modrigen Dachboden:

Sammeltassen und Engelshaar,
Großvaters Pariser Postkarten
(Oh là là!) und sein Koppelschloß
aus einem anderen Krieg,
löchrige Unterröcke, Orden,
Puppenhäuser, die Psyche aus Gips
und ein paar vergessene Gottesbeweise
in einer Zigarrenschachtel—

aber im Keller die Leichen
sind immer noch da.

HANS MAGNUS ENZENSBERGER

Autumn 1944

True, to the one who lay in the grass
they seemed glorious,
glittering there so high up
against the cloudless October sky,
the bomber chains, and he didn't care
about those mementos
that far away were burnt
in the mouldering loft:

antique cups and angel's hair,
Grandfather's postcards from Paris
(*Oh là là*) and his belt buckle
from another war,
petticoats with holes, decorations,
dolls' houses, the Psyche in plaster
and a few forgotten proofs of God
in a cigar-box—

but those corpses in the cellar
are still there.

    Michael Hamburger

Der Geist des Vaters

An manchen Abenden sitzt er da,
wie früher, leicht gebückt,
summend am Tisch
unter der eisernen Lampe.
Die Tuschfeder schürft
über das Millimeterpapier.
Ruhig zieht sie, unbeirrt,
ihre schwarze Spur.
Manchmal hört er mir zu,
den schneeweißen Kopf geneigt,
lächelt abwesend, zeichnet weiter
an seinem wunderbaren Plan,
den ich nicht begreifen kann,
den er niemals vollenden wird.
Ich höre ihn summen.

HANS MAGNUS ENZENSBERGER

His Father's Ghost

Some evenings he sits there
as he used to do, slightly bowed,
humming at his table
under the iron lamp.
The Chinese ink pen skims
the graph paper.
Quietly, sure of itself,
it traces its black course.
At times he listens to me,
his snow-white hair inclined,
absently smiles, goes on drawing
towards his wondrous plan
which I cannot understand,
which he'll never complete.
I hear him hum.

Michael Hamburger

Länderlexikon

Schade um das Drachenreich Druk-Yul,
von dem die wenigsten wissen, wo es liegt,
und um die Republik des Erlösers
mit ihren ergrauten Rollkommandos;
jammerschade um die verzweifelte Demokratische
und Populäre Algerische Republik;
schade auch, wennschon aus anderen Gründen,
um die Confœderatio Helvetica,
die mit Kontoauszügen und Spritzen bedeckt ist—
Kümmernisse, nicht zu verwechseln
mit den Plagen der Heimstatt des Friedens
und der Republik der Ehrbaren Männer;
schade, ewig schade um die Föderative Republik
Jugoslawien, samt ihren grambedeckten
ehemals autonomen Gebieten;
schade, wennschon aus anderen Gründen,
um die Vereinigten Staaten von Amerika
und um die zahlreichen Bewohner derselben,
die, jeder für sich, in ihrer Garage lauernd,
ihre ganz persönlichen Schrotflinten umklammern;
schade, in Gottesnamen, um Abu Dhabi Dubai Scharja
Ra al-Khaima Fujaira Um al-Kaiwain und Ajman,
die Vereinigten Arabischen Emirate! schade auch,
schade, wennschon in geringerem Maße,
um die Bundesrepubliken Deutschland und Mikronesien,
ja sogar um die unter ihren Souvenirläden ächzende
Serenissima Repubblica di San Marino,
um die untröstliche Hellenische Demokratie
und das mühselige und beladene Medinat Yisr' aél;
ganz zu schweigen von der unermeßlich verstörten

HANS MAGNUS ENZENSBERGER

Gazetteer

Pity about the Dragon Kingdom Druk-Yul
that hardly anyone could find on a map
and about the Republic of Our Saviour
with its grey-haired raiding parties;
and more still a pity about the desperate Democratic
and Popular Republic of Algeria;
a pity also, though for other reasons,
about the Confoederatio Helvetica
littered with bank statements and needles—
worries not to be likened to
the tribulations of the Homeland of Peace
and the Republic of Honourable Men;
a pity, a neverending pity about the Federal Republic
of Jugoslavia with all its stricken
once autonomous regions;
a pity, though for other reasons,
about the United States of America
and its numerous inhabitants who,
each man for himself, skulking in their garages
clutch at their personalised shotguns;
a pity, in God's name, about Abu Dhabi Dubai Ash-Shariqah
Ra's al-Khaymah al-Fujayrah Umm al-Qaywayn and Ajman,
the United Arab Emirates! a pity too
a pity, though to a lesser degree,
about the Federal Republics of Germany and Micronesia,
yes, even about the Most Serene Republic of San Marino
groaning under its souvenir shops
and about the Hellenic Republic that cannot be comforted
and the troubled and burdened Medinat Yisra'el;
to say nothing of the immeasurably distressed

Rußländischen Föderation
und dem noch weit unermeßlicheren
Zhongua Renmin Gonghe-guo;
und wehe, wehe über die rote, grüne, lehmfarbene
République Rwandaise mit ihren hinterbliebenen
6 211 518 Insassen, sowie über manche andere
in Sack und Asche gehüllte Gegenden,
derer wir selten gedenken.

Druk-Yul = Bhutan; Republik des Erlösers = República de El Salvador; Heimstatt des Friedens
= Myanmar, früher Burma; Republik der Ehrbaren Männer = Burkina Faso; Medinat Yisr'aél =
Israel; Zhonghua Renmin Gonghe-guo = China.

HANS MAGNUS ENZENSBERGER

Russian Federation
and the far more immeasurable
Zhongua Renmin Gonghe-guo;
and alas, alas for the red, green and clay-coloured
République Rwandaise and its 6,211,518
inmates left, and likewise many another
region enveloped in sackcloth and ashes
we rarely think about.

David Constantine

Druk-Yul: Bhutan; *Republic of Our Saviour*: El Salvador; *Homeland of Peace*: Myanmar, formerly Burma; *Republic of Honourable Men*: Burkina Faso; *Medinat Yisra'él*: Israel; *Zhonghua Renmin Gonghe-guo*: China.

Als der Krieg zu Ende war:

Da war ein Nest blutroten Schwalbenflaums,
Da war ein Nest gebaut aus nackten Knöchlein
Der kleinen Schwalben, die in diesem Nest,
Gebaut aus ihren Knöchlein, hausen wollten,
Sehr warm im Nest aus ihrem Flaum blutrot.

ADOLF ENDLER

ADOLF ENDLER, 1930–

When the war was over:

There was a nest of blood red swallow down,
there was a nest, built with the naked bones
of little swallows that wanted to live
in this nest built with their little bones,
so warm in the nest of their down blood red.

Charlotte Melin

Wechselnder Wind

Paestum. Oder war Birra Peroni gemeint . . . Keiner wußte
was, auf der Goulasch/Matratzen-Party; wer war
Raymond Roussel—
        Schatten seltener Wörter
                    (un-
bemerkt)
      wandern ab. Zugestempeltes Gedächtnis.
Wer fuhr den blauen Volkswagen, am Ende
                welcher
Kurzgeschichte? im Regen . . .
            Aber die günstige Zeit
für Schellack-Platten; die Neuigkeit des alten Geräuschs;
und die Straßen werden nicht
          leer und dunkel
sein—
    Wechselnder Wind, zum Vergleich; Wind
im Wechsel der Metaphern
          (das Ende der Metaphern, oder:
Ziele im Neuen Deutschunterricht)
           Die meisten merken
nichts
   (etwas bereitet sich vor); einige sind schon
von selber gegangen; andere still und zögernd.

A Shift in the Wind

Paestum. Or was the reference to Birra Peroni . . . No one
knew anything at the goulash/mattress party; who was
Raymond Roussel—
                    shadows of obscure words
                                    (un-
noticed)
        drift off. Memory sealed shut.
Who drove the blue Volkswagen, at the end of
                        what
short story? in the rain . . .
                      But the salad days
of shellac records; the novelty of old sounds;
and the roads won't be
                empty and dark.
A shift in the wind by way of comparison: wind
in the mutation of metaphor
                    (the end of metaphor, or:
objectives in the new teaching of German).
                        Most don't notice
anything
        (something's afoot); a few have already taken it
upon themselves to leave; others are silent and hesitating.

   Michael Hofmann

Hotel Belgica

Die Chefin löst Kreuzworträtsel.
Würde gern helfen, Blondine,
spreche kein Flämisch.
Gut der weiße Kabeljau.
Ihre Mädchen rauchen zuviel.
Ein Bier noch, noch eins.
Die Nacht wird sehr stürmisch,
wie die letzte; jetzt das Lexikon.
Kommt denn noch wer,
Matrose, Hotelgast, Gespenst.
Noch sind Sie schön; alternd
die Holzwände, Bänke und Spiegel.
Ausbeuterin, warum lächeln Sie nie?
Vorgestern auch schon mal hier,
ein Bier noch, am selben Tisch.
Hören Sie, ganz gewaltig, draußen,
die Brandung; oder was ist.
Buchstaben, Wörter; kein Flämisch
und lerne es nicht, ein Bier noch,
in dieser wortlosen Nacht.

JÜRGEN BECKER

Hotel Belgica

The cook is doing the crossword.
Wouldn't mind helping, blonde,
don't speak any Flemish.
Cod in white sauce was pretty good.
Her girls all smoke too much.
Another beer, one more.
Tonight's stormy, just like
last night; now the dictionary.
Will anyone else come,
sailor, hotel guest, ghost.
You are still beautiful; ageing
wood-panelled walls, benches and mirrors.
Exploitrix, smile, why don't you?
Here the day before yesterday too,
more beer, same table.
Do you hear it, crashing outside,
the surf, or whatever it is.
Letters, words; I've no Flemish
and I'll never learn now, one more beer
in this night without words.

Michael Hofmann

". . . Beerdigungen im Sommer"

. . . Beerdigungen im Sommer. Jetzt hört es
nicht mehr auf. Man trifft Bekannte, und
das Wiedererkennen, nach wenigstens zehn Jahren,
beginnt mit Verwechslungen; immerhin, man kennt sich
noch aus zwischen Eingang und Ausgang. Mit 19
die Weltbeste stöhnt: ich spüre mein Alter, und
Seerosen kamen vor in einem verramschten Gedicht.
Besser, man kommt nicht zurück in
diese und jene Gegend; dein Dorf ist
schöner geworden, das Pfarrhaus verkabelt, und
der Typ aus der Frittenbude hat
fortgemacht nach Lanzarote. Doch, langsam wieder
Plätze frei auf dem alten Friedhof;
der Leichenschmaus, gleich nebenan, beim Italiener . . .

JÜRGEN BECKER

". . . Funerals in summer"

. . . Funerals in summer. No let-up now.
You meet acquaintances, and after ten years
of not seeing each other, you always start off
on the wrong foot, with mistaken identities;
at least you're still able to make the exit
under your own steam. The world champion, 19,
moans about feeling her age, and you have water-lilies
in a crap poem. There are certain regions
you'd better stop going to; your village has got prettier,
the vicarage has cable now, and the man
who ran the chip shop has bunked off to Lanzarote.
Surprise, there are a few vacancies in the old cemetery;
the funeral feast is next door, at that handy Italian's . . .

Michael Hofmann

Herbstgeschichte

Eine Zeichnung, oder auch nur Gekritzel . . . ich hatte
versucht, dem alten, sich senkenden Birnbaum
einen Halt zu geben. Aber die Stütze aus
Bleistiftstrichen mißlang. Nun regiert hier, seit
ein paar Tagen, der Nebel, der es heute
fertiggebracht hat, daß man gar nichts mehr
sieht. So geht das all diese Jahre,
Strukturen, Fröste, Eulenflug, Kriege im September.

JÜRGEN BECKER

Autumn Story

A drawing, or just a scribble . . . I had tried
to prop up the old collapsing pear tree.
But the prop of pencil lines didn't hold up.
For a few days now, it's been all fog,
which finally today has obscured all visibility.
This is how it is every year, structures,
frosts, owl flight, wars in September.

Michael Hofmann

Die Bringer Beethovens

für Ludvik Kundera

Sie zogen aus, Beethoven zu bringen
jedermann
Und da sie auch eine schallplatte hatten
spielten sie zur rascheren einsicht
die sinfonie nr. 5 c-moll opus 67

Der mensch M. aber sagte,
es sei ihm zu laut, das
mache sein alter

Über nacht setzten die bringer Beethovens
maste an strassen und plätze
spannten drähte befestigten
lautsprecher und mit dem morgen
ertönte zur bessren gewöhnung
die sinfonie nr. 5 c-moll opus 67,
laut genug dass sie gehört ward
auch in der ferne

Der mensch M. aber sagte, ihn schmerze der kopf,
ging heim gegen mittag schloss
türen und fenster und lobte
die dicke der mauern

Herausgefordert, knüpften die bringer Beethovens
draht an die mauern und hingen
lautsprecher über die fenster dass
durch die scheiben drang
die sinfonie nr. 5 c-moll opus 67

Der mensch M. aber ging aus dem haus und zeigte an
die bringer Beethovens;

REINER KUNZE

The Bringers of Beethoven

for Ludvik Kundera

They set out to bring Beethoven
to everyone.
And as they had a record with them
they played for speedier understanding
Symphony no. 5, in C minor, opus 67

But the man M. said
it was too loud for him, he
was getting old

In the night the bringers of Beethoven put
up poles in streets and squares
hooked up cables, connected
loudspeakers, and with the dawn
for more thorough acquaintance came the strains of
Symphony no. 5, in C minor, opus 67,
came loud enough to be heard
in the mute fields.

But the man M. said he had a headache,
went home about noon, closed
doors and windows and praised
the thickness of the walls

Thus provoked, the bringers of Beethoven strung
wire on to the walls and hung
loudspeakers over the windows, and in
through the panes came
Symphony no. 5, in C minor, opus 67

But the man M. stepped out of the house and denounced
the bringers of Beethoven;

doch jeder fragte ihn, was er habe
gegen Beethoven

Angegriffen, klopften die bringer Beethovens
am tore des menschen M., stellten als er es auftat
hinter die schwelle den fuss; die sauberkeit lobend
traten sie ein
Zufällig kam auch die rede
auf Beethoven
und zur belebung des themas hatten sie
zufällig bei sich
die sinfonie nr. 5 c-moll opus 67

Der mensch M. aber schlug mit der eisernen schöpfkelle
ein auf die bringer Beethovens
Er wurde verhaftet zur zeit

Mörderisch nannten die tat des M.
anwalt und richter der bringer Beethovens
Doch hoffnung sei immer
Er wurde verurteilt
zur sinfonie nr. 5 c-moll opus 67
von Ludwig van Beethoven

Da trommelte M. und schrie
bis stille war

Er war schon zu alt, sagten die bringer Beethovens
Am sarge des M. aber, sagten sie,
stehn seine kinder

REINER KUNZE

they all asked him what he had
against Beethoven

Thus attacked, the bringers of Beethoven knocked
on M.'s door and when he opened up they
forced a foot inside; praising the neatness of the place
they went in.
The conversation happened to turn
to Beethoven,
and to enliven the subject they happened
to have with them
Symphony no. 5, in C minor, opus 67

But the man M. hit the bringers of
Beethoven with an iron ladle.
He was arrested just in time.

M.'s act was called homicidal
by lawyers and judges of the bringers of Beethoven.
But they must not give up hoping.
He was sentenced
to Symphony no. 5, in C minor, opus 67,
by Ludwig van Beethoven

M. kicked and screamed,
until the loudspeakers stopped
beyond the mute fields

He was just too old, the bringers of Beethoven said.
But by M.'s coffin, they said,
are his children

Und die kinder verfügten
dass gespielt werde
am sarge des menschen M.
die sinfonie nr. 5 c-moll opus 67

REINER KUNZE

And his children demanded
that over the coffin of
the man M. should be played
Symphony no. 5, in C minor, opus 67

Gordon and Gisela Brotherston

Zimmerlautstärke

Dann die
zwölf jahre
durfte ich nicht publizieren sagt
der mann im radio

Ich denke an X
und beginne zu zählen

REINER KUNZE

With the Volume Turned Down

Then came
twelve years
when I wasn't allowed to publish
says the man on the radio

I think of X
and start counting

Ewald Osers

In memoriam Johannes Bobrowski

Sein foto
an den anschlagsäulen

Jetzt

Der nachlaß ist
gesichtet, der dichter
beruhigend tot

REINER KUNZE

In Memoriam Johannes Bobrowski

His photograph
on the hoardings

Now

His papers have been
examined, the poet is
reassuringly dead

Ewald Osers

Trauriger Tag

Ich bin ein Tiger im Regen
Wasser scheitelt mir das Fell
Tropfen tropfen in die Augen

Ich schlurfe langsam, schleudre die Pfoten
die Friedrichstraße entlang
und bin im Regen abgebrannt

Ich hau mich durch Autos bei Rot
geh ins Café um Magenbitter
freß die Kapelle und schaukle fort

Ich brülle am Alex den Regen scharf
das Hochhaus wird naß, verliert seinen Gürtel
(ich knurre: man tut was man kann)

Aber es regnet den siebten Tag
Da bin ich bös bis in die Wimpern

Ich fauche mir die Straße leer
und setz mich unter ehrliche Möwen

Die sehen alle nach links in die Spree

Und wenn ich gewaltiger Tiger heule
verstehn sie: ich meine es müßte hier
noch andere Tiger geben

Sad Day

I am a tiger in the rain
water parts my hide
drops drop into my eyes

I shuffle slowly, slide my paws
along Friedrichstrasse
and am stone-broke in the rain

I fight my way through cars on red
walk into the café for bitters
eat the band and swing out

I bellow sharply at the rain on Alex-Platz
the high-rise gets wet, loses its belt
(I snarl: one does what one can)

But it rains the seventh day
Then I'm angry up to the eyelashes

I hiss the street empty
and sit down among honest seagulls

They all look left into the Spree

And when I mighty tiger howl
they understand: I mean there should
still be other tigers here

Wayne Kvam

Winter

Ich lerne mich kennen, zur Zeit
die Wohnung die
wenigstens drei Generationen von Leuten
sah, immer hatten die Fenster
oben die Wölbung, die Bretter schmal
kaum geeignet für Blattwerk in Töpfen
die Wände
wie Bäume Jahresringe
tragen Tapetenschichten
ganz unten Jugendstil, dazwischen
Makulatur Zeitungsberichte
empörte Leser zu Freudenhäusern
zwei Zeilen Reichstagsbrand dann
bloß noch Tapeten, das Handwerk
ließ nach. Oder den Ausblick
auf Dächer (kaum ein Stück Himmel) das
hatten sie vor mir im Aug, vermutlich
ähnlichen Regen und Schnee, schwärzte
den Asphalt im Hof machte das Mauerwerk rot
andre
solln es noch sehn, eine Katze
begleitet mich ein paar Jahre was
weiß sie von mir sie liebt mein Parfüm
oder einfach den Platz, auf dem
ich hier sitze ich bin nicht sehr gut, aber
lernte Geduld als ich klein war bei
Wasserfarben:
wartet man nicht, verliert man das Bild—
und manchmal
bewegt sich mein Herz in den Aufhängebändern
das ist, wenn ich eine fremde Gegend seh

SARAH KIRSCH

Winter

I learn to know myself, at present
the lodging that saw
at least three generations of people,
always the windows had
an arch above, the sills small
hardly suited to foliage in pots
the walls
like annual rings of trees
bear layers of wallpaper
on the bottom Jugendstil, in between
wastepaper newspaper reports
enraged readers on brothels
two lines Reichstag's fire then
only more wallpaper, the handicraft
slackened. Or the outlook
onto roofs (hardly a piece of sky) they
had that before me in their view, likely
similar rain and snow blackened
the asphalt in the yard made the masonry red
others
are still to see it, a cat
has accompanied me a few years what
does she know of me she loves my perfume
or simply the spot on which
I'm sitting I am not very good, but
learned patience at water-coloring when
I was little:
if one doesn't wait, one loses the picture—
and sometimes
my heart moves in its suspension bands
that is, when I see a strange countryside

von mutigen Menschen höre oder
einer was fragt;
ich liebe meinen Bauernpelz meine Stiefel
und mein trauriges Gesicht

SARAH KIRSCH

hear of courageous people or
someone asks a question;
I love my peasant's fur my boots
and my sad face

    Wayne Kvam

Allein

Die alten Frauen vor roten Häusern
Roten Hortensien verkrüppelten Bäumen
Brachten mir Tee. Würdevoll
Trugen sie die Tabletts zurück, bezogen
Horch- und Beobachtungsposten
Hinter Schnickschnackschnörkel-Gardinen.

SARAH KIRSCH

Alone

The old women before red houses
Red hydrangea crippled trees
Brought me tea. Worthily
They carried the trays back, resumed
Listening- and observation posts
Behind tittle-tattle-ornamental curtains.

Wayne Kvam

Brief

Ich bin glücklich in Italien, in diesem
Frühen Dezember. Morgens Sterne, dann
Nebel unter den grünen Bäumen. Der Steinvogel
Klirrt Kiesel aneinander mit seiner Stimme, ihr seht mich
Auf roten Fliesen und obgleich
Der Herd ein Elektroherd ist tu ich
Die einfachen Dinge von vor dreihundert Jahren.
Ich brate—ja ich habe Pompeji gesehen und zweitausend
Säulen und alle Kirchen, abgeschiedene Gärten—ich brate
Den Hasen im Topf und er kriegt
Einen Whisky am Schluß und ich auch ich hab
Das Schreibzeug aufm Küchentisch und lebe und lebe
Und lebe immer noch und mein Geliebter
Hat Locken und Kleider aus Samt und Seide und schöne
Achtfüßige Hunde, die bringen
Mir Stiefel und Feuer und Flamme, was zu rauchen und dann
Kommt er selbst

SARAH KIRSCH

Letter

I am happy in Italy, in this
Early December. Mornings the stars, then
Fog under the green trees. The stone bird
Clinks pebbles together with his voice, you see me
On red tiles and although
The stove is an electric stove I do
The simple things of three hundred years past.
I roast—yes I have seen Pompeii and two thousand
Pillars and all the churches, secluded gardens—I roast
The rabbit in a pot and he gets
A whiskey after and I too I have
The writing stuff on the kitchen table and live and live
And live still and my lover
Has curls and clothes of velvet and silk and fine
Eight-footed hounds, they bring
Me boots and light and fire, something to smoke and then
Comes himself

Wayne Kvam

aus **Säure**

Und ich warte immer noch, daß du von der Küste
                                        raufkommst in diesem
alten Omnibus, der einmal am Tag hier hält
                        und lauter Leute abläd, die kein Mensch erwartet.
Deine Koffer sind angekommen, die Shawls, die Schuhe
                        und die bunten Gläser, die wir am Rialto klauten
das Bett ist schon hier, dein Bademantel, und erst der Tod
nur du selber fehlst noch, dein Atem, dein Lachen für zwei

                        . . .

Ihre Telefonnummer. Als ich sie schließlich
                                verloren hatte, dachte ich: das bist du los:
rumstehn in einer Telefonzelle im Winter, endlich
                                        hast du das wieder: Zeit
und Winterzeit in rauhen Mengen
Ruhe in einer dunklen Bar mit einem Sherry
                        und Iris entfernt sich auf dem Regenbogen.
Na schön; in der Jackentasche find ich sie wieder
zwei Wochen später, und alles beginnt von vorn:
das Ja, das Nein, das Vielleicht
                                        die gurrende Hölle.

                        . . .

Ende des Sommers, und Julia ist heute morgen
                                abgereist mit einem gewissen Hopkins.
Wenn sie wieder hier auftaucht, abgebrannt
und bereit zu weinen, hat sie den dunklen
                                süßen, feuchten, duftenden Mund verloren
und gehört nicht mehr zu den schönen Sachen.
Das Ende, wie immer, macht irgend ein Mister Hopkins.

                        . . .

CHRISTOPH MECKEL

from Acid

And I'm still waiting for you to come up
                                        from the coast in that
clapped out bus that stops here once a day
                        and drops loads of people that no one's waiting for.
Your suitcases have come, your scarves, your shoes
                        and the coloured glasses that we stole on the Rialto
the bed is here, and your robe, and death never left,
only you're missing, your breathing, your laughter, for two.

. . .

Her telephone number. When I finally lost her,
                            I thought: well, you're shot of that at least:
standing around in a callbox in winter, and you've gained
                                                something: time
and winter in loose handfuls
quiet in a dark bar over a sherry
                            and Iris takes off on a rainbow.
All right; then I find it in my jacket pocket
two weeks later, and the whole thing starts over again:
yes, no, maybe
                        the whole purring inferno.

. . .

End of summer, and Julia left this morning
                        with someone by the name of Hopkins.
By the time she comes back, shattered
    and weepy, she'll have lost her dark
                                sweet, moist, fragrant mouth
and will no longer be reckoned among the beautiful things.
The end, as always, is brought about by some Hopkins or other.

. . .

Ich fand den Gürtel ihres roten
                      Bademantels unter der Treppe nachdem sie
lange schon abgereist war, und nachts. Ich hatte
keinen Tiefschlag mehr erwartet.
                      Anfangen zu leben mit nichts
und einem Gürtel.
                 . . .

Jahre des Schlafs, der Unbrauchbarkeit
                      und des Vergessens.
Aber plötzlich: ihr Gesicht im himmeloffenen Morgen
die nackten Schultern, der Kaffeegeruch
                      und das Laub auf den Treppen
ein altes Feuerzeug im Regenstiefel
ein Lachen ohne Grund
                      die Rufe der Dohlen im Flußland
                 die Schreie der Dohlen und ein ganzes Leben.

CHRISTOPH MECKEL

I found the belt of her red
                    dressing-gown under the stairs long after she was gone,
and at night. I hadn't expected any more
low blows.
                              Imagine, having to start a life with
                                    nothing
and a belt.

                              . . .

Years of sleep, uselessness
                              and forgetting.
Then one day: her face in the clear morning sky
her bare shoulders, smell of coffee
                              and the leaves on the stairs
an old cigarette lighter in a wellington boot
laughter for no reason
        the cries of the jackdaws filling the valley
        screams of the jackdaws filling a lifetime.

Michael Hofmann

Tränen

Als offenbar wurde
Der schändliche Charakter des
Unlängst Verstorbenen
Schämten sich einige
Ihrer Tränen an seinem Grab
Und sprachen, sie
Hätten vor Freude geweint.

Tears

When the unpleasant character
Of the deceased
Was made known
Some mourners felt ashamed
Of the tears they had shed
At his graveside and claimed
They had been weeping for joy.

Michael Hofmann

G.

Meine Schwester mit dem Kopf im Gasherd.
Was mag sie gedacht haben als sie starb.
Was mag sie gedacht haben als sie lebte.
Ich glaube, die Welt hat in vierzig Jahren
Keinen besondren Eindruck auf sie gemacht.
Krieg Hunger Kälte. Zwei Kinder, der Mann
Ein Säufer. Sie liebt ihn aber. Er lebt
Auf ihrem Rücken, von ihrer Arbeit
Die sie, ein stilles Tier, still verrichtet.
Als der Mann sie verläßt, versucht sie zweimal
Die Welt zu verlassen. Beim drittenmal klappt es.
Ihr Grabstein sagt aus, daß sie gelebt hat.

KURT BARTSCH

G.

My sister with her head in the gas oven.
What was going through her mind as she died.
What was going through her mind when she was alive.
I think the world didn't make any particular
impression on her in forty years.
War hunger cold. Two children, her husband
a drunk. She loves him, though. He lives
off her back, off the work she performs quietly,
like a quiet animal. When he leaves her,
she twice tries to do away with herself.
The third time she is successful.
On the gravestone, it says she was alive.

Michael Hofmann

Besuch Enzensberger

52 Grad 31 nördlicher Breite, 13 Grad 25 östlicher Länge
Auf meinem Sofa Herr Enzensberger
Trägt einen Gehrock, ein Stück *fin de siècle*
Zeichen der Zukunft, in seinen Augen
(Hellblau) schwimmt etwas Weißes, ich denk noch
Wie schön sich der Zucker spiegelt, der weiß
Auf silbernem Löffel gereicht wird, da
Hör ich dies feine Klirren. Ein Knirschen
Scharren, wasweißich. Dann wieder Stille.
Wir lächeln. Wir trinken Tee. Es ist
19 Uhr 43 MEZ, vor dem Fenster
Ist alles schwarz, auch der Schnee. WIR BITTEN
WEITERE NACHFORSCHUNGEN EINZUSTELLEN.
WER ETWAS TUT ODER UNTERLÄSST MACHT SICH STRAFBAR.
Es überkommt mich, ich weiß nicht warum
Eine große Ruhe. Es ist, seh ich
Kein Eisberg zu sehen. Der Anfang vom Ende
Sagt Enzensberger, ist immer diskret.

KURT BARTSCH

A Visit from Enzensberger

Position 52′ 31″ North, 13′ 25″ East,
on my sofa Herr Enzensberger
is wearing a cutaway, a touch of *fin de siècle*
in deference to the future, I have a sense of something white
floating in his eyes (which are light-blue),
and I remember thinking how prettily
the sugar is reflected in them, on the silver
tongs, when I hear a faint tinkle. A creak,
a scrape, what do I know. Then silence.
We smile. We drink tea. It's 19:43
Central European Time, outside the window
everything, even the snow, is black. WE ADVISE
YOU TO INQUIRE NO FURTHER.
BY ACTING OR FAILING TO ACT
YOU ARE IN BREACH OF THE LAW.
I don't know why, a great feeling of peace
overcomes me. There is, I see,
no iceberg in sight. The beginning of the end,
says Enzensberger, is always discreet.

Michael Hofmann

Frage Antwort Frage

für Volker Braun

Warum kalke ich meine Wände?
Ich will hier nicht wohnen bleiben.
Wenn die Tünche aufgebraucht ist
Gehe ich fort hier, sage ich. Ach
Warum dann die Mühe, frage ich
Listig lächelnd. Damit, wenn ich gehe
Ich nicht etwas Unbewohnbares hinterlasse
Kein sinkendes Schiff, von dem bekanntlich
Sogar die Ratten abhauen. Warum
Wenn es bewohnbar ist, gehst du?

KURT BARTSCH

Question Answer Question

for Volker Braun

Why am I painting the walls?
I don't want to go on living here.
When the paint's all finished up,
I'll be on my way, I say. Oh,
why go to so much trouble, I ask
with a canny smile. So that,
when I go, I don't leave behind
something uninhabitable,
no sinking ship, as deserted by
proverbial rats. Then why,
if it's so habitable, are you leaving?

Michael Hofmann

Marktlage

Was ist los?
Die Hunde gebärden sich heute
wie toll.
Die Bewegungen der Hauswartsfrau
ergeben wieder Reglosigkeit.

Auf dem Markt ist Leben
all die frischen Gemüse und Kräuter
sollen gekauft werden.
Der Fischstand geschlossen
das Angebot an Frischfleisch groß.
Südfrüchte billiger
Schlangengurken Kopfsalat billiger
erstaunlich wie Bananen
verschleudert werden.
Kohl billig Tomaten teuer
Paprikaschoten gehn aus
Chicorée erst in 14 Tagen.

Die leeren Flaschen müssen
gestapelt werden, die Winterkleider
gesichtet. Bald werden
die oberen Knöpfe geschlossen.
Die Hunde streunen
die Autos parken länger im Dunkeln.
Über den ersten Schnee gehen alte Damen
an der Seite alter Herren.
Merkwürdig ist der Winter
bevor er kommt.

Market Position

What's going on?
The dogs are carrying on like crazy
today.
It takes the movements of the janitor's wife
to restore torpor.

In the market there's life
all those fresh vegetables and herbs
there to be bought.
The fish-stall is closed
but a great array of fresh meat.
Tropical fruit cheaper
snaky cucumbers lettuces cheaper
amazing how bananas
are just being given away.
Cabbages cheap tomatoes dear
bell peppers almost gone
endives not for another two weeks.

The empty bottles
have to be stacked the winter clothes
pulled out. Soon
top buttons will be done up.
The dogs stray
cars spend longer parked in the dark.
In the first snow old ladies
walk at the side of old gentlemen.
Curious thing winter
before it's there.

Michael Hofmann

Selbstbildnis

Oft für kompakt gehalten
für eine runde Sache
die geläufig zu leben versteht—
doch einsam frühstücke ich
nach Träumen
in denen nichts geschieht.
Ich mein Ärgernis
mit Haarausfall und wunden Füßen
einssechsundachtzig und Beamtensohn
bin mir unabkömmlich
unveräußerlich kenne ich
meinen Wert eine Spur zu genau
und mach Liebe wie Gedichte nebenbei.
Mein Gesicht verkommen
vorteilhaft im Schummerlicht
und bei ernsten Gesprächen.
Ich Zigarettenraucher halb schon Asche
Kaffeetrinker mit den älteren Damen
die mir halfen
wegen meiner sympathischen Fresse und
der Rücksichtslosigkeit mit der
ich höflich bin.

NICOLAS BORN

Self-Portrait

Often thought of as stout
and well-set
with a fluent gift for life
but I breakfast alone
after uneventful
dreams.
I my trouble
with hair-loss and sore feet
six-two and the son of a civil servant
indispensable to myself
not for sale I know
my worth a tad too exactly
and make love and poems on the side.
My dilapidated face
to best advantage in halflight
and in serious discussions.
I cigarette smoker half ash myself
drinker of coffee with elderly ladies
who help me out
on account of my pleasant expression and
my ruthless deployment
of good manners.

Michael Hofmann

Grimms Märchen

Eine graue Sau in einem Winkel. Nachdem wir lange gegangen sind, mit schmutzigen Schuhen, nach einer schon endlosen Fahrt im Vorortzug, frierend, in einem Winkel des Hofs, am Ende der Welt, zeig uns doch deine Tiere, Karl, steht sie im fahlen Licht, linst über das Gitter aus Knüppeln, eine graue Sau, umgeben vom niedrigen Stall am Ende der Welt.

Grimm's Fairytales

A grey sow in a corner. After a long walk in muddy shoes, after an already endless ride in the local, freezing, in a corner of the yard, at the end of the world, why don't you show us your animals, Karl, there she stands in the pale light, peers over the fence posts, a grey sow, in a low pen, at the end of the world.

Rosmarie Waldrop

N.s Identität

"Situation!!" FRIEDRICH HEBBEL, Tagebücher

N.s Frau hatte sich, noch vor dem Krieg, von N. getrennt und einen an-
deren geheiratet. Bei der Zerstörung Dresdens wurde seine Straße Schutt
und Asche, später Wiese. Ein Luftangriff auf Nordhausen ermordete N.s
Eltern. Seine beiden Schwestern starben auf der Flucht gottweißwo, sie
waren kinderlos. Ein Freund wurde vergast, ein anderer war und blieb
vermißt. Sein Bruder fiel in Holland. N. selbst geriet in Kriegsgefangen-
schaft nach England. Er hatte Villen mitgebaut, nicht eine stand noch. Das
einzige, was nach dem Krieg an N. erinnerte, war N.

ELKE ERB

N.'s Identity

"Situation!!" FRIEDRICH HEBBEL, Diaries

N.'s wife had, even before the war, left him and married somebody else. The destruction of Dresden turned his street into rubble and ashes, later into a field. A bombing of Nordhausen murdered N.'s parents. Both his sisters died fleeing, God knows where, they had no children. One friend was gassed, another was and remained missing. His brother fell in Holland. N. himself was a prisoner of war in England. He had helped build villas, not a single one remained standing. The only thing that, after the war, reminded us of N., was N.

Rosmarie Waldrop

O Chicago! O Widerspruch!

Brecht, ist Ihnen die Zigarre ausgegangen?
Bei den Erdbeben, die wir hervorriefen
In den auf Sand gebauten Staaten.
Der Sozialismus geht, und Johnny Walker kommt.
Ich kann ihn nicht an den Gedanken festhalten
Die ohnehin ausfallen. Die warmen Straßen
Des Oktober sind die kalten Wege
Der Wirtschaft, Horatio. Ich schiebe den Gum in die Backe
Es ist gekommen, das nicht Nennenswerte.

O Chicago! O Dialectic!

Now, Brecht, did you let your cigar go out?
In the course of the earthquakes we provoked
In those states that were built on sand.
Socialism takes its hat, never mind, here's Johnnie Walker.
I can't grab it by its principles
Which are falling out anyway. The warm streets
Of October are the chilly routes
Of market economics, Horatio. I wedge my gum in my cheek
And there it is, your nothing-much-worth-mentioning.

Michael Hofmann

Das Theater der Toten

Die Toten führen sich auf wie immer.
Sie treten nachts heraus auf den Friedhof in Rotoli
Die alten Waffen und Worte. Sie können nicht anders.
Das Blut fließt ins Mittelmeer. Sie bauen Ruinen
KARTHAGO NEW YORK. Der gewaltige
Linke Ellbogen Jupiters im Museum von Tunis
Er gebrauchte beide für die siegreiche Sache.
Aber die Lebenden einmal könnten . . . ach was
PRIVATPÖBEL. WENN MAN IHNEN NUR ANGENEHM DAS MAUL STOPFT
Und das Spiel ist gelaufen. Im übrigen bin ich der Meinung
Daß der Sozialismus zerstört werden muß, und
Mir gefällt die Sache der Besiegten.

VOLKER BRAUN

The Theatre of the Dead

The dead conduct themselves the way they always do.
At night they step out onto the graveyard at Rotoli
For ritual exchanges of weapons and words. It's all they know.
The blood drains away into the Mediterranean. They erect ruins
CARTHAGE NEW YORK. The colossal
Left elbow of Jupiter in the museum at Tunis
He needed both of them to secure victory.
If only the living would . . . never mind.
YUPPIE RABBLE. ALL THEY WANT IS THEIR MOUTHS STUFFED WITH
   SOMETHING TASTY
And game over. In general, I'm of the opinion
That socialism must be destroyed, and
I like my causes lost.

Michael Hofmann

Landschaft

    1 verrußter Baum,
nicht mehr zu bestimmen
        1 Autowrack, Glasscherben
        1 künstliche Wand, schallschluckend

verschiedene kaputte Schuhe
im blätterlosen Gestrüpp

        "was suchen Sie da?"

    1 Essay, ein Ausflug in die Biologie
das Suchen nach Köcherfliegenlarven, das gelbe

        Licht 6 Uhr nachmittags

        1 paar Steine

        1 Warnschild "Privat"
        1 hingekarrtes verfaultes Sofa
        1 Sportflugzeug

mehrere flüchtende Tiere,
der Rest einer Strumpfhose an
einem Ast, daneben

        1 rostiges Fahrradgestell

        1 Erinnerung an
        1 Zenwitz

Landscape

1 soot-covered tree
of a type no longer ascertainable
1 wrecked car
1 manmade wall, soundproofed

various defunct shoes
in the leafless shrubs

"what do you think you're doing there?"

1 essay, one excursion into biology
the quest for caddis fly larvae, the yellow

light of 6 p.m.

1 pair of stones

1 warning sign "Private"
1 fly-tipped rotten sofa
1 Cessna

several fleeing animals,
the rest of a pair of stockings on
a bough, next to

1 rusty bicycle frame

1 recollection of
1 Zen joke

Michael Hofmann

Hommes à femme

Wenn eine kleine unscheinbare Frau
lange kluge und ein wenig
lispelnde Reden hält
über Don Juan und Casanova
dann stehen so Männer auf
und zischen Herrgottnochmal
was soll das überhaupt
die ist doch viel zu fipsig dafür

Hommes à femme

When a small inconspicuous woman
delivers long, clever, and slightly
lisping speeches
about Don Juan and Casanova
then these men just get up
and hiss forchristsake and
what's the point of it all—
she's too much of a shrimp anyhow

Charlotte Melin

Fußnote

Wir kommen zurück, die Reste
zu holen: Kissen, Überzug, Laken,
eine Zeichnung, die ungeschützt
über dem Herd hing: *Hermes,*
der Totengeleiter, der vier Jahre
lang das Essen würzte. Noch ist Gott
nicht geboren, die Uhr bleibt hängen,
auch der Spiegel im Flur: wie groß
die Wohnung wird, je mehr sie sich
leert, und wie klein die Zeit,
die in den kahlen Zimmern brütet.
Es ist jetzt dunkel, weil wir
die Lampen entfernt haben, alles
geht sanft durch uns hindurch. Dort,
wo früher mein Schreibtisch stand,
versuche ich auf der Wand eine Notiz
zu entziffern: Dein Zorn ist Liebe,
eine Fußnote in der Geschichte
der Eitelkeit, die noch zu schreiben ist.

MICHAEL KRÜGER, 1943–

Footnote

We're coming back to fetch
what remains: pillow; pillow-case; pall;
a drawing which hung unprotected
above the stove: *Hermes, the Guide
of the Dead* who, for the space of four years,
added spice to our meals. God has still
not been born; the clock stays hanging there;
so, in the hall, does the mirror. How
the flat grows and grows, the more it
empties, and how small is Time,
brooding away in the tomb-like rooms.
All is now dark, we've
removed the lamps: everything
passes softly through us. From where
my writing-desk once was,
I try to decipher a note
on the wall: Your Anger is Love.
A footnote in the history
of vanity, still to be written.

    Richard Dove

Meister

In den Dingen
die Augen,
noch vor der Sprache.
Gleich, wo du bist,
du kehrst zurück:
Stein, Schwelle, Haus,
du wirst erwartet.
Es gibt
einen dritten Raum,
neben Innen und Außen:
so bleibst du
am Leben,
immer im Blick.

MICHAEL KRÜGER

Ernst Meister in Memoriam

In things
the eyes, Ernst,
prior to language.
Wherever you are
you return:
stone, threshold, house
are watching you closely.
Therefore, Ernst,
you remain alive,
always in view.

Richard Dove

Mein junges Leben

Ich will so groß werden
wie die Männer, wenn sie die Daumen
an den Hosenträgern reiben.
Der Rauch aus den Zigarren mischt sich
mit dem Staub abgerissener Ruinen
und den blauen Schwaden der BASF
die von Ludwigshafen herüberziehen.
Auf dem Messeplatz spannt die Traber-Familie
ein Seil von Haus zu Haus und zeigt, wie man grazil
über die Nachkriegsjahre kommt.
Unten drehen allmählich die Lieder
der Arbeiter ab, die roten Fahnen
verschwinden in der Menge, und
die Gewerkschaftsführer schauen auf die Uhr.
Der Fernseher läuft ohne Ton
schon den ganzen Nachmittag, jetzt ist
der keusche Sheriff dran und Gottlob
er läßt sich nicht kriegen
von dieser raffinierten Lady aus Boston.
Wenn ich noch einmal geboren werde,
möchte ich als Zigarette
auf die Welt kommen und dann
zwischen deinen Lippen langsam verbrennen.
Während der Fernseher immer noch läuft,
zeigt mir meine Cousine im Schlafzimmer
ihre Muschi. Das rosa Zäpfchen
zwischen ihren Schamlippen ist eine Entdeckung,
die ich nicht für mich behalten kann.
Ein Brief vom Klassenlehrer, den
meine ganze Verwandschaft liest, bedroht mich

My Young Life

I want to grow up as big
as the men, when they rub their
thumbs on their suspenders.
The smoke of cigarettes mixes
with the dust of torn-down ruins
and the blue swaths of gases from BASF*
that drift over from Ludwigshafen.
Near the fairgrounds the Traber family suspends
a line from house to house and shows how to make it
gracefully through the postwar years.
Below wind-down gradually the songs
of the working class, the red flags
disappear in the crowd, and
the union leaders look at their watches.
The television runs without sound
the whole afternoon already, now it's
the chaste sheriff's turn and thank god
he doesn't let himself get hooked
by this artful lady from Boston.
If I'm ever born again,
I want to come to the world
as a cigarette and then
burn out slowly between your lips.
While the television is still on,
in the bedroom my cousin shows me
her pussy. The pink uvula
between its lips is a revelation
that I can't keep to myself.
A letter from the teacher, which
all my relatives read, threatens me

*BASF—Badische Anilin und Soda Fabrik, a chemical factory.

mit dem Jugendheim. Onkel Karl kommt von der Schicht,
ißt seinen Kartoffelsalat, übernimmt die Bank
und gewinnt zum ersten Mal in seinem Leben.
Wäre dies ein Film, wir hätten ihn
kurz nach Mitternacht erschossen. Lieber Onkel Karl,
alles in allem waren wir eine friedliche
Verwandtschaft. Jetzt sind wir ziemlich auseinander,
meine Cousine hat sich scheiden lassen
und Cousin Willi auch. Viele Grüße
aus Österreich, das Wetter ist sehr schön.
Meine Mutter bringt mir einen Kuli mit,
worauf ein Schiffchen immerzu
über den Wolfgangsee fährt. In der BASF
explodiert ein Kessel, und jeder Arbeiter
bekommt sein eigenes Grab, obwohl niemand weiß,
welche Reste von wem darin liegen.
Onkel Karl lebt noch und nimmt mich mit
zu den Reihengräbern. Sie erinnern mich
an den Krieg, ich beschließe
Pazifist zu werden und höre mir Platten
von Pete Seeger an. Vorher ist Kirmes,
wir drücken uns in die dunkleren Gänge
der Raupenbahn und knutschen die Mädchen ab,
die immer zu zweit sind. Heute arbeiten sie
bei BASF oder bei Daimler-Benz auf dem Waldhof,
ihre Brüste sind größer geworden, die Hintern,
die Arme. Ich erfahre aus dem Wirtschaftsteil
der FAZ, daß meine Lehrfirma bankrott gemacht hat:
Damals stand sie mir so groß gegenüber,
und heute habe ich sie überlebt. Lieber Cousin,

JÜRGEN THEOBALDY

with reform school. Uncle Karl comes from nightshift,
eats his potato salad, plays the banker,
and wins for the first time in his life.
If this were a film, we would have
murdered him just after midnight. Dear Uncle Karl,
all in all we were a peaceful
family. Now we are pretty much apart,
my cousin got a divorce
and Cousin Willy too. Greetings
from Austria, the weather is beautiful.
My mother brings me a ballpoint pen
on which a little ship keeps
sailing on Wolfgangsee. In BASF
a cauldron explodes, and each worker
gets his own grave, although no one knows
which pieces from whom lay in it.
Uncle Karl still lives and takes me along
to the grave-rows. They remind me
of the war, I decide
to become a pacifist and listen to Pete Seeger
records. But before that, it's the Kirmes festival,
we hide in the darker passages of the
funhouse and smooch the girls
who always come in twos. Today they work
at BASF or at Daimler-Benz in Waldhof,
their breasts are grown larger, their behinds,
their arms. I learn from the business section
of the FAZ* that the firm where I apprenticed has
gone bankrupt: Back then it seemed so much bigger than me,
and now I've outlived it. Dear cousin,

*FAZ—Frankfurter Allgemeine Zeitung, a conservative newspaper.

alle zusammen sind wir immer noch ärmer
als jeder ihrer Teilhaber. Sie ziehen
ihre Einlagen ab, du wechselst die Einlegesohlen
und suchst eine neue Stelle. Ich habe schon
1963 gekündigt und fahre zum ersten Mal
nach Paris. Es ist eine Sensation.
Hans und ich finden zwei Huren für 17 Francs,
anschließend trinken wir Rotwein am Tresen,
reden über Rimbaud und stellen uns ab jetzt
unser Leben ganz toll vor.

JÜRGEN THEOBALDY

all of us put together are still poorer
than every one of its stockholders. They change
their investments, you change arch-supports
and look for a new job. I already
quit in 1963 and go for the first time
to Paris. It is a sensation.
Hans and I find two whores for 17 francs,
afterwards we drink red wine at the counter,
talk about Rimbaud and from now on imagine
how really far out our life will be.

   Mitch Cohen

Alexandria

Dort hinten saß er, an diesem Marmortisch,
sagte der alte Kellner, unter den altmodischen Ventilatoren,
die sich damals schon träge drehten,
unter dieser Decke, Stuck des Art Nouveau,
la vie était confortable: Stanley Beach,
Glymenopoulo, und das anmutige
kleine Zizinia, ein Kino heute,
wo in der Saison Tosca gespielt wurde,
La Bohème und Lohengrin (das Strengste
von Wagner, das damals südlich von Neapel
akzeptierbar war). Dort saß er, ein Grieche
von ein paar zehntausend Griechen,
der eine halbe Million Ägypter nicht wahrnahm.
Er lebte in einem imaginären Europa,
stehengeblieben bei Strabo: "das großartigste
Emporium in der bewohnten Welt,"
das jetzt aus Steinen ist und der See
und einem Gefühl der allergrößten Erschöpfung.

Alexandria

Back here is where he once sat, at this marble table,
said the old waiter, under the old-fashioned ventilators
that slowly revolved even in his lifetime,
under this ceiling with its art nouveau stucco,
la vie était confortable: Stanley Beach,
Glymenopoulo, and the pleasant little
Cicinia, a cinema today, where they gave *Tosca*
in season, and *La Bohème* and *Lohengrin*
(the only Wagner that was then found acceptable
south of Naples). There he sat, a Greek,
one of a couple of tens of thousands of Greeks,
steadfastly ignoring half a million Egyptians.
He lived in an imaginary Europe,
that stopped with Strabo: "the most magnificent
emporium in the inhabited world,"
which is now nothing but stone and sea,
and a feeling of millennial exhaustion.

Michael Hofmann

Vieux Jeu

Jedem Wanderer
sein verlederter Frosch
jedem Café
sein Sotto-voce-Streit
jeder Katze
ihr Mäuseleben unterm Buchs
jedem Barbier
das eigene Klingenspiel

Jedem:
seine Hökerin
mit den süßesten Trauben

JOACHIM SARTORIUS

Vieux Jeu

To every traveller
his wizened leather frog
to every café
its sotto voce argument
to every cat
its mouse-life under the box tree
to every barber
his own sharpening antics

To every one:
his own market seller
with her grapes sweeter than anyone's.

Michael Hofmann

Metamorfosis

Ich könnt doch ein Parkett sein
Kein Problem ein Parkett zu sein oder
Pflastersteinfarben als Straße als Dreck drauf.
Ich könnt auch der Mann sein im Anzug
Hätte die steifen Kniee und Kalk am Gesicht
Wäre ein laufendes Mädchen, vor ihm davon
Ich könnt einschlafen in der U-Bahn
Und wär der Beamte in farbiger Uniform
Im Dienste höherer Gewalt und schmiß
Den Penner raus veranlaßte das Wischen
Der Wischfrau am Hingekotzten.
Ich könnt der Plasteboden sein, weiß nicht
Würdst du mich noch erkennen?
Der Mann aus Borges' Geschichte mit dem Hirn
Worein alles woheraus nichts mehr geht.
Ich wäre glücklich damit und flöge ab
Vom Fensterbrett die Straße lang danach
Nachdem ich ein freundliches Bild weitergab
An eine freundliche weibliche Stimme.
Ich versuchte zu leben damit schwarz
Zu malen wie alle Teufel unterm Kreuz.
Ich wär dieser Große Herr dessen Hand
Kaum der Ahnung erreichbar ich hätt
Mich in der Gewalt benutzte alle Moden
Aller Tyrannen Weisheit ich Uwe Kolbe
Hab alle diese Möglichkeiten offen
Die des kleinen täglichen Faschisten
Die des Verworrenen der Plastik der Bühne.
Gern zu gern auch die Märchenfigur
Anstelle drei goldener Haare den harten Satz.
Alles könnt gewonnen sein durch mich
So viel weiß ich bereits soviel
Vergesse ich wie die Fliege den Libellentraum.

UWE KOLBE

Metamorphosis

I could be a wooden floor
I'd have no problem being a wooden floor or
Cobblestonecolored as the street or its dirt.
Or I could be the man in the suit
With the stiff knees and the whey face
I could be the girl running away from him
I could fall asleep in the subway
And be the official in the fantasy uniform
In the service of a higher power and throw
The bum out and get the cleaning woman
To mop up the up-chuck.
I could be the plastic floor, I dunno,
Would you still recognize me?
The man from Borges' story with the brain
That everything enters and nothing leaves.
I'd be happy with that and would fly away
From the windowsill along the street
In pursuit of it, then pass along
A friendly picture to a friendly female voice.
I would try to live with it to paint it
Black like all the devils under the cross.
I would be this great master with the
Almost imperceptible hand I'd have
Myself in hand would follow every fashion
Every tyrant's wisdom I Uwe Kolbe
Have all these possibilities open
Those of the little daily fascist
Those of the confused of the sculpture of the stage.
Happily too happily the fairytale figure too
Instead of three golden hairs the hard phrase.
Everything could be won through me
So much I know already so much
I forget like the fly the dragonfly-dream.

Mitch Cohen/Michael Hofmann

Trilce, César

An manchen Tagen wußten wir einfach
    nichts Bessres zu sagen als
        "Gleich passierts" oder "Geht
      schon in Ordnung . . ." gelangweilt in

überheizten Bibliotheken wo unsere Blicke
    bevor sie glasig wurden wie
        Rauchringe schwebten
      unter den hohen Kassettendecken
        alexandrinischer Lesesäle. Die
      meisten von uns

    wollten fort (nach New York oder
        sonstwohin): Studenten mit

komisch flatternden Stimmen
    gescheiterte Pläne umkreisend immer im
      Aufwind und manche vor

      melancholischer Anarchie süchtig
      nach neuen Totems, Idolen
        gestriger Revolutionen und dem
        zum x-ten Mal
akupunktierten Leib der Magie. Man kam
    ziemlich billig wenn man den ganzen Tag
      dort verbrachte (besonders
    im Winter) zwischen den
        kurzen Pausen allein

mit seinen postlagernden Sorgen miets-
    schuldig, die Stille wie
      Nervengas aus den Büchern
      saugend all dieser
sanften Bestien (. . .) und manchmal

DURS GRÜNBEIN

Trilce, César

There were days it was all we could manage
       to say "It may never happen" or
           "Something will turn up . . . " bored in

overheated libraries where, in moments
       before they completely glazed over
           our glances found themselves drifting
           like smoke-rings
           under the lofty coffered ceilings
              of Alexandrian reading-rooms.
              Most of us

     wanted to get away (to New York
       or someplace): we were students

with funny cracked voices
       enthusiastically turning
           failed projects in our heads, and some of us

           in melancholy anarchy
              were in thrall to new totems, idols
       of gone revolutions and the
multiply acupunctured body of magic.
       If you spent the whole day there
           (especially in winter),
           it was pretty cheap, alone
              between the short intervals

with our poste restante worries, owing
       for the rent, sucking the silence
           from books like nerve gas
of all these mild beasts (. . .) and sometimes

gab es selbst dort im Einerlei
dieses Treibhausklimas ein wenig
lebendige Überraschung—
(Trilce, César!). Ich

erinnere noch genau eines Nachmittags
im Sommer das
raschelnde Zwielicht als ich
beim Scheißen aus einer Nebenzelle der
Bibliothekstoilette
gedämpftes Atmen und Stoß auf Stoß
schnell sich steigern hörte: mein Herz
flog plötzlich auf und ich
erschrak wie ein ganzer
Schmeißfliegenschwarm vor dem

Liebesspiel zweier Männer die stumm
aneinander arbeiteten
schwitzend und selbst-
vergessen wie fremde
kentaurenartige Wesen auf einer

überbelichteten Fotografie.
Schwer zu vergessen mit welcher
Erleichterung sie nachher
frischgekämmt jeder
hochrot und mit cremigem Teint

einzeln an mir vorübergingen und nur
ein Augenzwinkern (durch mich
hindurch) verriet mir:
Sie hatten sich kennengelernt.

DURS GRÜNBEIN

even in the monotonous
                    hothouse climate there was a
                            somewhat living surprise
                                    (Trilce, César!). I

remember one particular
        summer afternoon
                the rustling dusk
        I was in the toilet taking a dump
                when I heard rapid breathing
from another cubicle and an accelerated thumping
        suddenly my heart
            skipped a beat
        and I was alarmed as an entire
                                    swarm of blowflies at the

love of two men silently belabouring
                            one another
                sweating and oblivious like strange
                centaur-like creatures on an

                        overexposed photograph.
            Hard to forget
                    the relief with which,
            with freshly combed hair
    red faces and creamy complexions

they separately walked past me and only
        a wink (a wink that went
                through me) assured me:
        they had gotten acquainted.

Michael Hofmann

Dieser Tag gehört dir

Undurchdringliche Augenblicke eng
    aneinandergereiht wie
Gerüchte im Schein einer immerfort
                gestrigen Politik, eine

Folge schnell wechselnder Grau-
    samkeiten, das
            Nonsens-Ping-Pong-
      Geschwätz einiger Zeitungs-
leser auf einer Parkbank und du
          wie du die Windstille

genießt unter niedrigem Himmel (im
    Schauspielhaus gegenüber proben sie
          Shakespeare . . . "Wir Hu-
manisten . . .")
         Du wartest und
      beugst dich vor zwischen
           Kinderwagen und
    Scharen räudiger Tauben die

einen Wirbel machen beim Füttern—
      Du siehst ihre Köpfe ab-
    getrennt
         blutig im Rinnstein, ein
    schillernder Tagtraum, ringsum

bespritzte Statisten in einem
        Attentatsfilm (Der
Mord an Leo Trotzki) oder das übliche

DURS GRÜNBEIN

All About You

A series of impenetrable instants
　　jammed up together like
rumours by the light of an insistently
　　　　　ancestral politics, a

sequence of rapidly changing grue-
　　　somenesses, the moronic ping-pong
　　　　chatter of a few newspaper-
readers on a park bench, and you
　　　　　you're just enjoying the calm

under a low sky
　　(in the theatre opposite they're rehearsing
　　　Shakespeare . . . "We
humanists . . .").

　　　You wait and then
　　you choose your moment between
　　　　the baby carriages
　　and the flock of mangy pigeons that

fly up in a sort of *haute volée* gobbling—
　　　　You can picture them
　　　　with se-
　　　　vered
　　　bloody heads in the gutter, a
　　vivid daydream,

　　　the bespattered extras in an
　　　　assassination flic (*The
Murder of Leon Trotsky*) or the usual

Kino des Status Quo
        Minus . . . , aber dann
            schlenderst du einfach
    ein wenig weiter zur
        nächsten Kreuzung sehr
            langsam, denn
dieser Tag gehört dir.

DURS GRÜNBEIN

BBBBBB films . . . but instead you just
    gander on very slowly
  to the next crossing, because
today is all about you.

  Michael Hofmann

Ohne Titel

Ein neues Gedicht hat
begonnen an diesem
Nebelmorgen von García
Lorcas Ermordungstag. Eis
essende Kinder und alte
Männer mit komisch
geschwollenen Köpfen
begegnen uns auf der
Straße zum Standesamt wo

unser Kreuzschiff vom
Stapel gelassen wird ohne
das übliche Winken ganz
und gar ungeweiht aber
dennoch von allen bösen
Familiengeistern besetzt.

Wir hatten das Schweigen
gelernt mühlos vorm
Abend wie eine dunkle
Sehne zu spannen: man
sah uns nicht an wie
uns zumute war beim
Verlöschen der Ziele.
Westwärts zog ein Paar
kleiner Wolken, die
Stadt färbte den Himmel
über sich grau und
ich sagte, es hätte mir
Freude gemacht über
Müllhalden mit dir zu
schlendern. Du aber

DURS GRÜNBEIN

Untitled

A new poem began
on this foggy morning
of the anniversary of García
Lorca's murder. Children
eating ices and old
men with strangely swollen
heads passed us on our
way to the registry office

where our cruise ship
was launched without any
of the usual waving and cheering
unblessed but for all that
occupied by all the evil
spirits of both families.

We had learned to span
silence quite effortlessly
in the evening like a taut
sinew: they couldn't see
what we felt like
as the targets were wiped.
Two small clouds
moved off
in a westerly direction,
the city dyed the heavens
grey overhead and
I said I had enjoyed
wandering over the garbage
heaps with you. But you

trugst die verrückten
Schuhe: knallgelb und
wir hatten es eilig als
ein besonders kühler
Nieselregen begann.

DURS GRÜNBEIN

were wearing those crazy
shoes: bright yellow, and
we were in a hurry as
a particularly cool drizzle
started to fall.

Michael Hofmann

MonoLogisches Gedicht no. 2

Zwischendurch gibt es dann
manchmal Tage an denen

habe ich wieder Lust ein
Gedicht anzufangen der Art

wie sie noch immer nicht
sehr beliebt sind. Ich meine

eins ohne alle meta-
physischen Raffinessen oder

was als Ersatz neuerdings
dafür gilt . . . diese Tour

zynisch abzuknien vor dem
Stelzengang der Geschichte

oder gebrochenen Blicks im
harten Ost-West-Marathon
wie nur je ein verdammter

Schatten Dantes von Seiten-
stechen zu klagen. Gedichte

sagte mir neulich jemand

reizten ihn nur wenn sie
voller Überraschungen sind

aufgeschrieben in diesen
seltsamen Augenblicken da

DURS GRÜNBEIN

MonoLogical Poem no. 2

From time to time
I have these days when

I feel like embarking
on a poem again

of a kind that still isn't
all that popular. I mean

one without any meta-
physical refinements or

that thing that lately has stood in
for such . . . that type of

cynical genuflecting
at the stilted progress of history

or standing gasping akimbo
in the tough East-West marathon
as if you were one of

Alighieri's damned
with a stitch. Poems

someone said to me the other day

only attracted him if they
were full of surprises

written at those
odd times when

irgendetwas noch Ungewisses
ein Tagtraum eine einzelne

Zeile von neuem anfängt und

dich verführt.

DURS GRÜNBEIN

something still inchoate
a daydream a single

line begins somewhere and

undoes you.

Michael Hofmann

Tizians neue Zimmer

All die Sitzkissen schwitzen. All die Zierfische japsen
Hinter Panzerglas, wo das Wasser wie von Brausetabletten schäumt
Und die Algen sich Blut zufächeln. Mit zerfressenen Flossen
Ging der Krieg im Aquarium zuende. Der dickliche Guppy träumt.
Vor dem Sofa, verrenkt, liegt ein Strumpfpaar mit Strapsen,
In den letzten Zügen im Kristall die Zigarre. Wie hingegossen
Breiten sich Stoffbahnen aus um die Fenster, knöcheltief, Kelims.
Im ganzen Apartment schmelzen, an den Wänden in goldenen Tiegeln,
Pastose Farben zu etwas, das Rosen ähnelt, Mondgebirgen,
    Phlegmonen,—
Ein Frauenakt hier, dort eine Bibelszene. Pro Glasschrank drei Spiegel
Decken den Rückzug ins Labyrinth. Was da klirrt als *Klimbim*,
Die Fayencen, die Lüster schmeicheln den feisten, kinderlosen
    Bewohnern,
Die auf Kommoden von Photos lächeln, auf Kreuzfahrt, die ewige Crew.
Im Radio liest jemand, sich klösterlich räuspernd, das Decamerone,
Und nur der Afghane, sein Fell eins mit den Teppichfransen, hört zu.
"Wie es war, willst du wissen, *chérie*? Wie mit himmlischen Geigen . . .
Gespielt? War das Stöhnen gespielt? Frag die Fische, sie schweigen."

DURS GRÜNBEIN

Titian's New Pad

Heaving with throw cushions. All the ornamental fish are yapping
Behind thickened glass, in water effervescing like Alka Seltzer.
Algae fan themselves with fresh blood. Peace returns to the aquarium,
At the expense of a few chewed up fins. The guppy stoutly dreams.
A pair of stockings plus garters is writhing at the foot of the sofa,
A portly cigar, with cummerbund, blows smoke rings from the massy
    ashtray.
Kilims, ankle-deep, unroll clear to the windows, like red carpets.
In golden palettes all over the apartment, glutinous colours
Are melting to the likeness of a rose, moon mountains, phlegmons—
Female nude here, Old Testament scene there. Three mirrors per glass-
    fronted cabinet
To cover your retreat into the labyrinth. Kickshaws on the mantelpiece,
Faience pottery and candelabra flatter the dependably childless denizens,
Smiling from framed photographs on tallboys, cruise snaps, captain and
    crew.
On the wireless someone with a nasty monastic cough is reading the
    Decameron,
Though only the afghan hound, blending in so nicely with the carpet
    tassels, seems to be attending.
"Shall I describe it to you, sweetness? The music of the spheres . . .
    Faked?
I suppose your orgasm was faked too? Don't take my word for it then,
    ask the fishes."

Michael Hofmann

Klage eines Legionärs aus dem Feldzug des Germanicus an die Elbe

Nichts ist schlimmer als dieser tödliche Rückweg
Nach einer Schlacht, und der Gedanke daran
Wochen bevor der Feind sich gezeigt hat.
Todfinster ist das Gesicht des Feldherrn,
Die Truppe erschöpft, kein Eilmarsch mehr möglich.
Hinter den Schilden geht schweißnaß, die Füße wund
Der Rest der noch Unverletzten. Im Dauerregen
Sind die Pfade im Schlamm versunken, die Wälder
Ein einziger Hinterhalt, und die Barbaren in Rudeln
Beißen sich Stücke aus unseren Rücken, die Wölfe.
Wer nicht im Nordmeer ertrank, fern der Heimat,
Den schlucken die Sümpfe, weit weg von Rom.
Über Nacht hält Morast die ganze Legion,
Tags sind es morsche Dämme, brüchige Leitern,
Von deren Rand mit gebrochenen Fingern
Der Einzelne abrutscht. Das Land liegt im Nebel
Wie eine Inselgruppe im Meer . . . *Germania Magna*,
Wo die Wälder noch dicht sind, kein Baum
Auf dem Ozean treibt als Galeerenbank
Oder als brennender Schiffsrumpf. Aussichtslos
Ist der Krieg um Provinzen groß wie ein Erdteil,
Um Gebiete, die nicht zu halten sind,
Außer durch neuen Krieg. In den waldigen Tiefen
Verliert der Triumph sich, die lateinische Ordnung.
Und kommst du endlich, um Jahre gealtert, nach Haus,
Steht der Germane in deiner Tür, und es winkt dir
Das strohblonde Kind deiner Frau.

DURS GRÜNBEIN

Lament of a Legionnaire on Germanicus's Campaign to the Elbe River

There's nothing worse than this deadly retreat
following a battle, except the same retreat in prospect
weeks before . . .
Black as death the expression on the general's face,
the shambling, exhausted troops.
Behind the shields are the remnants of those unhurt,
footsore, running
with sweat. Incessant rain
has softened the tracks, the woods are one long ambush,
and the barbarians in packs, the wolves,
bite pieces out of our rearguard.
Whoever did not drown in the North Sea, far from home,
goes down in the swamps, as remote from the eternal city.
Overnight, morasses detain the whole legion,
by day it's rotten causeways, mouldering ladders,
from whose rungs a man slips to his death
with fingers crushed. This land merely punctuates fog
like some archipelago at sea . . . Germania Magna,
where the forests are still integral and dense,
no tree bobs on the sea cut to a bank of oars—
or a blazing hulk. The futility of fighting
over provinces as vast as continents, and territories
that can only be defended by further wars.
In the depths of the forest there is no triumph, and no Latin order.
And when, aged by many years, you finally make it home,
it will be to see the German installed under your lintel,
and waving to you your wife's towheaded offspring.

Michael Hofmann

Täglich weht ein leichter Wind hier durchs Gedächtnis.
   Schleift die Eigenschaften ab, hält das Gewissen rein.
Unbeschwert geht man, gebräunt, durchs Leben. Den Besucher
   Lädt das Lächeln weißer Zähne nicht zum Essen ein,

Nein, zum Vergessen. Und den Strand am Ufer der Phäaken
   Säumen Palmen, grüne Säulenreihn. In hellen Villen
Wohnen Leinwand-Engel, diese Ewigschönen, Immerjungen.
   Jeder Friedhof duftet, im WC die Seife, nach Vanille.

. . .

Selbst der Sternenhimmel ist hier anders. Zu den neuen Bildern,
   Funkelnd zwischen Leier, Schwan und Schütze,
Zählt ein Cabrio in voller Fahrt, verfolgt von einem Saurier.
   Über dem *Revolver* kreist, verkehrtherum, die *Mütze*.

Auf den Hügeln strecken Weltraumteleskope ihre Segelohren
   Ufo und Komet entgegen. Eher hier als anderswo
Bäckt man für Besucher aus dem All Begrüßungskuchen.
   Kinos sind hier Planetarien, und in manchem Bungalow

Steckt ein Flugleitzentrum für die ersten Raumpatrouillen.
   Suchscheinwerfer kreuzen ihre Strahlen nachts zu Chiffren.
Schon vom Flugzeug aus scheint diese Stadt ein Text zu sein,
   Den nur Leute mit Facettenaugen einst entziffern.

Nicht zum Baden laden diese Strände, wüste Landebahnen.
   Beim Spazieren schrickt man auf, wenn da ein Telephon
An der Uferpromenade läutet. Weit und breit kein Mensch . . .
   Durch die Palmenreihen streicht vom Mars ein Celloton.

DURS GRÜNBEIN

from **Greetings from Oblivion City**

Here a light breeze soughs through your memory every day.
  Bears away singularities, keeps your conscience clear.
You stroll through life, bronzed, at ease. The shimmer
  Of white teeth doesn't invite the visitor to eat,

Rather to forget. And the beach where these Phaeacians consort
  Is lined by palms, green pillars' colonnades.
In pastel villas live screen divas, ever young, of unimpaired allure.
  Every cemetery breathes, like the soap in the comfort station, vanilla.

. . .

Even the (star-spangled) night sky is different here. Among the new
  Constellations, glittering alongside the Lyre, the Swan, and Sagittarius,
Is a Sports Car at full tilt, hounded by a Dinosaur.
  Over the *Revolver* hangs the back-to-front *Baseball Cap*.

On the hills radio telescopes stretch out their flapping ears
  For UFO and comet. People here will be quicker than elsewhere
To put out the welcome mat for little green visitors.
  Cinemas here double as planetaria, and the odd bungalow

Houses an air traffic control center for the first space patrols.
  At night, swivelling searchlights phase their beams in code.
Seen from the air, the city looks like a scrambled text anyway
  That only beings with polyhedron eyes could ever crack.

The desert landing strips of the beaches are not for swimming off.
  Taking a walk, you jump when a telephone shrills
On the promenade. No one around for miles . . .
  A *thrup* from Mars pulses through the palms.

  Michael Hofmann

LUTZ SEILER, 1963–

good evening kap

hier draussen lieben sie ihre
kleinen zersessenen hunde. es ist hier auch
nicht so weit
vom sofa bis zum zaun
wie in amerika. und abends
wenn das licht ausgeht
oben, in den bäumen
lehnt ein kleiner zersessener schatten am tor
und sagt:
hier draussen werde ich geliebt, verstehen sie, geliebt

LUTZ SEILER, 1963–

good evening skip

what they love out here are their
threadbare little dogs. it's not
so far either
from sofa to fence
like in america. and at night
when the lights go out
high up in the treetops
a threadbare little shadow
presses up against the gate
saying:
they love me out here, take my word for it, love me

Susan Bernofsky

fin de siècle

ich ging im schnee mit den nervösen
nachkriegs peitschen lampen im genick
über die wiener mozart brücke dort
hockte noch an einem strick ein müder
    irish setter er

war tot und wartete auf mich das
heisst ich band den strick
vom sockel des geländers und begann
das tier ein wenig hin & her
zu schwenken *haut & knochenleichtes*
glocken läuten schnee gestöber
    setzte ein ich sang

ein kleines lied über die donau hin
& z'rück (ich war ein kind) der tote
setter kreiste jetzt an meinem
rechten arm über die schöne
balustrade er rotierte
leicht & gross in das nervöse
nachkriegs lampen licht ein riss
am hals vertiefte sich ein pfeifen

kam in gang und seine steifen
augen schalen klappten
müde auf & zu: du

hättest die mechanik dieses blicks geliebt
und wärst noch einsamer gewesen
über dem schnee, der brücke & dem alten lied

LUTZ SEILER

fin de siècle

i walked through snow with nervous
postwar whip lamps at my neck
across vienna's mozart bridge a tired
irish setter squatted there still
on a rope he

was dead and waiting for me that's
to say i untied the rope
from the railing's base began
to swing the creature round
& round a little skin and bone light
tolling bells blowing snow
started I sang

a little song about the danube back
'n' forth (I was a boy) the dead
setter circled now from my right
arm above the lovely
balustrade he wheeled
light & large into the nervous
postwar street lamp light a cut
grew deeper on his neck a whistling

got into gear his solid
eyes tiredly peeled
opened & shut: you

would have loved the mechanism of that look
and would have been still lonelier
about the snow, the bridge & the old song

    Andrew Shields

"mein jahrgang, dreiundsechzig, jene"

mein jahrgang, dreiundsechzig, jene
     endlose folge von kindern, geschraubt
in das echo gewölbe der flure, verkrochen
beim gehen gebeugt in die tasche

eines anderen, fremden mantels, sieben
  voll wachs mit einer aus dielen
geatmeten schwere, acht

    mit einer aus piss-
becken zu kopf gestiegenen schwere, wir hatten
    gagarin, aber gagarin

hatte auch uns, morgens das gleiche, der schrift
folgende scharren der ärmel
über den bänken & mittags
das schlagwerk der löffel, wir hatten

den tischdienst, den milchdienst, den druck
  einer leerkraft in den augen gelee
    in den ohren bis
sie verstummte
die schwerkraft verstummte
    in unseren mützen
    das waren die schmerzen

beim urinieren, im schutzwald
beim sprechen, wir hatten
zitate: dass wir den schattenseiten des planeten
   wenigstens *eine lichte entgegenhielten*
    erst alle gemeinsam & dann
      jeder noch einmal
      still für sich, wir hatten

LUTZ SEILER

"my birth year, sixty-three, that"

my birth year, sixty-three, that

infinite series of children, attached
to the hallways' echo vault, creeping
with a stoop into the pocket

of another, unfamiliar coat, seven
full of wax with a weight inhaled
in corridors, eight

with a weight that had arisen
from urinals to heads, we had
gagarin, but gagarin

also had us, every morning the same scraping
of sleeves pursuing writing
over the benches & at noon
the clockwork of spoons, we had

table duty, milk duty, the pressure
of an empty lesson in our eyes jelly
in the ears until
it fell silent
gravity fell silent
that was the pain
in our caps

while urinating, in the protective wood
while speaking, we had
quotations: at least we held a light
up against the planet's shadow sides
first all together & then
each of us again
silently for himself, we had

kein glück. also zerfallen die häuser
            werden wir endlich
        wieder klein &
reiten zurück in die dörfer aus holz, aus
stroh, aus denen wir kamen, rissig & dünn
mit einem am wind

geschliffenen echo: wir grüssen gagarin, wir
hatten kein glück, abfahrt, zurück
in unsere dörfer
            & ausfahrt der dörfer
über die äcker bei nacht . . .

LUTZ SEILER

no luck. so the houses collapse
we finally become
small again &
ride back into the villages of wood, of
straw, from which we came, cracked & thin
with an echo sharpened

on the wind: we say hello to gagarin, we
have no luck, departure, back
to our villages
& departing the villages
across the fields at night . . .

Andrew Shields

müde bin ich

vorm schlafen sprach ich leise mit
dem haarteil meiner mutter ich
kann mich nicht erinnern wie

es sang von seinem bleichen
kopf aus styropor so leise
lieder loreleyn es sang

man müsste nochmal
zwanzig seyn & sagte dass
ich schlafen soll

LUTZ SEILER

now i lay me

before sleep a whispered conversation
with my mother's hairpiece I
cannot remember how

it sang from its pale
styrofoam head so softly
its lullabys loreleys sang

oh to be
twenty again & it told
me to sleep

    Susan Bernofsky

Jihad Klänge der Heimat

Jihad Klänge der Heimat spielen sie
unten im Hof, im Dunkeln, wie jeden
Abend, der Nachthimmel hält dich wach.

Sie spielen die Kairocassetten, die hat
der Cousin mitgebracht, du bist bei den
Schatten, beim Gestern, beim Schweigen

von letzter Nacht, du denkst an bestimmte
Kekse, an Sofas, du weißt nicht warum,
denkst an ungemachte Betten, und siehst,

wie sich Wolken verlagern, du denkst
an Blaufilm-Attrappen, du bist bei den
schattigen Bildern, bei Seifeflocken und

Schnee, während unten die Klänge
verwildern, da der Cousin mit rauher
Stimme im Hof, vor der Garage, den

nächsten Durchgang mitsingt, was bis
in die vierte Etage, bis in die Schlafstatt
dringt. Dem Jüngsten steckt es im Rachen,

er beherrscht solche Laute nicht mehr. Was
sollen die Eltern machen, das Flüstern fällt
ihnen schwer. Ich weiß nichts von ihren

Gesprächen, nur von diesem kehligen
Klang. Der Jüngste hat keine Schwestern,
ihm wird die Nacht zu lang. Das Rauhe, das

MARCEL BEYER

Jihad Sounds of Home

They're playing jihad sounds of home
down in the courtyard, in the dark, like every
evening, the night sky keeps you awake.

They're playing the Cairo cassettes their
cousin brought them, you are with the
shadows, with yesterday, with the silence

of last night, you're thinking of certain
cookies, of sofas, you don't know why,
you're thinking of unmade beds, and you see

how the clouds shift, you're thinking
of blue-film dummies, you are with the
shadowy images, with soap flakes and

snow, while the sounds below
grow wild because their cousin sings
along the next time, his rough

voice in the courtyard, in front of the garage, it
carries all the way to the fifth floor, to the
sleeping quarters. It sticks in the youngest one's throat,

he no longer has command of such sounds. What
are the parents to do, whispering is
hard for them. I know nothing of their

conversations, only that throaty
sound. The youngest has no sisters,
the night is too long for him. The hoarseness,

Kehlige: Gestern war stundenlang Blickangst
und ein taubes Gefühl im Arm. Seitdem ist
die Taubheit geblieben, oder der Halbschlaf

bricht an. Sie spielen bis gegen Sieben, zwischen
den Häusern dämmert es schon, das Kind wird
bald weinend erwachen, es kennt keinen anderen

Ton. Sie spielen bis gegen Sieben, dann hörst
du nichts mehr vom Hof. Auf der Straße die
ersten Wagen, du fällst in leichten Schlaf.

MARCEL BEYER

the gutturals: Yesterday was hours of glance-fear
and a numb feeling in my arm. Since then
the numbness has remained, or the doze

is coming. They play until almost seven, between
the houses it's already dawning, soon the child
will wake up crying, it knows no other

sound. They play until almost seven, then
the courtyard falls silent. On the street the
first cars, you pass into a light sleep.

Margitt Lehbert

Raps

Auf einer leeren Landstraße sitzt du am Mittag hinterm
Steuer, zwei polnische Sender wechseln sich ab, in
dir spricht nichts, du meinst schon bald, du bist ganz
ohne Wörter aufgewachsen, und dann das: Raps,

hart gezeichnet, klare Linie, gestreute, dichte Rapsarbeit,
das Feld läuft an, das Bild läuft voll mit Raps, Raps
bis zur Kante, bis zum Haaransatz, randvoll mit Raps,

Rapsaugen, Rapskopf, Rapsgeräusche, kein Preßzeug,
keine Margarine, nichts als Raps.

MARCEL BEYER

Rapeseed

It's noon, you're sitting behind the wheel
in an empty country road, a couple of Polish stations
are cutting in and out, nothing speaks in you, you're on the point
of thinking you grew up mute, and then this: rape,

hard edge, clean line, scattered, dense rape work,
hatched and cross-hatched rape, the field fills, the screen fills
with rape, rape up to your hairline, brim full of rape,

rape eyes, rape head, rape rustle, rape scrape, nothing cattle cake,
nothing margarine, nothing but rape.

Michael Hofmann

Schöpfungsmythos

Sie nimmt das Kleenex und säubert sich
die Scham. Die folgende Geste
ist bereits simuliert, auf
Wiederholung programmiert.

Sie sind
bestimmt nicht müde gewesen, soviel
dürfte klar sein. Vielleicht hat er
einfach nur an ihrer Seite gelegen, unter

dem Apfelbaum, oder er hat sich
was zu rauchen besorgt, son bißchen
traurig ist man ja immer
danach, oder etwa nicht?

Ich würds
glatt noch mal tun, sagt sie, hier
in dieser schönen Gegend. Wird uns schon keiner
sehn hier.

He, was ist jetzt mit dir?
Du kannst mir doch jetzt nicht einschlafen,
wos gerade
so schön gewesen ist!

Creation Myth

She takes a Kleenex
and wipes herself. The following gesture
is already borrowed
pre-programmed.

They were
certainly not tired, that much
should be understood. Maybe he just
stretched out beside her, under

the apple tree, or he went
looking for a cigarette, it's natural
to feel a little bit sad afterwards,
isn't that right?

I wouldn't mind
doing it again, she says, it's
so pretty here. I'm sure
no one can see us.

Hey, what's up?
I can't believe you're falling asleep on me,
when it was so nice
a moment ago!

Michael Hofmann

Schlaflos

Das Gezeter der Vögel
in den Bäumen viertel
nach drei.

Cioran
klagte über Schlaflosigkeit
zeit seines Lebens.

Ich
werfe mich diesem Morgen
blind in die Arme.

Keine Erfahrung
ist teilbar.

VOLKER SIELAFF

Sleepless

The racket of the birds
in the trees at a quarter
past three.

Cioran
complained of sleeplessness
all his life.

I
throw myself blindly
into the arms of the morning.

No experience
is communicable.

    Michael Hofmann

Platz der Befreiung

An diesem Platz, der Befreiung
oder Freundschaft hieß und mehr
an ein Rollfeld bei Nebel erinnert,
ist ein Handy der kleinste
gemeinsame Nenner für ein Hallo.
Die Wahl deiner Nummer klingt
wie *Für Elise* auf einer Triola.
Und nimmst du ab und sprichst oder
atmest dann, stelle ich mir vor,
wie du dich dabei im Spiegel erkundest

. . . eine Karo anzündend. Deine Stimme
macht noch immer dieses Abrakadabra,
an Wunder wie Super-8-Streifen zu erinnern.
Doch jene Rückblende läuft
auf das gleiche hinaus
wie die Masche am Strumpf . . .
dir wird dunkel vor Augen und
Mund: Anstelle eines Seufzers,
Besetztzeichen zu vernehmen,
ist ein Quasi-Bescheid, dein Trumpf.

Liberation Square

In this square, called
liberation or friendship
that seems more like a foggy airfield
a mobile phone is the lowest
common denominator of hello.
Your number sounds like
an ice cream van playing *Für Elise*.
And if you pick up and speak
or breathe, I picture you
consulting the mirror

as you light up a Karo . . . Your voice
still does these abracadabra stunts
like a ribboning Super-8.
But any flashback
winds up in the same place
as the ladder in your tights.
Your eyes and mouth go dark,
instead of a sigh, the busy tone
a communication of sorts,
your diamond trump.

    Michael Hofmann

Thema über eine Variation

Gould sitzt auf dem Stummel von einem Hocker,
vor seinem Flügel, Yamaha, und summt . . .
Die Haltung von Kopf und Händen,
die eines Spielzeugtischlers,
in einer Puppenstube Stühle rückend,
Fenster schließend. April,
die Eisberge ziehen vorüber,
die Stube wird davon empfindlich heller.
Über der zum Horizont auf Stoß gerückten,
silberfarbenen Tapetenleiste
das Foto in der Pose eines Arktikers
am Ausgangspunkt der Reise.
Die Wände dünn, man kann Gezwitscher
hören, Tellerscheppern, Telefongespräche,
einen Zug, so lang, daß sie in A und B
zugleich die Schranken schließen.

Goldberg-Variation 25, Einspielung N.Y., April/Mai 1981.

HAUKE HÜCKSTÄDT

Theme on a Variation

Gould sits on his stump of a stool,
in front of his Yamaha piano, and hums . . .
The position of head and hands
reminiscent of a toy-maker,
re-arranging the furniture in a doll's house,
shutting the windows after him.
April, the icebergs drifting past,
the room perceptibly brightened by them.
Over the silver dado rail
on the horizon, the picture of him
in the pose of an Eskimo
at the start of an expedition.
The walls so thin, you can hear birdsong,
clink of china, telephone conversations,
a train so very long that the level crossings
are simultaneously down in A and B.

Michael Hofmann

Goldberg variation 25, recorded NYC, April/May 1981.

Going Beck

zweimal zurück, für A.

Der Morgen war verhangen, troffschwer,
bereit, das Pflaster, die Markisen, die Dachbutzen—
dein Bonsai-Schwabing-Panorama, zu fluten.
In den Biergärten nippten die Stühle an den Tischen.
Ich benutzte Pläne, Straßenbahnen, nestelte am Gepäck
oder lächelte Menschen zu, Leuten mit Handikaps,
Berufen, Kindern, Marschrouten, Krücken.
Ein Kundschafter auf Rückzug, äußerlich devot,
aber mit Samen in seinen ausgebeulten Hosentaschen.
Es kam wirklich nicht darauf an, in einem Roman aufzuwachen.
Pascal meinte, es sei leichter, ein schönes Mädchen
als ein Gedicht zu begutachten.
Ich ging all die Planquadrate zurück. Wieder im Zug,
preschte der Regen über das Fenster.
Tropfen tränten an den Rand und zitterten.
Ich korrigierte im Buch, das mit dem Traum beginnt,
sich das Ding abzuschneiden und einzugraben.

HAUKE HÜCKSTÄDT

Going Beck*

for A, two times

The morning was obscure and drippy,
all set to drench the sidewalks, the marquees, the garrets—
your bonzai Schwabing panorama.
In the beer-gardens, the chairs were sipping at the tables.
I took maps and trams, leaned on suitcases
or smiled at people, people with handicaps,
jobs, children, itineraries, crutches.
A withdrawn scout, seemingly reputable,
but with semen stains in his clapped-out pockets.
I really didn't want to wake up in someone's novel.
Pascal reckoned it was easier to describe
a pretty girl than a poem.
I retraced all my steps. Back on the train,
the rain thrashed against the windows.
Drops teared against the edge and hung trembling.
I took out my book which began with a man's dream
of slicing off his prick and burying it.

Michael Hofmann

*The Munich publisher C. H. Beck.

Im Hause

Das Zimmer, das wir zu zweit bewohnten,
war menschenleer.

Ausgestreckt und blind verharrte ich
am Fenster—ein Pfosten, der dir Leselicht raubte.

Du warst eins mit dem Ohrensessel,
in dem ich diese Sätze bilde,

in dem du wochenlang die Abnormitäten
menschlicher Anatomie vor dich her murmeltest:

Bücher, aufgemacht und stimulierend
wie Packungen Psychopharmaka oder Kopfschmerztabletten.

Der stockende Sex erinnerte
die Verletzungen, deren Behandlung er war.

Am Morgen obduzierten wir den Kleiderschrank,
sperrten die Flügel auf und griffen

in das Skelett der Bügel, an dem wir schlaff
und dicht aneinander hinunterhingen.

HAUKE HÜCKSTÄDT

No One Home

The room we lived in together
was deserted.

I hung around in front of the window—
a piece of wood getting in your light.

You were at one with the grandfather chair
in which I write these lines,

where you spent whole weeks muttering
litanies of human physical deficiencies to yourself:

books cracked open and stimulating
like packets of prescription medicine or distalgesics.

Our halting intercourse
called to mind the injuries it was intended to treat.

In the morning, we conducted an autopsy on the wardrobe,
yanked open its doors, and reached

in among the small bones of the coathangers
where we dangled together.

Michael Hofmann

MATTHIAS GÖRITZ, 1969–

Für Wolodja in Moskau

Ich gehe ans Fenster
und werde ein schöner Abend

Was macht man im Himmel?
Wer stirbt ist nicht mehr auf der Welt

Im Himmel essen sie Eiscreme
Und wenn es die Farbe gibt?

Ist die Farbe nur ein geträumter Raum
Ich bin im Bauch von Mama

Gott macht dort Pizza
Wenn ich rauskomm, gibt's Lärm

Mama schreit
Ich schreit

Die Hölle stell ich mir lieber gar nicht erst vor
Ich bin mir ziemlich sicher, daß es sie gibt

Im Unterschied zu den vielen Dingen
hat das Nichts die Farbe weiß

Meine Mütter kommen vom Affen
Ich kann keine Banane mehr sehn

All das macht Lärm
Und das Fegefeuer ist, glaube ich, wie die chemische Reinigung

MATTHIAS GÖRITZ

MATTHIAS GÖRITZ, 1969–

For Volodya in Moscow

I go over to the window
and turn into a fine evening

What do people get up to in heaven?
If you die you're no longer in the world

In heaven they eat ice cream—
Or they will do if they have colour, at any rate

Is colour just a dreamspace
I'm in Mama's belly

God is making pizza there
When I get out, there'll be hell to pay

Mama yells
I say hello

I prefer not to imagine hell
I'm pretty sure it exists

Unlike a lot of things
Nothing is coloured white

My mothers are descended from apes
I'm sick of the sight of bananas

It all makes noise
And purgatory must be something like a chemical laundry

Alles was auf der Welt ist, stirbt
Und wenn wir dann weiterleben, zum Beispiel im Himmel

regnet es

MATTHIAS GÖRITZ

Everything in the world must die
And if we live on afterwards, for instance in heaven,

I bet it'll be raining

Michael Hofmann

JAN WAGNER, 1971–

Frösche

das zimmer—ein chaos. was noch nicht verkauft ist
formt auf dem boden die schwer zu entziffernde formel

seines bestrebens: drähte, instrumente
und bücher. leere flaschen. seine frau

ist lange fort. und auch der letzte zahn:
"ohne ehrfurcht vorm eigenen körper" wie achim

von arnim meinte, kämpft er mit dem wein
und mit der prämisse: alles leben besteht

aus elektrizität. draußen am see
ist es plötzlich unheimlich still—die frösche geben

einander heimlich das neue codewort durch.

Von 1800 bis zu seinem frühen Tod im Jahre 1810 unternahm der Naturwissenschaftler Johann
Wilhelm Ritter—angeregt durch die Entdeckungen Luigi Galvanis—zahlreiche Selbstversuche
mit der sogenannten Voltaschen Säule.

JAN WAGNER

Frogs

the room—a chaos. what's not yet been sold
forms on the floor the scarcely decipherable formula

of his endeavour: wires, instruments
and books. empty bottles. his wife

is long since gone. and so is his last tooth:
"undeterred by respect for his own body" as achim

von arnim said, he battles with the wine
and with the premise that all life consists

of electricity. outside on the lake
it is suddenly uncannily still—the frogs are in secret

transmitting the new codeword to each other.

Georgina Paul

From 1800 until his early death in 1810 the scientist Johann Wilhelm Ritter—inspired by the discoveries of Luigi Galvani—undertook numerous experiments on himself with the so-called Voltaic Pile.

1960, 2005 by Arche Literatur Verlag AG, Zürich-Hamburg. Translation courtesy of Harriett Watts.

Ernst Stadler: "On Crossing the Rhine Bridge at Cologne by Night" courtesy of Michael Hamburger.

Gottfried Benn: *Sämtliche Werke*, Stuttgarter Ausgabe. Volume I/ Volume II: *Gedichte 1/Gedichte 2*, copyright © 1986 by J. G. Cotta'sche Buchhandlung Nachfolger GmbH, Verlag Klett-Cotta. "Chopin," from Gottfried Benn, *Statische Gedichte*, copyright © 1948, 1983, 2006 by Arche Literatur Verlag AG, Zürich-Hamburg. "Morgue I, II," and "Express Train," translated by Michael Hamburger, and "The Evenings of Certain Lives" and "People Met," translated by Christopher Middleton, from *Primal Vision: Selected Writings of Gottfried Benn*, edited by E. B. Ashton (Marion Boyars, 1976), courtesy of the publisher. "Night Café," "Chopin," "Little Sweet Face," "Fragments," "Blue Hour," "Par ci, par là," and "Listen" courtesy of Michael Hofmann.

Georg Heym: Translation of "Umbra Vitae" courtesy of Christopher Middleton. "Poet à la Mode" and "Dead Girl in the Water" from *Georg Heym: Poems*, translated and introduced by Antony Hasler (Libris, 2004).

Jakob van Hoddis: "Weltende" copyright © Erbengemeinschaft Jakob van Hoddis. "End of the World" courtesy of Christopher Middleton.

Georg Trakl: "Dream of Evil," translation of "De Profundis," and "Landscape" courtesy of Robert Firmage. "The Rats," "Psalm III," and "Grodek" from *Georg Trakl: Poems and Prose* (Libris, 2001), translated by Alexander Stillmark, used by permission of the publisher. "Eastern Front" courtesy of Christopher Middleton. "Childhood" courtesy of Michael Hofmann. "The Rats," "Psalm III," and "Grodek" from *George Trakl: Poems and Prose* (Libris, 2001), translated by Alexander Stillmark, used by permission of the publisher.

Hans Arp: "Kaspar ist tot," copyright © 1963 by Limes Verlag, Wiesbaden, by permission of F. A. Herbig Verlagsbuchhandlung GmbH, Munich. "Kaspar Is Dead," translation by Christopher Middleton, from *Faint Harps and Silver Voices* (Carcanet Press, 2000), reprinted by permission of the publisher and translator.

Kurt Schwitters: "Die Raddadistenmaschine," "Es ist Herbst," and "Gesetztes Bildgedicht" from Kurt Schwitters, *Das literarische Werk*, © DuMont Literatur und Kunst Verlag, Cologne, 1973. "The Dadaro-

"Perspective from the Spezial-Keller," "Tips from the Posthumous Papers," and "Confined to Bed" courtesy of Michael Hofmann.

Ernst Meister: "Monolog der Menschen" from *Ernst Meister: Ausstellung. Gedichte*. Aachen, 1985. Copyright © Rimbaud Verlag. "Human Monologue" from *Room Without Walls: Selected Poems by Ernst Meister*, translated by Georg M. Gugelberger (Red Hill Press, 1980).

Johannes Bobrowski: All German texts from *Gesammelte Werke in sechs Bänden*, Volume I, copyright © 1998 by Deutsche Verlags-Anstalt, Munich, Verlagsgruppe Random House GmbH. Translation of "Trakl" courtesy of Michael Hamburger. "Childhood," "Mozart," "Report," "Latvian Songs," and "Unsaid," translated by Ruth and Matthew Mead, from *Shadowlands: Selected Poems*, copyright © 1984 by Ruth and Matthew Mead. Reprinted by permission of New Directions Publishing Corp.

Rainer Brambach: All German texts from Rainer Brambach, *Gesammelte Gedichte*. Copyright © 2003 Diogenes Verlag AG, Zürich. Translations courtesy of Michael Hofmann.

Paul Celan: " 'Schläfenzange' " and " 'Schreib dich Nicht' " copyright © Suhrkamp Verlag, Frankfurt am Main. All rights reserved. "Erinnerung an Frankreich," "Corona," "Todesfuge," and " 'Zähle die Mandeln' " from Paul Celan, *Mohn und Gedächtnis*, copyright © 1952 by Deutsche Verlags-Anstalt, Munich, Verlagsgruppe Random House GmbH. "Tenebrae," "Matière de Bretagne," " 'Es war Erde in Ihnen,' " and "Tübingen, Jänner" from Paul Celan, *Sprachgitter. Die Niemandsrose. Gedichte*, copyright © 1986 S. Fischer Verlag GmbH, Frankfurt am Main. "Deathfugue," translation of "Tenebrae," " 'There was earth inside them,' " "Tubingen, January," " 'Temple-pincers,' " and " 'Don't write yourself' " from *Selected Poems and Prose of Paul Celan*, translated by John Felstiner. Copyright © 2001 by John Felstiner. Used by permission of W. W. Norton & Company, Inc. "Memory of France," "Corona," "Matière de Bretagne," and "Count the Almonds" from *Poems of Paul Celan*, translated by Michael Hamburger. Translation copyright © 1972, 1980, 1988, 1994, 2002 by Michael Hamburger. Reprinted by permission of Persea Books, Inc. (New York).

Friederike Mayröcker: "Ostia wird dich empfangen" and "Verlust und Nähe" copyright © Suhrkamp Verlag, Frankfurt am Main. All rights reserved. "Ostia Will Receive You," translation by Reinhold Grimm, from *German 20th Century Poetry*, edited by Reinhold Grimm and Imgard Hunt. Copyright © 2001 by Continuum International Pub-

"Film Put in Backwards," translation by Christopher Middleton, from *Faint Harps and Silver Voices* (Carcanet Press, 2000), reprinted by permission of the publisher and translator. "Shelley Plain" courtesy of Michael Hofmann. "About Some Who Survived" from *German Poetry in Transition, 1945–1990*, edited and translated by Charlotte Melin. Copyright © 1999 by University Press of New England, Hanover, N.H. Reprinted by permission.

Heiner Müller: All German texts copyright © Suhrkamp Verlag, Frankfurt am Main. All rights reserved. "Brecht," translation by Reinhold Grimm, and "Heart of Darkness adapted from Joseph Conrad," translation by Margitt Lehbert, reprinted from *German 20th Century Poetry*, edited by Reinhold Grimm and Imgard Hunt, copyright © 2001 by Continuum International Publishing Group, Inc. Reprinted by permission. "The Hyena" courtesy of Michael Hofmann.

Hans Magnus Enzensberger: All German texts and Enzensberger's translations of "Valse triste et sentimentale," "Fetish," "Identity Check," and "In Memory of Sir Hiram Maxim" copyright © Suhrkamp Verlag, Frankfurt am Main. All rights reserved. "Autumn 1944" and "His Father's Ghost" translations by Michael Hamburger, from *Kiosk* (Bloodaxe Books, 1997) by permission of the publisher and Suhrkamp Verlag. "Gazeteer," translation by David Constantine, from *Lighter Than Air* (Bloodaxe Books, 2002) by permission of the publisher and Suhrkamp Verlag. "In Memory of William Carlos Williams," translation by Reinhold Grimm and Felix Pollak, from *German 20th Century Poetry*, edited by Reinhold Grimm and Imgard Hunt, copyright © 2001 by Continuum International Publishing Group, Inc. Reprinted by permission. "At Thirty-three," "The Holiday," "Visiting Ingres," and "Karl Heinrich Marx," translations by Michael Hamburger, from *Selected Poems of Hans Magnus Enzensberger* (Bloodaxe, 1994), by permission of the publisher and translator. "the end of the owls" and "foam" courtesy of Jerome Rothenberg.

Adolf Endler: "Als der Krieg zu Ende war:" reprinted with the permission of the author. "When the war was over:" from *German Poetry in Transition, 1945–1990*, edited and translated by Charlotte Melin. Copyright © 1999 by University Press of New England, Hanover, N.H. Reprinted by permission.

Jürgen Becker: All German texts copyright © Suhrkamp Verlag, Frank-

lotte Melin. Copyright © 1999 by University Press of New England, Hanover, N.H. Reprinted by permission.

Michael Krüger: "Fußnote" and "Meister" copyright © Suhrkamp Verlag, Frankfurt am Main. All rights reserved. "Footnote" and "Ernst Meister in Memoriam," translations by Richard Dove, from *Diderot's Cat* (Carcanet Press, 1994), reprinted by permission of the publisher and translator.

Jürgen Theobaldy: "Mein junges Leben" appears courtesy of the author. "My Young Life," from *Contemporary Writing from East and West Berlin*, edited by Mitch Cohen (Bandanna Books, 1983).

Joachim Sartorius: "Alexandria" from *Keiner gefriert anders.* Copyright © 1966 by Verlag Kiepenheuer & Witsch, Cologne. "Vieux Jeu" from *Der Tisch wird kalt.* Copyright © 1992 by Verlag Kiepenheuer & Witsch, Cologne. Translations courtesy of Michael Hofmann.

Uwe Kolbe: "Metamorfosis" copyright © Suhrkamp Verlag, Frankfurt am Main. All rights reserved. "Metamorphosis" from *Contemporary Writing from East and West Berlin*, edited by Mitch Cohen (Bandanna Books, 1983).

Durs Grünbein: All German texts copyright © Suhrkamp Verlag Frankfurt am Main. All rights reserved. "All About You," "Greetings from Oblivion City," "Lament of a Legionnaire," "Monological Poem no. 2," "Titian's New Pad," "Trilce, César," and "Untitled," from *Ashes for Breakfast* by Durs Grünbein, translations by Michael Hofmann. Translation copyright © 2005 by Michael Hofmann. Reprinted by permission of Farrar, Straus and Giroux, LLC.

Lutz Seiler: All German texts copyright © Suhrkamp Verlag, Frankfurt am Main. All rights reserved. "fin de siècle" and "'my birth year, sixty-three, that'" courtesy of Andrew Shields. "good evening skip" and "now I lay me" courtesy of Susan Bernofsky.

Marcel Beyer: "Jihad Klänge der Heimat" and "Raps" copyright © Suhrkamp Verlag, Frankfurt am Main. All rights reserved. "Jihad Sounds of Home" courtesy of Margitt Lehbert. "Rapeseed" courtesy of Michael Hofmann.

Volker Sielaff: "Schöpfungsmythos" from *Postkarte für Nofrete: Gedichte*, Springe: Klampen Verlag, 2003, p. 11. "Schlaflos" from *Postkarte für Nofretete. Gedichte*, Springe: Klampen Verlag, 2003, p. 16. Translations courtesy of Michael Hofmann.

Hauke Hückstädt: "Platz der Befreiung" from *Neue Heiterkeit: Gedichte*, Lüneburg: Klampen Verlag, 2001, p. 8. "Thema über eine